STARBRAND
AND
NIGHTMASK

ETERNITY'S CHILDREN
(ATTEND UNIVERSITY)

E.S.U. DAILY BULLETIN

Jul. 12, 2016 — Vol. 76, Issue 1

WHO IS EMPIRE STATE UNIVERSITY'S
NEW SUPER DUO?

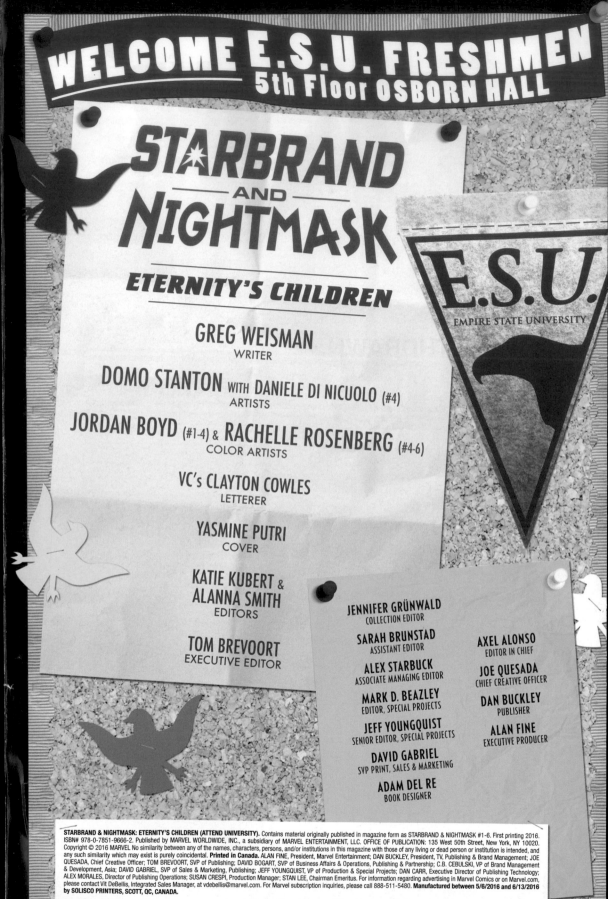

WELCOME E.S.U. FRESHMEN
5th Floor OSBORN HALL

STARBRAND AND NIGHTMASK
ETERNITY'S CHILDREN

GREG WEISMAN
WRITER

DOMO STANTON WITH **DANIELE DI NICUOLO** (#4)
ARTISTS

JORDAN BOYD (#1-4) & **RACHELLE ROSENBERG** (#4-6)
COLOR ARTISTS

VC's CLAYTON COWLES
LETTERER

YASMINE PUTRI
COVER

KATIE KUBERT &
ALANNA SMITH
EDITORS

TOM BREVOORT
EXECUTIVE EDITOR

E.S.U.
EMPIRE STATE UNIVERSITY

JENNIFER GRÜNWALD
COLLECTION EDITOR

SARAH BRUNSTAD
ASSISTANT EDITOR

ALEX STARBUCK
ASSOCIATE MANAGING EDITOR

MARK D. BEAZLEY
EDITOR, SPECIAL PROJECTS

JEFF YOUNGQUIST
SENIOR EDITOR, SPECIAL PROJECTS

DAVID GABRIEL
SVP PRINT, SALES & MARKETING

ADAM DEL RE
BOOK DESIGNER

AXEL ALONSO
EDITOR IN CHIEF

JOE QUESADA
CHIEF CREATIVE OFFICER

DAN BUCKLEY
PUBLISHER

ALAN FINE
EXECUTIVE PRODUCER

STARBRAND & NIGHTMASK: ETERNITY'S CHILDREN (ATTEND UNIVERSITY). Contains material originally published in magazine form as STARBRAND & NIGHTMASK #1-6. First printing 2016. ISBN# 978-0-7851-9666-2. Published by MARVEL WORLDWIDE, INC., a subsidiary of MARVEL ENTERTAINMENT, LLC. OFFICE OF PUBLICATION: 135 West 50th Street, New York, NY 10020. Copyright © 2016 MARVEL No similarity between any of the names, characters, persons, and/or institutions in this magazine with those of any living or dead person or institution is intended, and any such similarity which may exist is purely coincidental. **Printed in Canada.** ALAN FINE, President, Marvel Entertainment; DAN BUCKLEY, President, TV, Publishing & Brand Management; JOE QUESADA, Chief Creative Officer; TOM BREVOORT, SVP of Publishing; DAVID BOGART, SVP of Business Affairs & Operations, Publishing & Partnership; C.B. CEBULSKI, VP of Brand Management & Development, Asia; DAVID GABRIEL, SVP of Sales & Marketing, Publishing; JEFF YOUNGQUIST, VP of Production & Special Projects; DAN CARR, Executive Director of Publishing Technology; ALEX MORALES, Director of Publishing Operations; SUSAN CRESPI, Production Manager; STAN LEE, Chairman Emeritus. For information regarding advertising in Marvel Comics or on Marvel.com, please contact Vit DeBellis, Integrated Sales Manager, at vdebellis@marvel.com. For Marvel subscription inquiries, please call 888-511-5480. **Manufactured between 5/6/2016 and 6/13/2016 by SOLISCO PRINTERS, SCOTT, QC, CANADA.**

10 9 8 7 6 5 4 3 2 1

CHAPTER 1: MATRICULATION

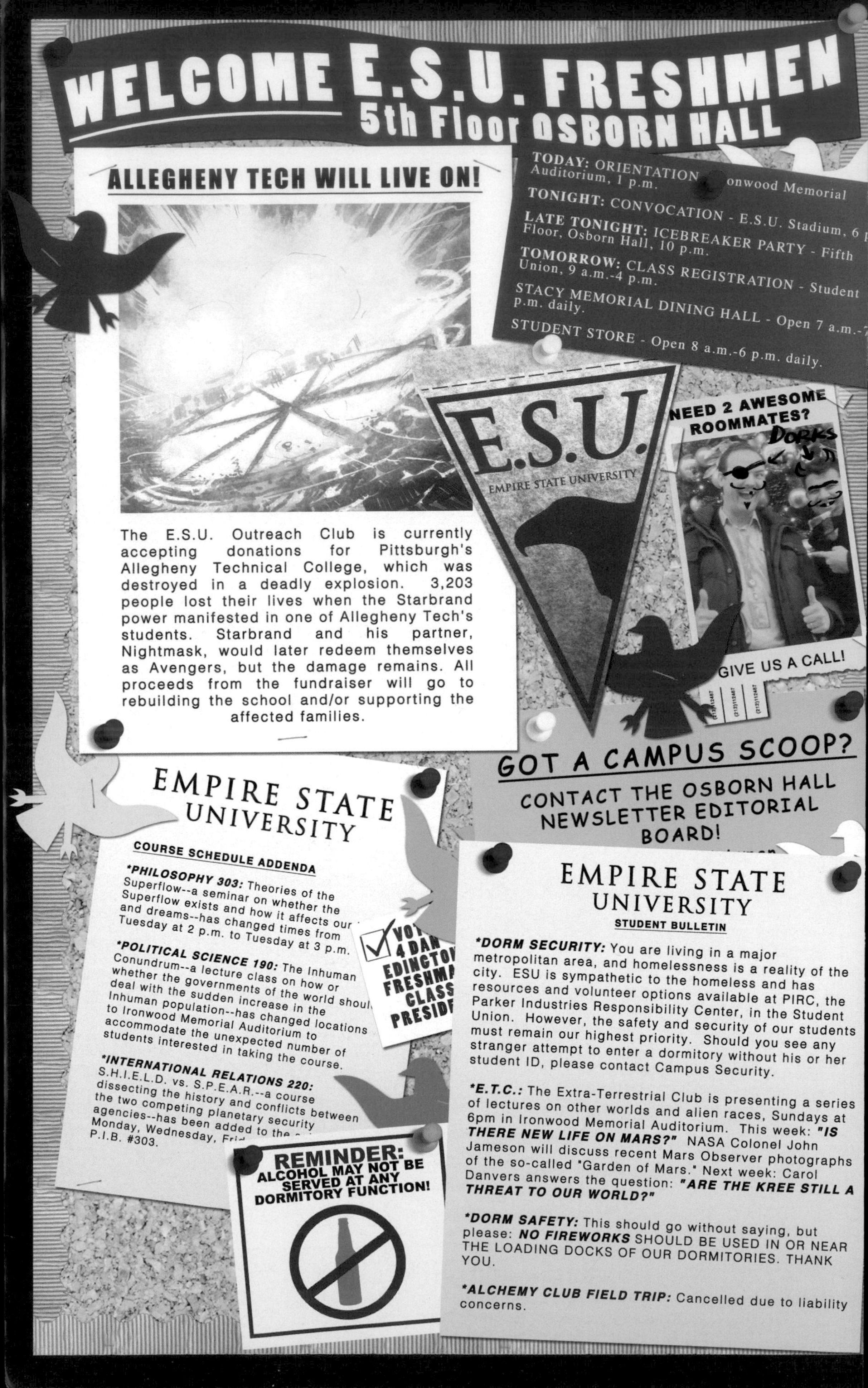
WELCOME E.S.U. FRESHMEN
5th Floor OSBORN HALL
ALLEGHENY TECH WILL LIVE ON!
The E.S.U. Outreach Club is currently accepting donations for Pittsburgh's Allegheny Technical College, which was destroyed in a deadly explosion. 3,203 people lost their lives when the Starbrand power manifested in one of Allegheny Tech's students. Starbrand and his partner, Nightmask, would later redeem themselves as Avengers, but the damage remains. All proceeds from the fundraiser will go to rebuilding the school and/or supporting the affected families.
TODAY: ORIENTATION onwood Memorial Auditorium, 1 p.m.
TONIGHT: CONVOCATION - E.S.U. Stadium, 6 p
LATE TONIGHT: ICEBREAKER PARTY - Fifth Floor, Osborn Hall, 10 p.m.
TOMORROW: CLASS REGISTRATION - Student Union, 9 a.m.-4 p.m.
STACY MEMORIAL DINING HALL - Open 7 a.m.-7 p.m. daily.
STUDENT STORE - Open 8 a.m.-6 p.m. daily.
E.S.U.
EMPIRE STATE UNIVERSITY
NEED 2 AWESOME ROOMMATES?
DORKS
GIVE US A CALL!
GOT A CAMPUS SCOOP?
CONTACT THE OSBORN HALL NEWSLETTER EDITORIAL BOARD!
EMPIRE STATE UNIVERSITY
COURSE SCHEDULE ADDENDA
*PHILOSOPHY 303: Theories of the Superflow--a seminar on whether the Superflow exists and how it affects our and dreams--has changed times from Tuesday at 2 p.m. to Tuesday at 3 p.m.
*POLITICAL SCIENCE 190: The Inhuman Conundrum--a lecture class on how or whether the governments of the world shoul deal with the sudden increase in the Inhuman population--has changed locations to Ironwood Memorial Auditorium to accommodate the unexpected number of students interested in taking the course.
*INTERNATIONAL RELATIONS 220: S.H.I.E.L.D. vs. S.P.E.A.R.--a course dissecting the history and conflicts between the two competing planetary security agencies--has been added to the Monday, Wednesday, P.I.B. #303.
VOT 4 DAN EDINGTO FRESHMA CLASS PRESID
REMINDER: ALCOHOL MAY NOT BE SERVED AT ANY DORMITORY FUNCTION!
EMPIRE STATE UNIVERSITY
STUDENT BULLETIN
*DORM SECURITY: You are living in a major metropolitan area, and homelessness is a reality of the city. ESU is sympathetic to the homeless and has resources and volunteer options available at PIRC, the Parker Industries Responsibility Center, in the Student Union. However, the safety and security of our students must remain our highest priority. Should you see any stranger attempt to enter a dormitory without his or her student ID, please contact Campus Security.
*E.T.C.: The Extra-Terrestrial Club is presenting a series of lectures on other worlds and alien races, Sundays at 6pm in Ironwood Memorial Auditorium. This week: "IS THERE NEW LIFE ON MARS?" NASA Colonel John Jameson will discuss recent Mars Observer photographs of the so-called "Garden of Mars." Next week: Carol Danvers answers the question: "ARE THE KREE STILL A THREAT TO OUR WORLD?"
*DORM SAFETY: This should go without saying, but please: NO FIREWORKS SHOULD BE USED IN OR NEAR THE LOADING DOCKS OF OUR DORMITORIES. THANK YOU.
*ALCHEMY CLUB FIELD TRIP: Cancelled due to liability concerns.

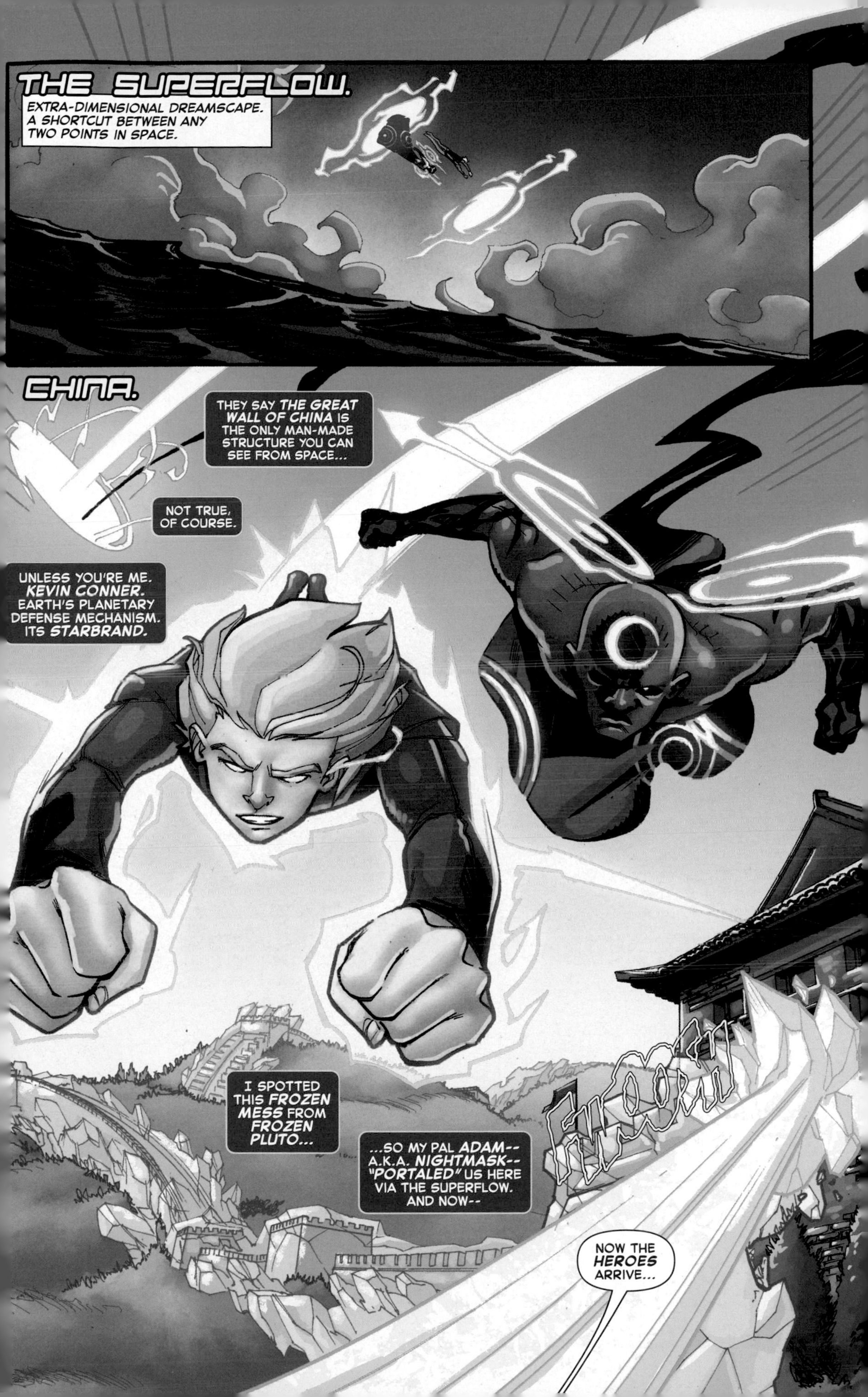
THE SUPERFLOW.
EXTRA-DIMENSIONAL DREAMSCAPE. A SHORTCUT BETWEEN ANY TWO POINTS IN SPACE.
CHINA.
THEY SAY THE GREAT WALL OF CHINA IS THE ONLY MAN-MADE STRUCTURE YOU CAN SEE FROM SPACE...
NOT TRUE, OF COURSE.
UNLESS YOU'RE ME. KEVIN CONNER. EARTH'S PLANETARY DEFENSE MECHANISM. ITS STARBRAND.
I SPOTTED THIS FROZEN MESS FROM FROZEN PLUTO...
...SO MY PAL ADAM-- A.K.A. NIGHTMASK-- "PORTALED" US HERE VIA THE SUPERFLOW. AND NOW--
NOW THE HEROES ARRIVE...

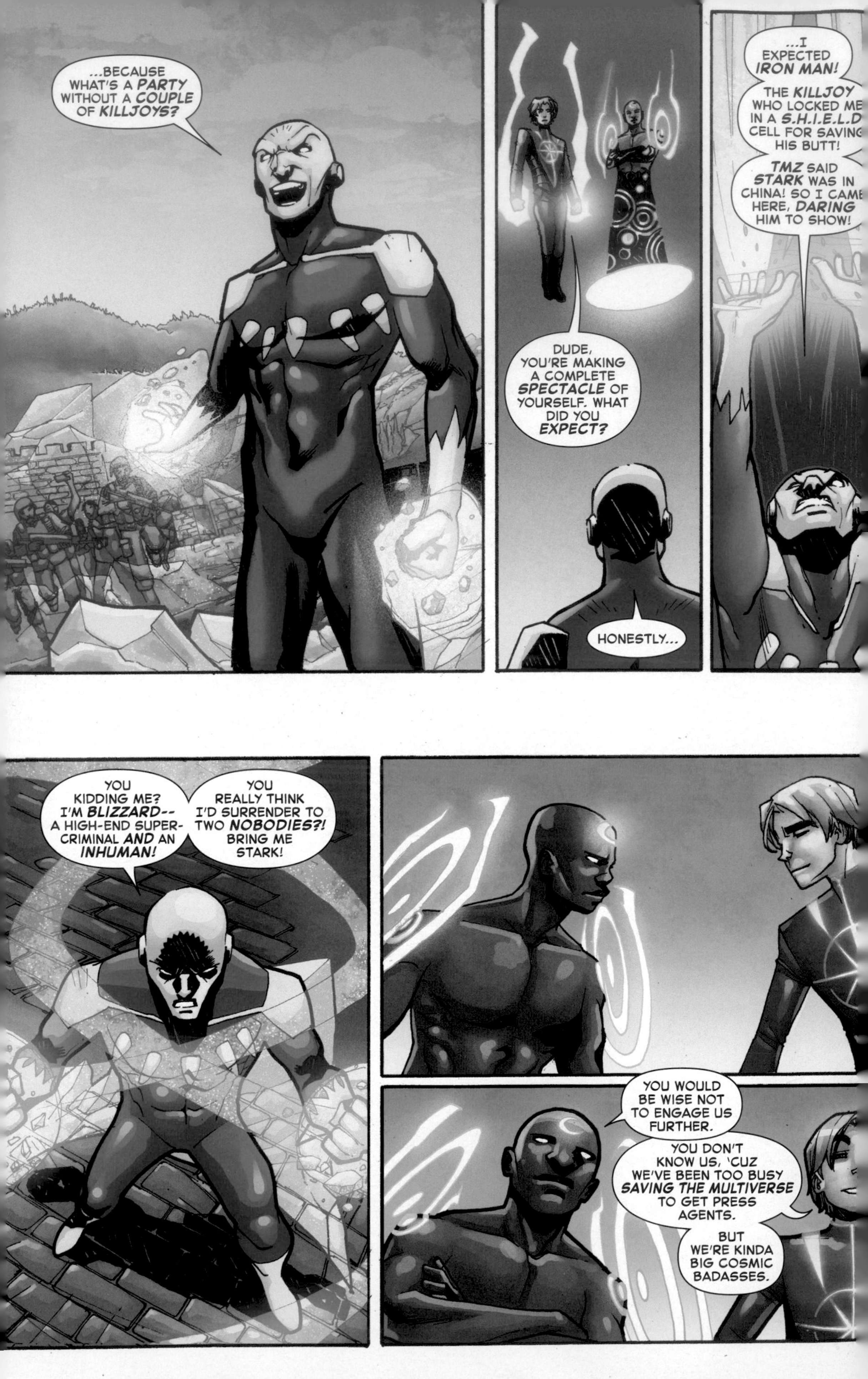
...BECAUSE WHAT'S A PARTY WITHOUT A COUPLE OF KILLJOYS?
DUDE, YOU'RE MAKING A COMPLETE SPECTACLE OF YOURSELF. WHAT DID YOU EXPECT?
HONESTLY...
...I EXPECTED IRON MAN!
THE KILLJOY WHO LOCKED ME IN A S.H.I.E.L.D. CELL FOR SAVING HIS BUTT!
TMZ SAID STARK WAS IN CHINA! SO I CAME HERE, DARING HIM TO SHOW!
YOU KIDDING ME? I'M BLIZZARD-- A HIGH-END SUPER-CRIMINAL AND AN INHUMAN!
YOU REALLY THINK I'D SURRENDER TO TWO NOBODIES?! BRING ME STARK!
YOU WOULD BE WISE NOT TO ENGAGE US FURTHER.
YOU DON'T KNOW US, 'CUZ WE'VE BEEN TOO BUSY SAVING THE MULTIVERSE TO GET PRESS AGENTS.
BUT WE'RE KINDA BIG COSMIC BADASSES.

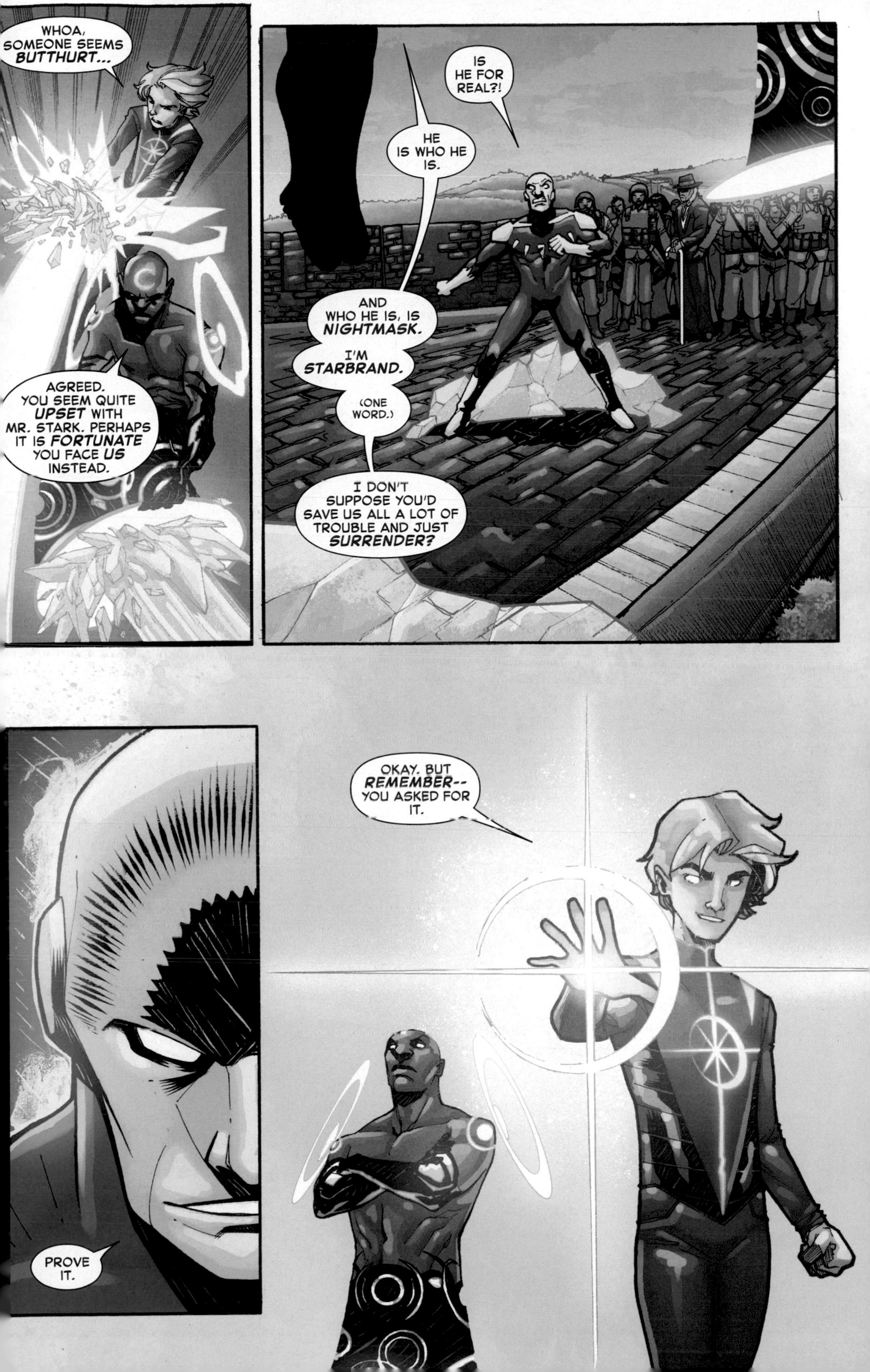
WHOA, SOMEONE SEEMS BUTTHURT...
AGREED. YOU SEEM QUITE UPSET WITH MR. STARK. PERHAPS IT IS FORTUNATE YOU FACE US INSTEAD.
IS HE FOR REAL?!
HE IS WHO HE IS.
AND WHO HE IS, IS NIGHTMASK.
I'M STARBRAND.
(ONE WORD.)
I DON'T SUPPOSE YOU'D SAVE US ALL A LOT OF TROUBLE AND JUST SURRENDER?
PROVE IT.
OKAY. BUT REMEMBER-- YOU ASKED FOR IT.

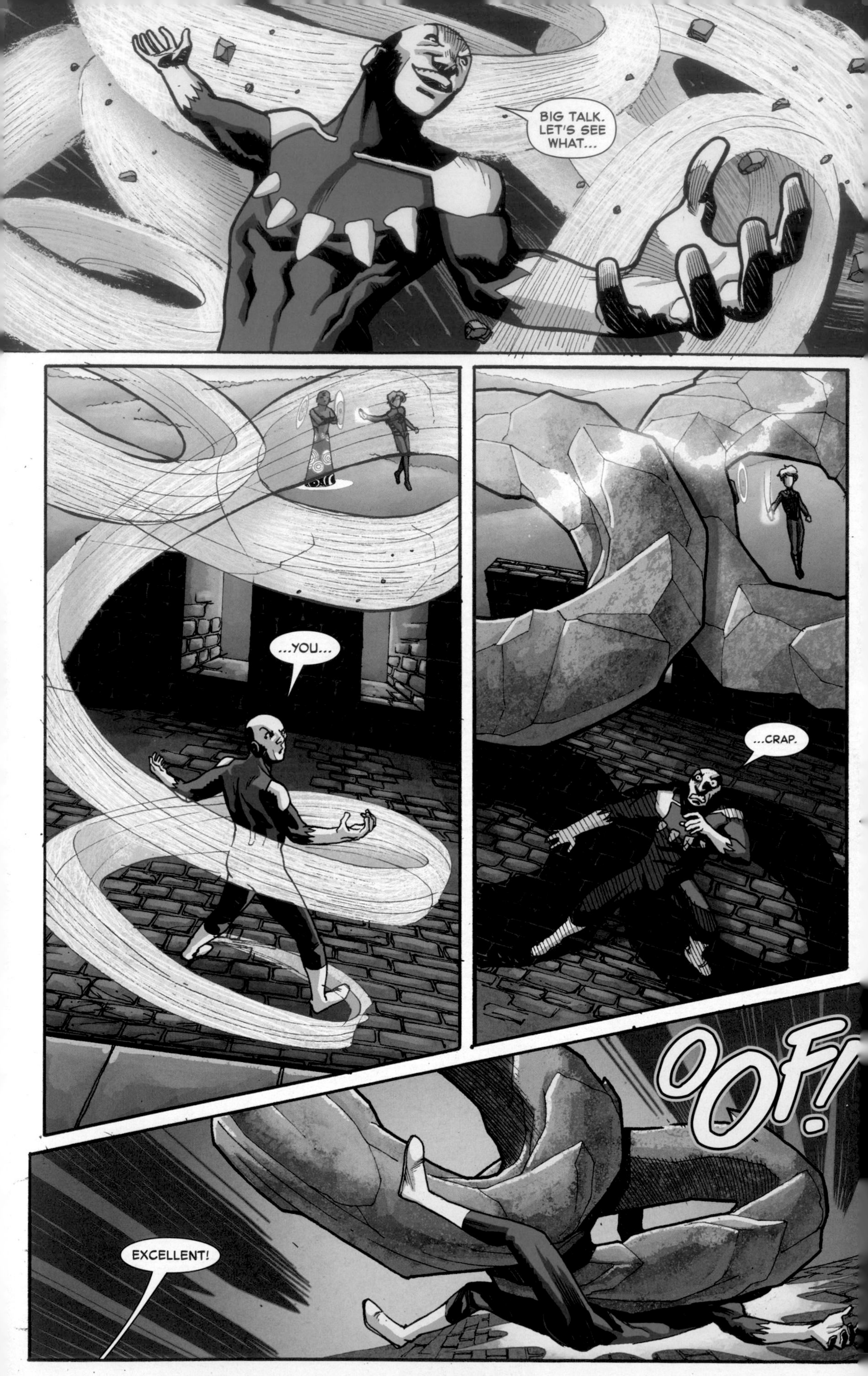
BIG TALK. LET'S SEE WHAT...
...YOU...
...CRAP.
OOF!
EXCELLENT!

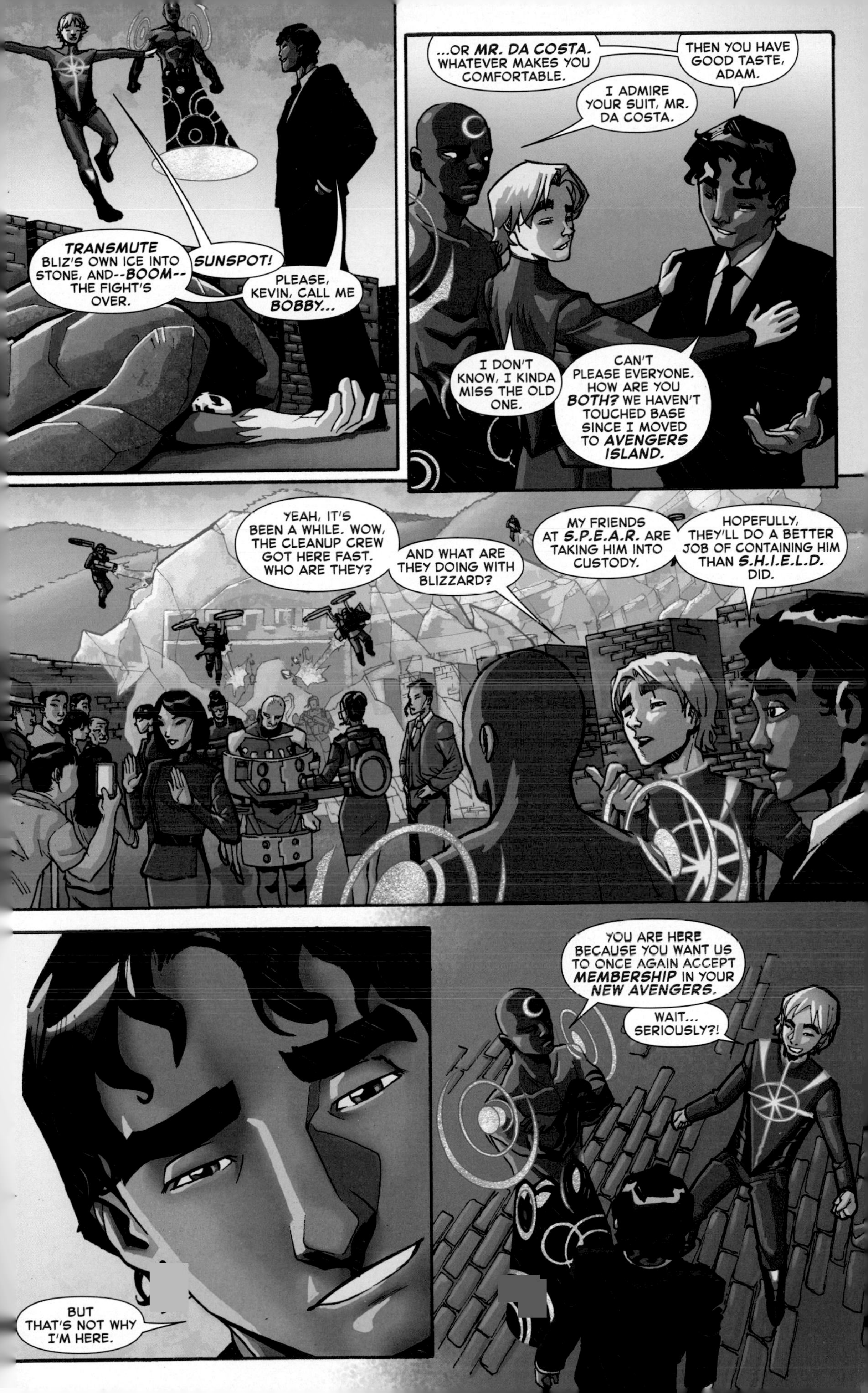
TRANSMUTE BLIZ'S OWN ICE INTO STONE, AND--BOOM--THE FIGHT'S OVER.
SUNSPOT!
PLEASE, KEVIN, CALL ME BOBBY...
...OR MR. DA COSTA. WHATEVER MAKES YOU COMFORTABLE.
THEN YOU HAVE GOOD TASTE, ADAM.
I ADMIRE YOUR SUIT, MR. DA COSTA.
I DON'T KNOW, I KINDA MISS THE OLD ONE.
CAN'T PLEASE EVERYONE. HOW ARE YOU BOTH? WE HAVEN'T TOUCHED BASE SINCE I MOVED TO AVENGERS ISLAND.
YEAH, IT'S BEEN A WHILE. WOW, THE CLEANUP CREW GOT HERE FAST. WHO ARE THEY?
AND WHAT ARE THEY DOING WITH BLIZZARD?
MY FRIENDS AT S.P.E.A.R. ARE TAKING HIM INTO CUSTODY.
HOPEFULLY, THEY'LL DO A BETTER JOB OF CONTAINING HIM THAN S.H.I.E.L.D. DID.
BUT THAT'S NOT WHY I'M HERE.
YOU ARE HERE BECAUSE YOU WANT US TO ONCE AGAIN ACCEPT MEMBERSHIP IN YOUR NEW AVENGERS.
WAIT... SERIOUSLY?!

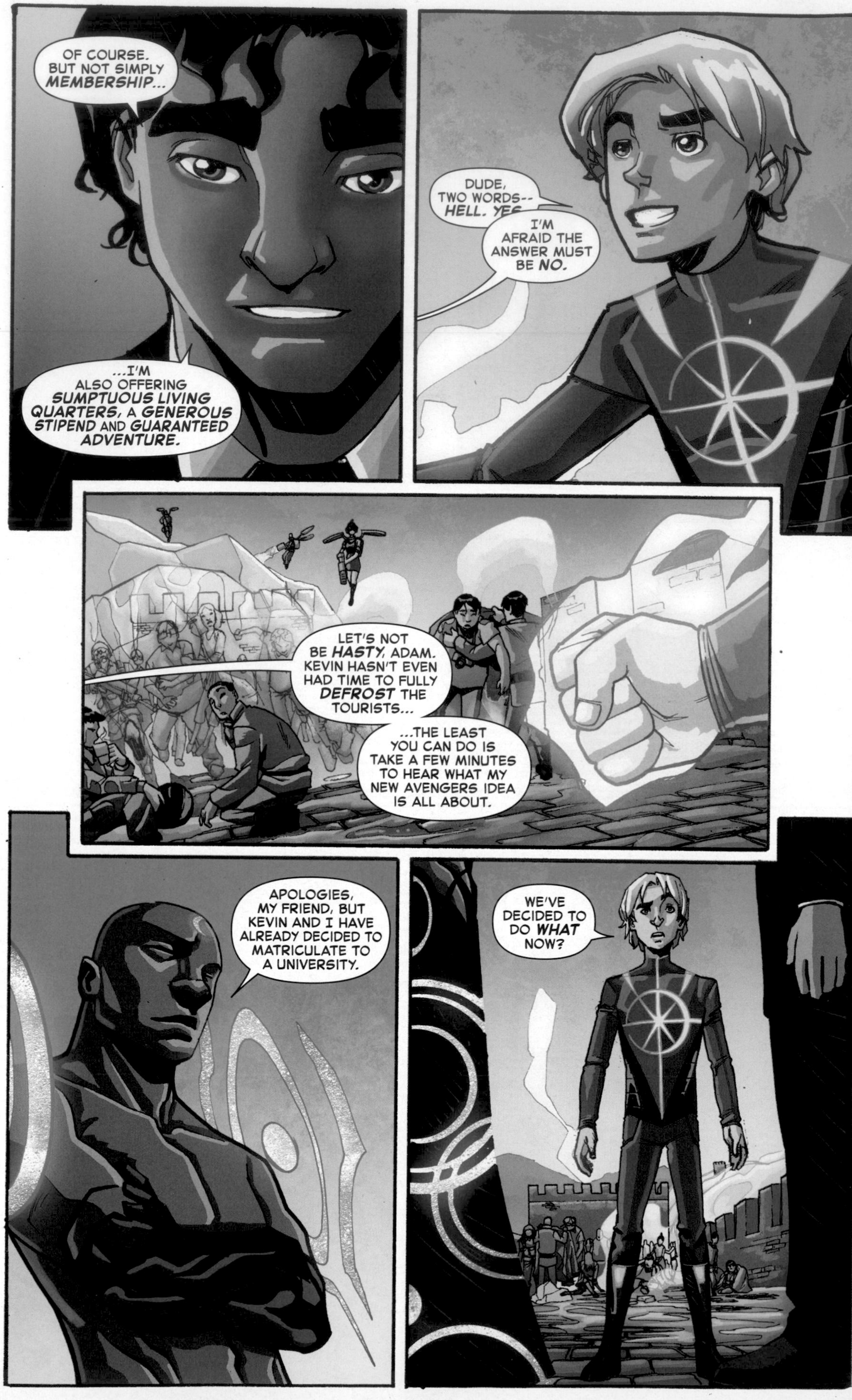
OF COURSE. BUT NOT SIMPLY MEMBERSHIP...
...I'M ALSO OFFERING SUMPTUOUS LIVING QUARTERS, A GENEROUS STIPEND AND GUARANTEED ADVENTURE.
DUDE, TWO WORDS-- HELL. YES.
I'M AFRAID THE ANSWER MUST BE NO.
LET'S NOT BE HASTY, ADAM. KEVIN HASN'T EVEN HAD TIME TO FULLY DEFROST THE TOURISTS...
...THE LEAST YOU CAN DO IS TAKE A FEW MINUTES TO HEAR WHAT MY NEW AVENGERS IDEA IS ALL ABOUT.
APOLOGIES, MY FRIEND, BUT KEVIN AND I HAVE ALREADY DECIDED TO MATRICULATE TO A UNIVERSITY.
WE'VE DECIDED TO DO WHAT NOW?

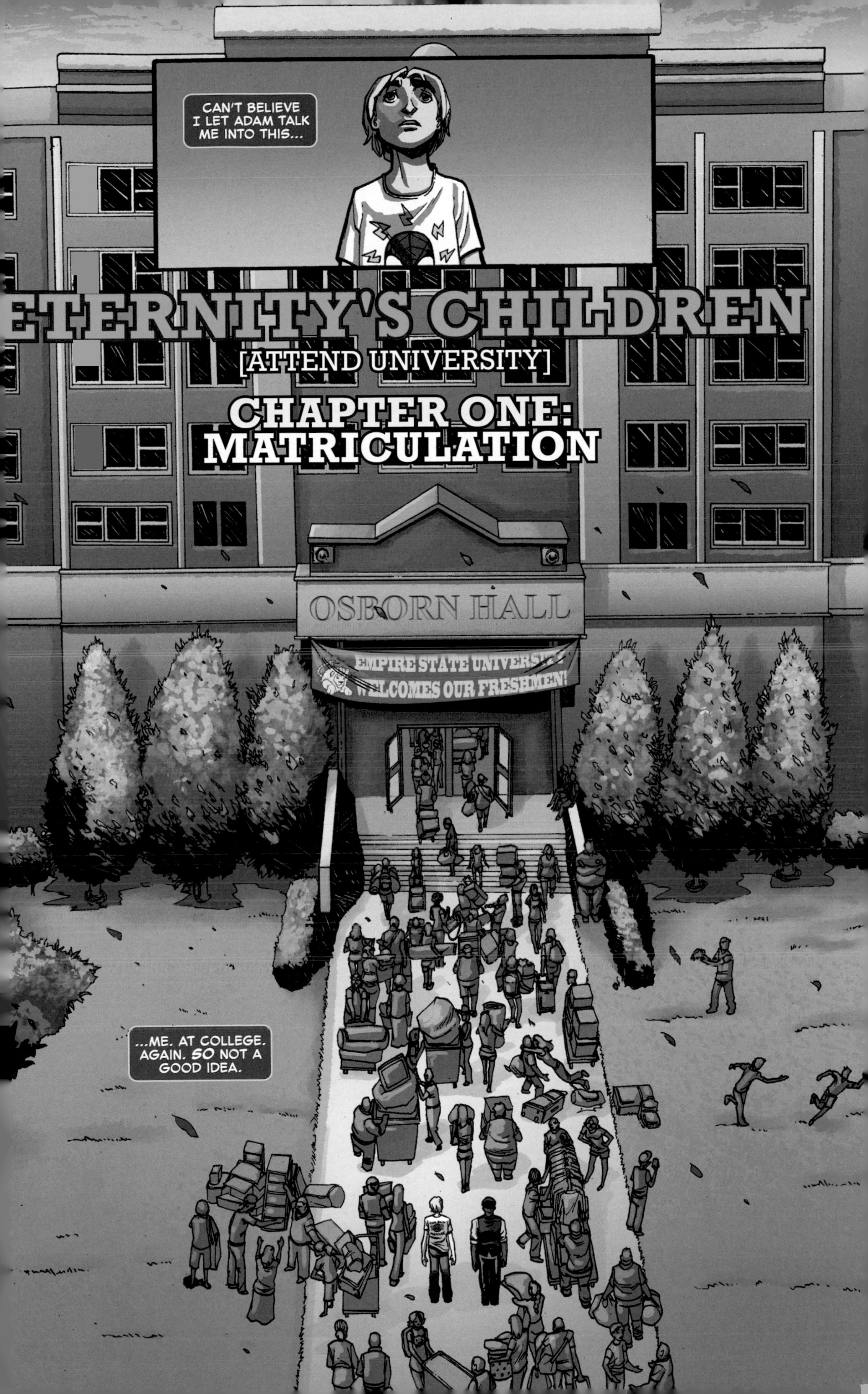
CAN'T BELIEVE I LET ADAM TALK ME INTO THIS...
ETERNITY'S CHILDREN
[ATTEND UNIVERSITY]
CHAPTER ONE: MATRICULATION
OSBORN HALL
EMPIRE STATE UNIVERSITY WELCOMES OUR FRESHMEN!
...ME. AT COLLEGE. AGAIN. SO NOT A GOOD IDEA.

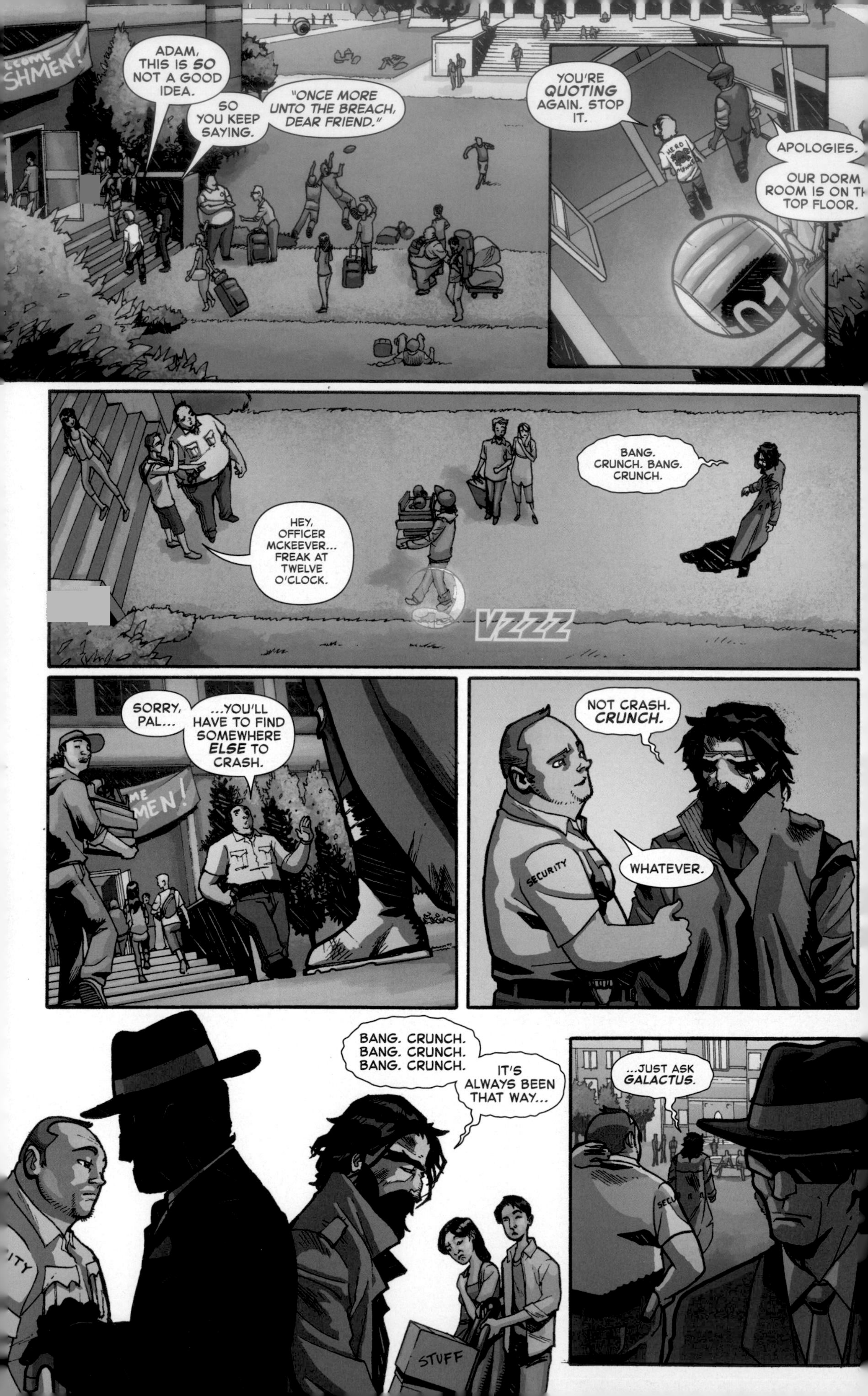

SHMEN!
ADAM, THIS IS SO NOT A GOOD IDEA.
SO YOU KEEP SAYING.
"ONCE MORE UNTO THE BREACH, DEAR FRIEND."
YOU'RE QUOTING AGAIN. STOP IT.
APOLOGIES.
OUR DORM ROOM IS ON THE TOP FLOOR.
HEY, OFFICER MCKEEVER... FREAK AT TWELVE O'CLOCK.
BANG. CRUNCH. BANG. CRUNCH.
VZZZ
SORRY, PAL...
...YOU'LL HAVE TO FIND SOMEWHERE ELSE TO CRASH.
NOT CRASH. CRUNCH.
SECURITY
WHATEVER.
BANG. CRUNCH. BANG. CRUNCH. BANG. CRUNCH.
IT'S ALWAYS BEEN THAT WAY...
STUFF
...JUST ASK GALACTUS.

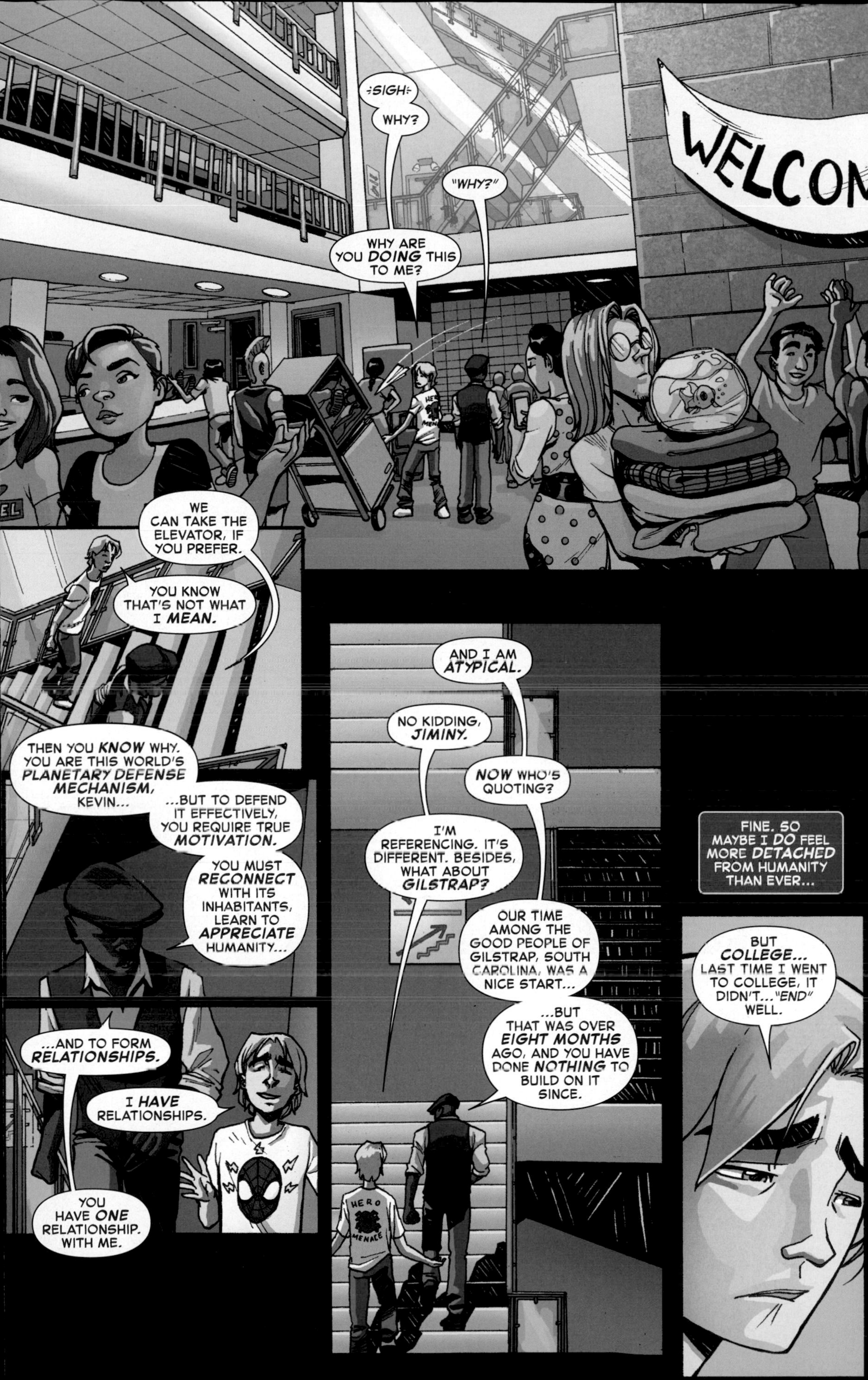

:SIGH:
WHY?
"WHY?"
WHY ARE YOU DOING THIS TO ME?
WELCOM
WE CAN TAKE THE ELEVATOR, IF YOU PREFER.
YOU KNOW THAT'S NOT WHAT I MEAN.
THEN YOU KNOW WHY. YOU ARE THIS WORLD'S PLANETARY DEFENSE MECHANISM, KEVIN...
...BUT TO DEFEND IT EFFECTIVELY, YOU REQUIRE TRUE MOTIVATION.
YOU MUST RECONNECT WITH ITS INHABITANTS, LEARN TO APPRECIATE HUMANITY...
...AND TO FORM RELATIONSHIPS.
I HAVE RELATIONSHIPS.
YOU HAVE ONE RELATIONSHIP. WITH ME.
AND I AM ATYPICAL.
NO KIDDING, JIMINY.
NOW WHO'S QUOTING?
I'M REFERENCING. IT'S DIFFERENT. BESIDES, WHAT ABOUT GILSTRAP?
OUR TIME AMONG THE GOOD PEOPLE OF GILSTRAP, SOUTH CAROLINA, WAS A NICE START...
...BUT THAT WAS OVER EIGHT MONTHS AGO, AND YOU HAVE DONE NOTHING TO BUILD ON IT SINCE.
FINE. SO MAYBE I DO FEEL MORE DETACHED FROM HUMANITY THAN EVER...
BUT COLLEGE... LAST TIME I WENT TO COLLEGE, IT DIDN'T..."END" WELL.

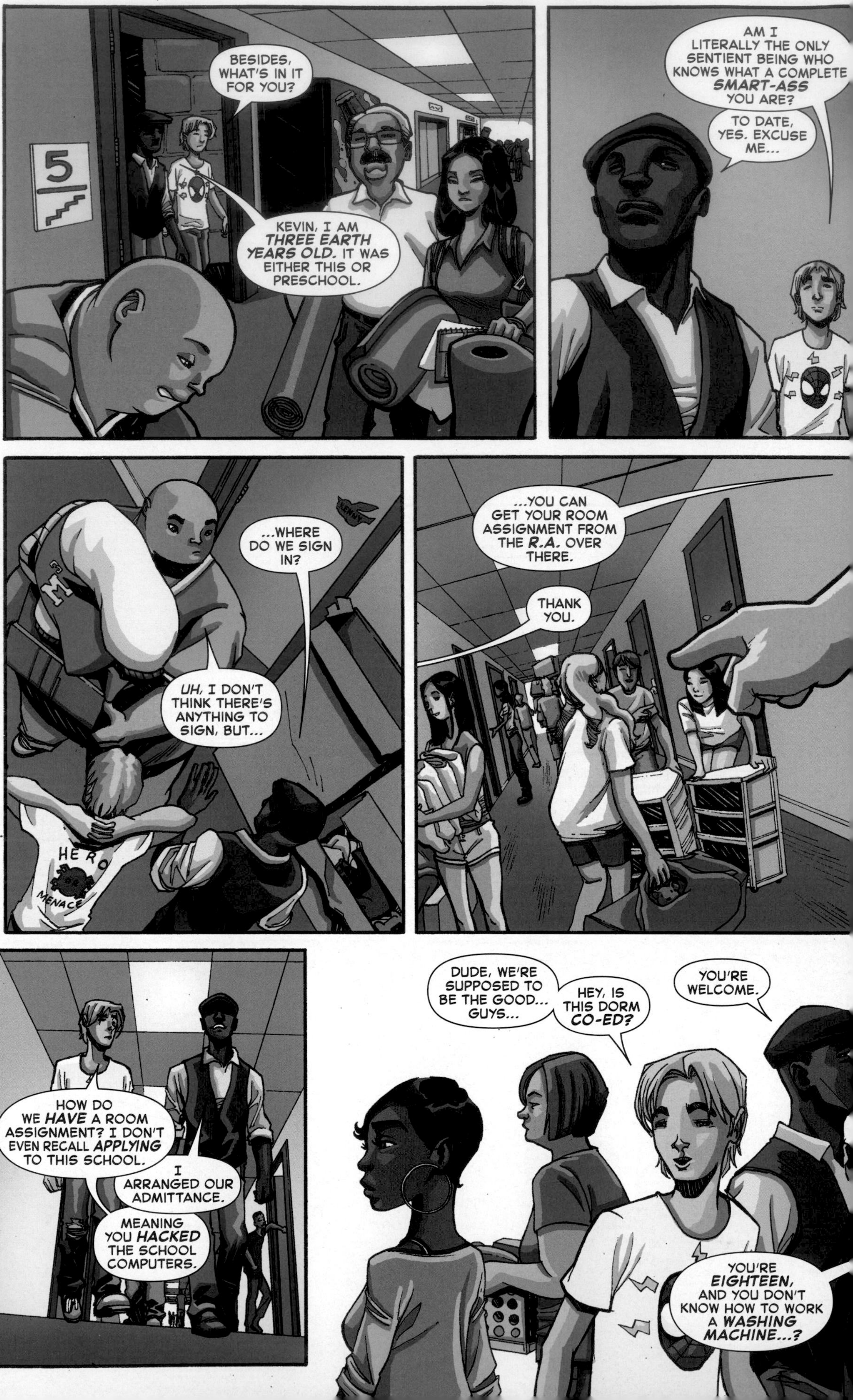

BESIDES, WHAT'S IN IT FOR YOU?
KEVIN, I AM THREE EARTH YEARS OLD. IT WAS EITHER THIS OR PRESCHOOL.
5
AM I LITERALLY THE ONLY SENTIENT BEING WHO KNOWS WHAT A COMPLETE SMART-ASS YOU ARE?
TO DATE, YES. EXCUSE ME...
...WHERE DO WE SIGN IN?
UH, I DON'T THINK THERE'S ANYTHING TO SIGN, BUT...
HERO
MENACE
...YOU CAN GET YOUR ROOM ASSIGNMENT FROM THE R.A. OVER THERE.
THANK YOU.
HOW DO WE HAVE A ROOM ASSIGNMENT? I DON'T EVEN RECALL APPLYING TO THIS SCHOOL.
I ARRANGED OUR ADMITTANCE.
MEANING YOU HACKED THE SCHOOL COMPUTERS.
DUDE, WE'RE SUPPOSED TO BE THE GOOD... GUYS...
HEY, IS THIS DORM CO-ED?
YOU'RE WELCOME.
YOU'RE EIGHTEEN, AND YOU DON'T KNOW HOW TO WORK A WASHING MACHINE...?

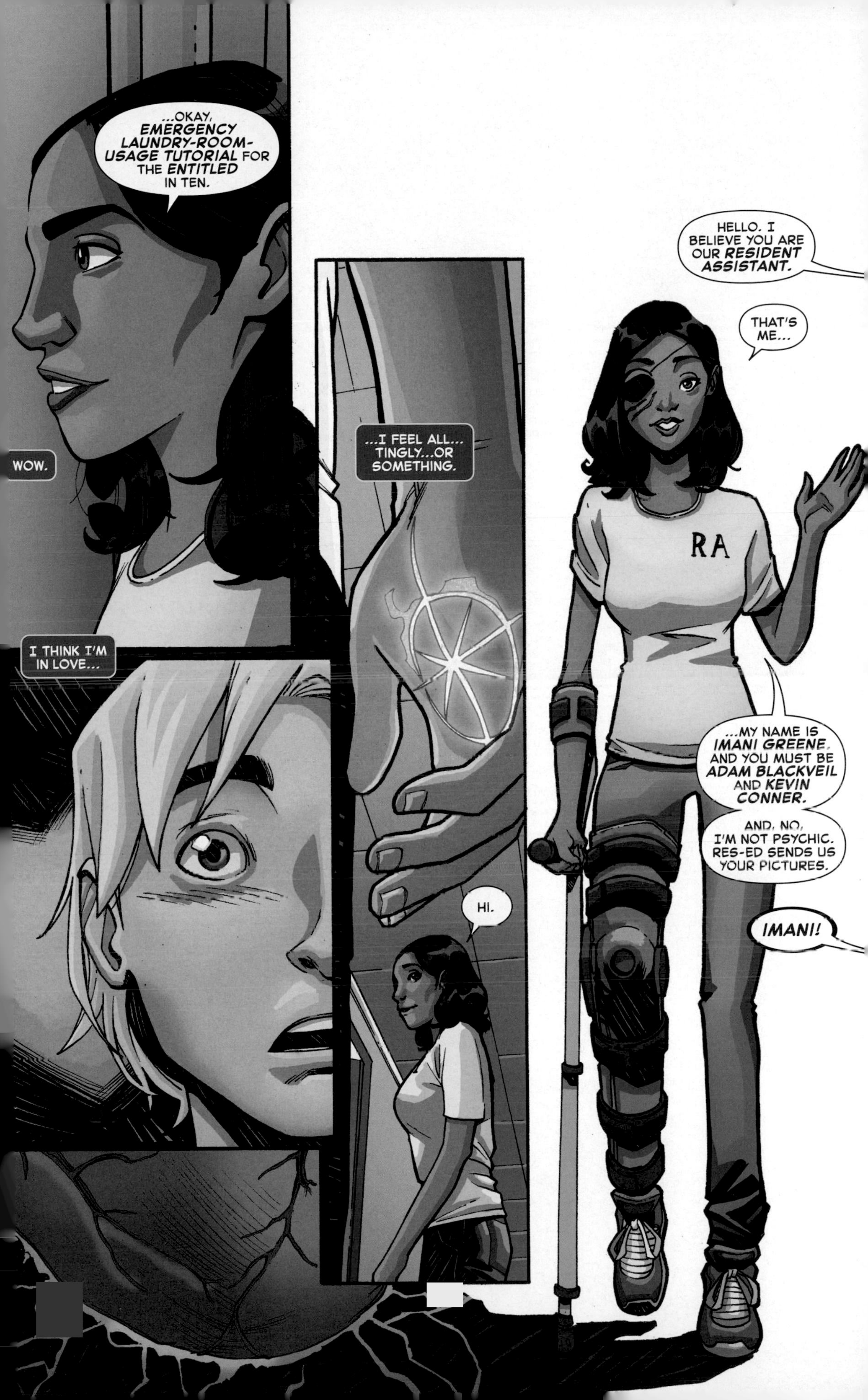
...OKAY, EMERGENCY LAUNDRY-ROOM-USAGE TUTORIAL FOR THE ENTITLED IN TEN.
WOW.
I THINK I'M IN LOVE...
...I FEEL ALL... TINGLY...OR SOMETHING.
HI.
HELLO. I BELIEVE YOU ARE OUR RESIDENT ASSISTANT.
THAT'S ME...
RA
...MY NAME IS IMANI GREENE, AND YOU MUST BE ADAM BLACKVEIL AND KEVIN CONNER.
AND, NO, I'M NOT PSYCHIC. RES-ED SENDS US YOUR PICTURES.
IMANI!

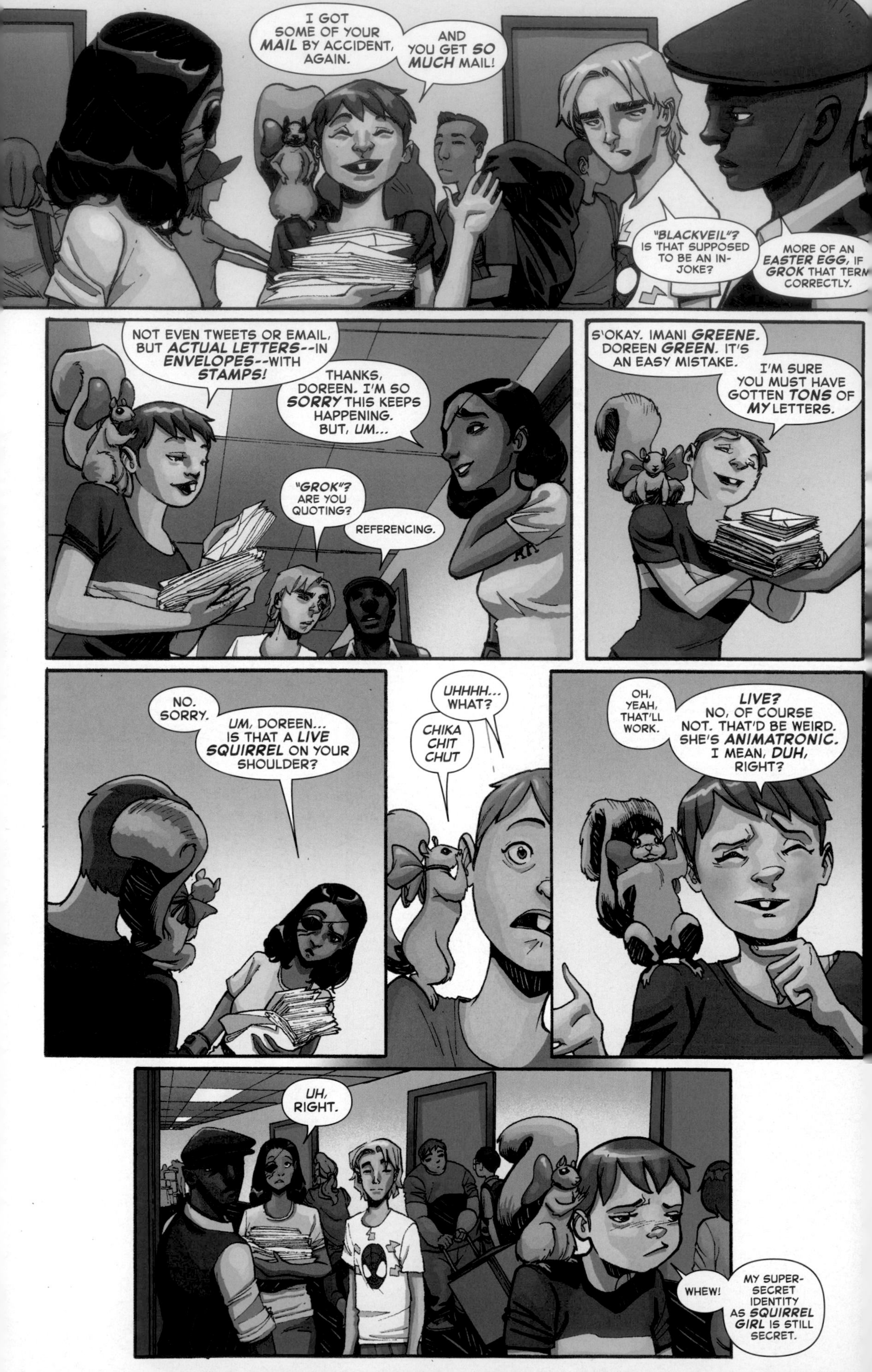
I GOT SOME OF YOUR MAIL BY ACCIDENT, AGAIN.
AND YOU GET SO MUCH MAIL!
"BLACKVEIL"? IS THAT SUPPOSED TO BE AN IN-JOKE?
MORE OF AN EASTER EGG, IF GROK THAT TERM CORRECTLY.
NOT EVEN TWEETS OR EMAIL, BUT ACTUAL LETTERS--IN ENVELOPES--WITH STAMPS!
THANKS, DOREEN. I'M SO SORRY THIS KEEPS HAPPENING. BUT, UM...
"GROK"? ARE YOU QUOTING?
REFERENCING.
S'OKAY. IMANI GREENE. DOREEN GREEN. IT'S AN EASY MISTAKE.
I'M SURE YOU MUST HAVE GOTTEN TONS OF MY LETTERS.
NO. SORRY.
UM, DOREEN... IS THAT A LIVE SQUIRREL ON YOUR SHOULDER?
UHHHH... WHAT?
CHIKA CHIT CHUT
OH, YEAH, THAT'LL WORK.
LIVE? NO, OF COURSE NOT. THAT'D BE WEIRD. SHE'S ANIMATRONIC. I MEAN, DUH, RIGHT?
UH, RIGHT.
WHEW!
MY SUPER-SECRET IDENTITY AS SQUIRREL GIRL IS STILL SECRET.

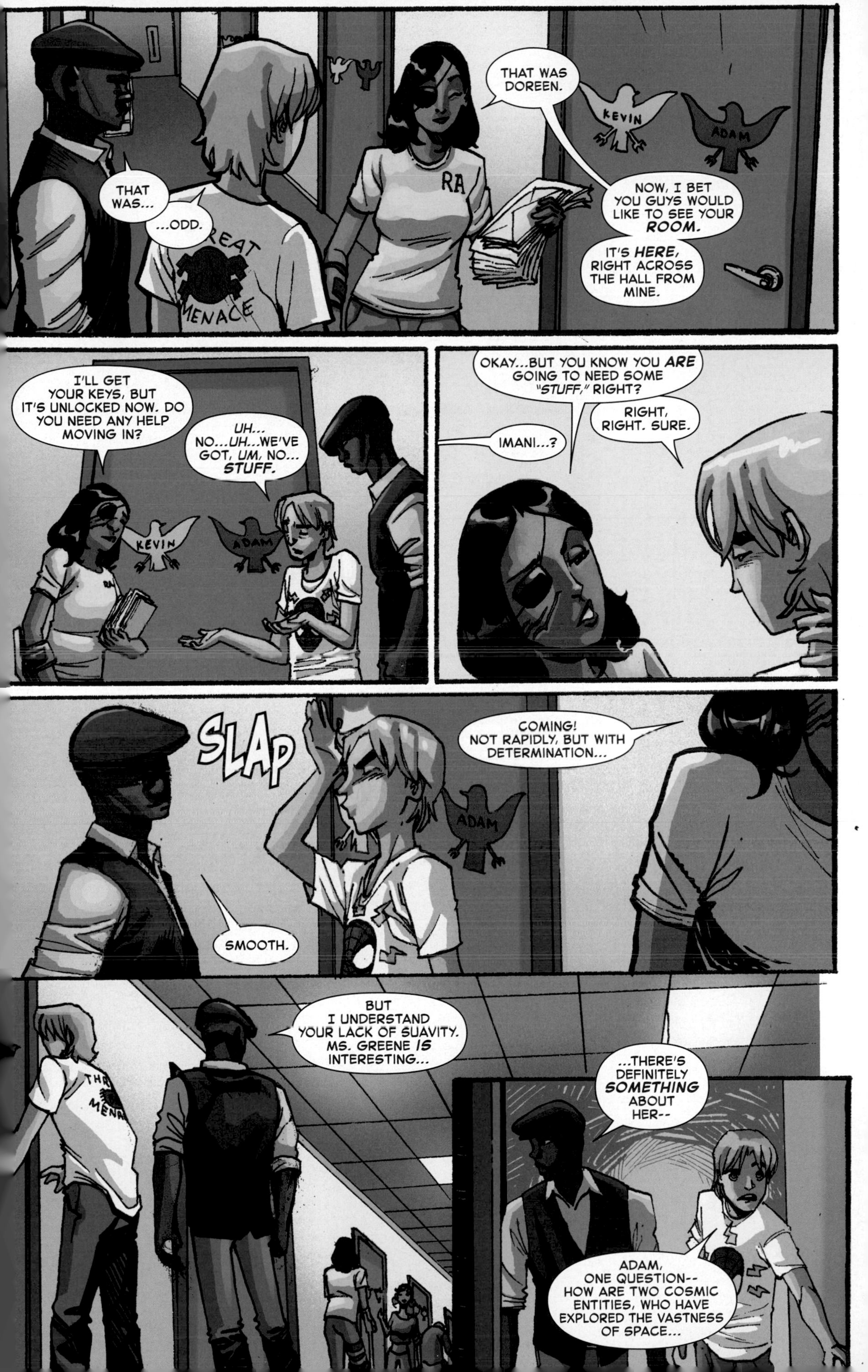
THAT WAS...
...ODD.
THAT WAS DOREEN.
NOW, I BET YOU GUYS WOULD LIKE TO SEE YOUR *ROOM.*
IT'S *HERE,* RIGHT ACROSS THE HALL FROM MINE.
I'LL GET YOUR KEYS, BUT IT'S UNLOCKED NOW. DO YOU NEED ANY HELP MOVING IN?
UH... NO...*UH...*WE'VE GOT, *UM,* NO... *STUFF.*
OKAY...BUT YOU KNOW YOU *ARE* GOING TO NEED SOME *"STUFF,"* RIGHT?
RIGHT, RIGHT. SURE.
IMANI...?
SLAP
COMING! NOT RAPIDLY, BUT WITH DETERMINATION...
SMOOTH.
BUT I UNDERSTAND YOUR LACK OF SUAVITY. MS. GREENE *IS* INTERESTING...
...THERE'S DEFINITELY *SOMETHING* ABOUT HER--
ADAM, ONE QUESTION-- HOW ARE TWO COSMIC ENTITIES, WHO HAVE EXPLORED THE VASTNESS OF SPACE...

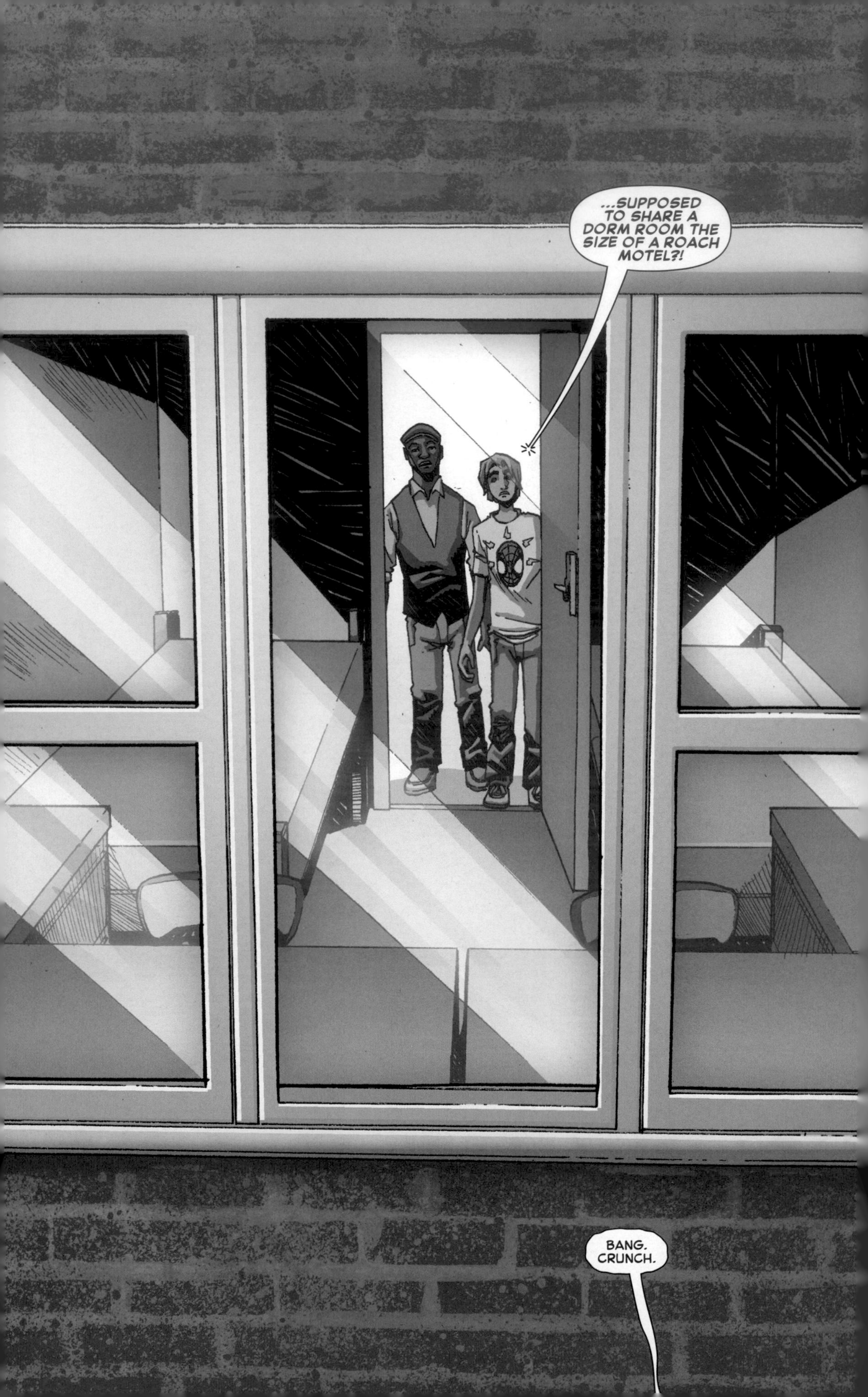
...SUPPOSED TO SHARE A DORM ROOM THE SIZE OF A ROACH MOTEL?!
BANG. CRUNCH.

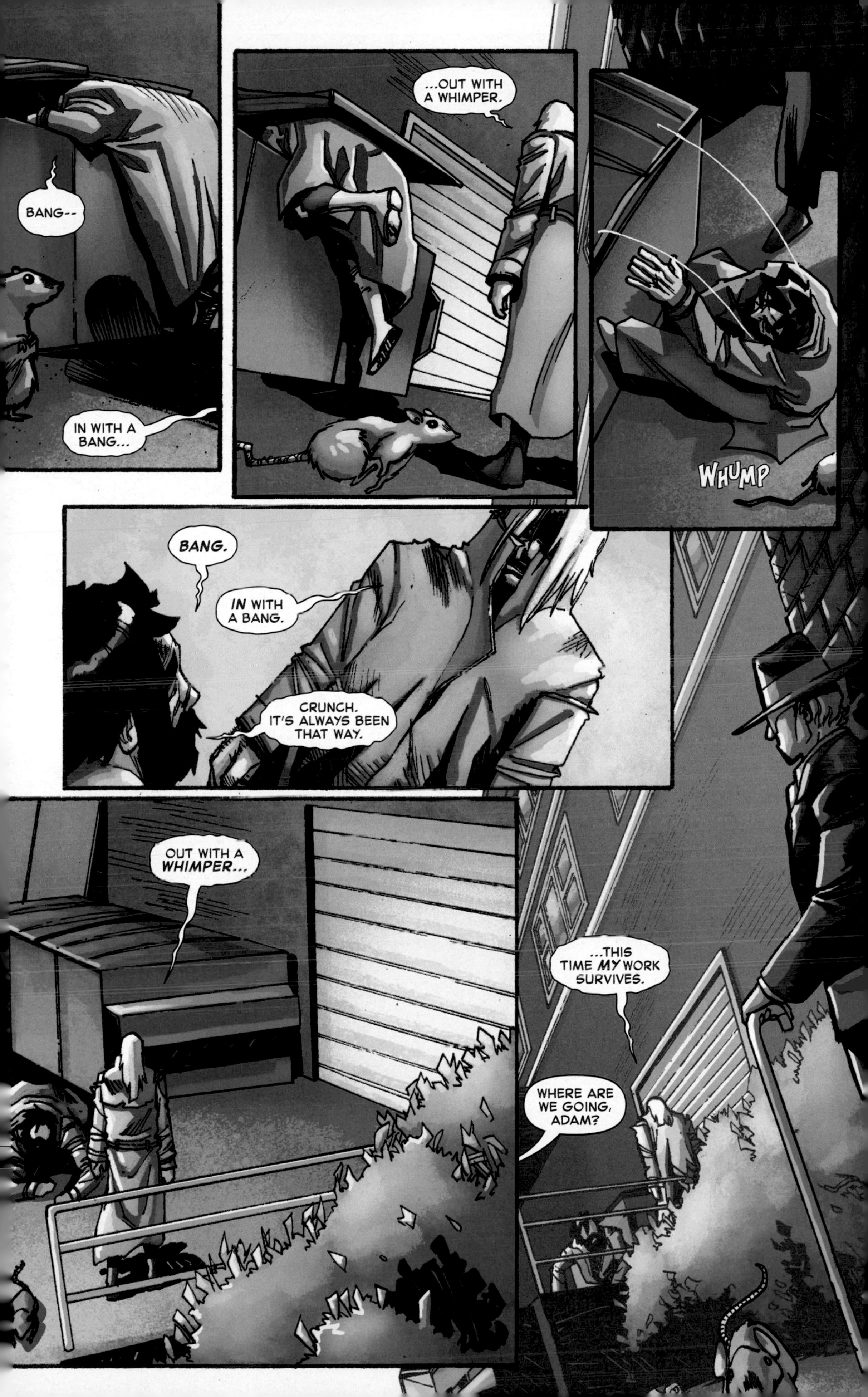
BANG--
IN WITH A BANG...
...OUT WITH A WHIMPER.
WHUMP
BANG.
IN WITH A BANG.
CRUNCH. IT'S ALWAYS BEEN THAT WAY.
OUT WITH A WHIMPER...
...THIS TIME MY WORK SURVIVES.
WHERE ARE WE GOING, ADAM?

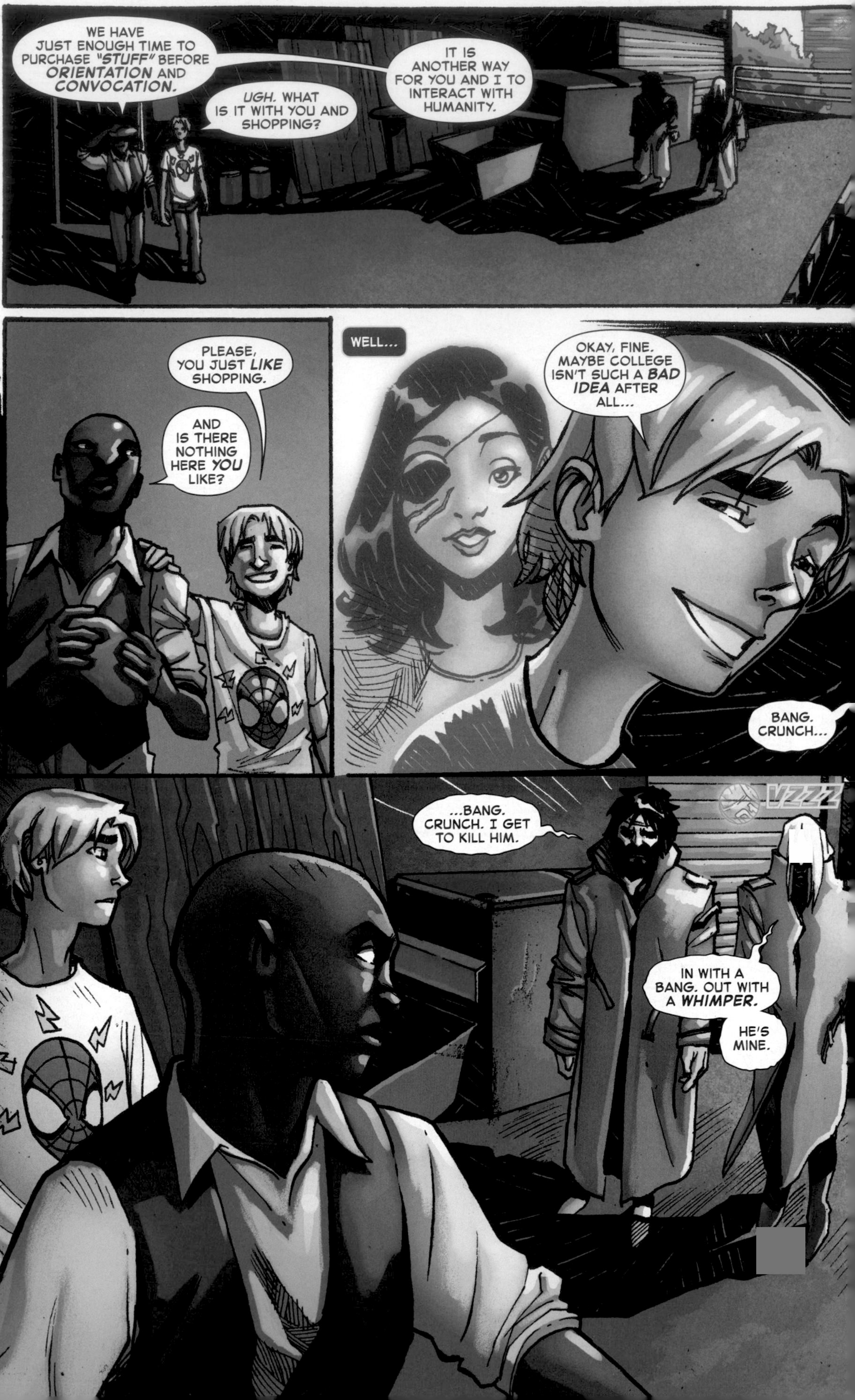
WE HAVE JUST ENOUGH TIME TO PURCHASE "STUFF" BEFORE ORIENTATION AND CONVOCATION.
UGH. WHAT IS IT WITH YOU AND SHOPPING?
IT IS ANOTHER WAY FOR YOU AND I TO INTERACT WITH HUMANITY.
PLEASE, YOU JUST LIKE SHOPPING.
AND IS THERE NOTHING HERE YOU LIKE?
WELL...
OKAY, FINE. MAYBE COLLEGE ISN'T SUCH A BAD IDEA AFTER ALL...
BANG. CRUNCH...
...BANG. CRUNCH. I GET TO KILL HIM.
VZZZ
IN WITH A BANG. OUT WITH A WHIMPER.
HE'S MINE.

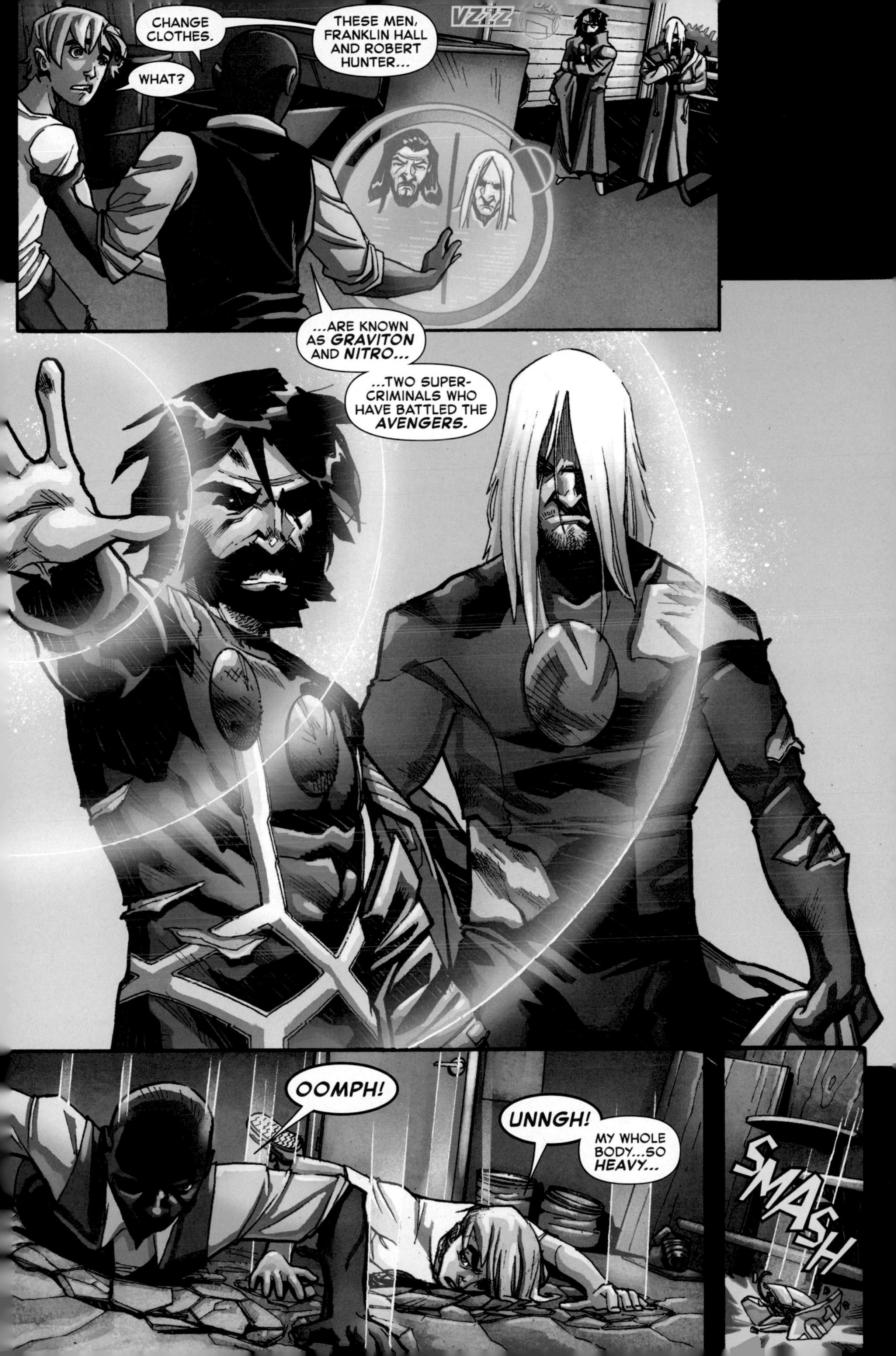
CHANGE CLOTHES.
WHAT?
THESE MEN, FRANKLIN HALL AND ROBERT HUNTER...
VZZZ
...ARE KNOWN AS GRAVITON AND NITRO...
...TWO SUPER-CRIMINALS WHO HAVE BATTLED THE AVENGERS.
OOMPH!
UNNGH!
MY WHOLE BODY...SO HEAVY...
SMASH

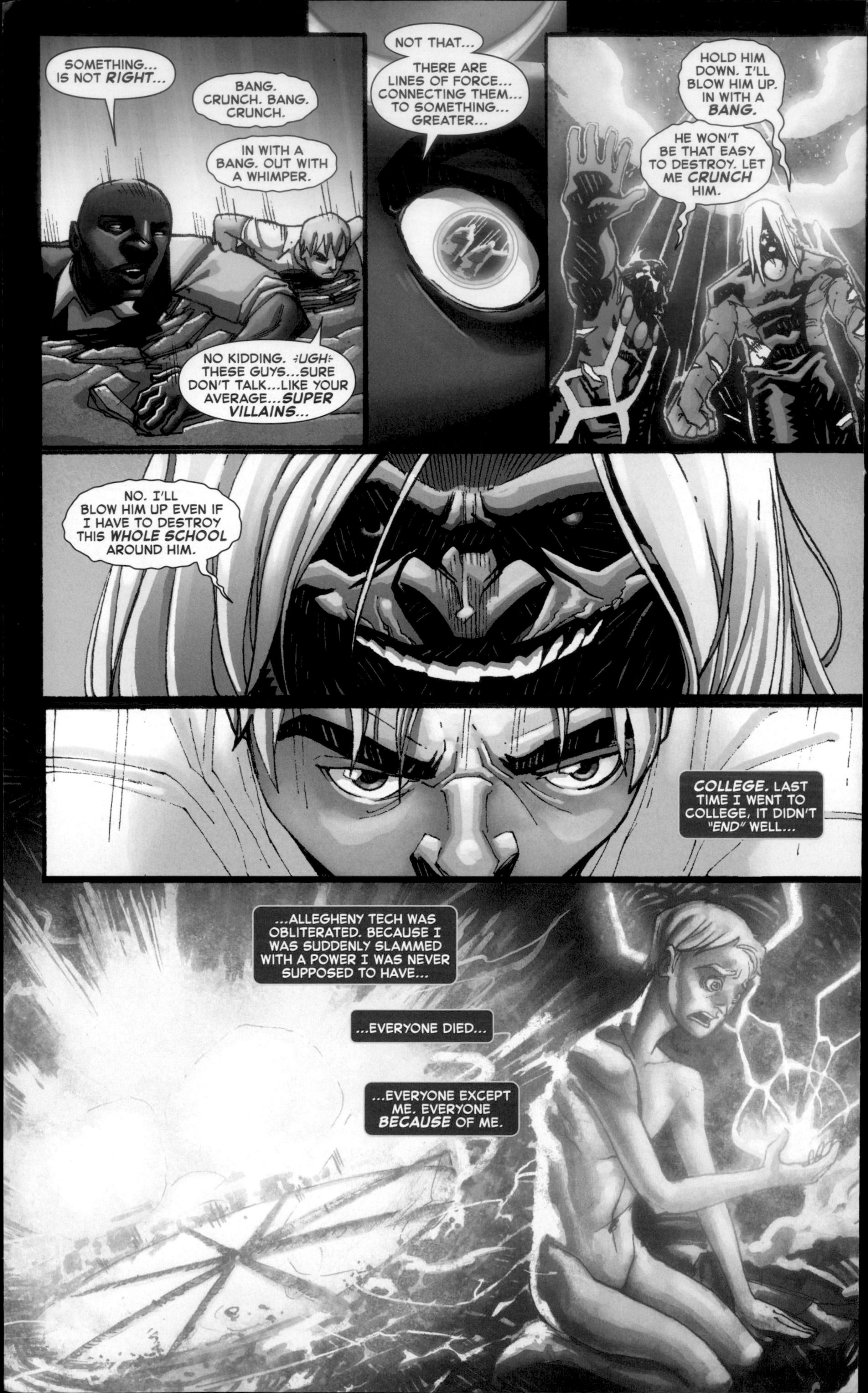
SOMETHING... IS NOT RIGHT...
BANG. CRUNCH. BANG. CRUNCH.
IN WITH A BANG. OUT WITH A WHIMPER.
NO KIDDING. ÷UGH÷ THESE GUYS...SURE DON'T TALK...LIKE YOUR AVERAGE...SUPER VILLAINS...
NOT THAT...
THERE ARE LINES OF FORCE... CONNECTING THEM... TO SOMETHING... GREATER...
HOLD HIM DOWN. I'LL BLOW HIM UP. IN WITH A BANG.
HE WON'T BE THAT EASY TO DESTROY. LET ME CRUNCH HIM.
NO. I'LL BLOW HIM UP EVEN IF I HAVE TO DESTROY THIS WHOLE SCHOOL AROUND HIM.
COLLEGE. LAST TIME I WENT TO COLLEGE, IT DIDN'T "END" WELL...
...ALLEGHENY TECH WAS OBLITERATED. BECAUSE I WAS SUDDENLY SLAMMED WITH A POWER I WAS NEVER SUPPOSED TO HAVE...
...EVERYONE DIED...
...EVERYONE EXCEPT ME. EVERYONE BECAUSE OF ME.

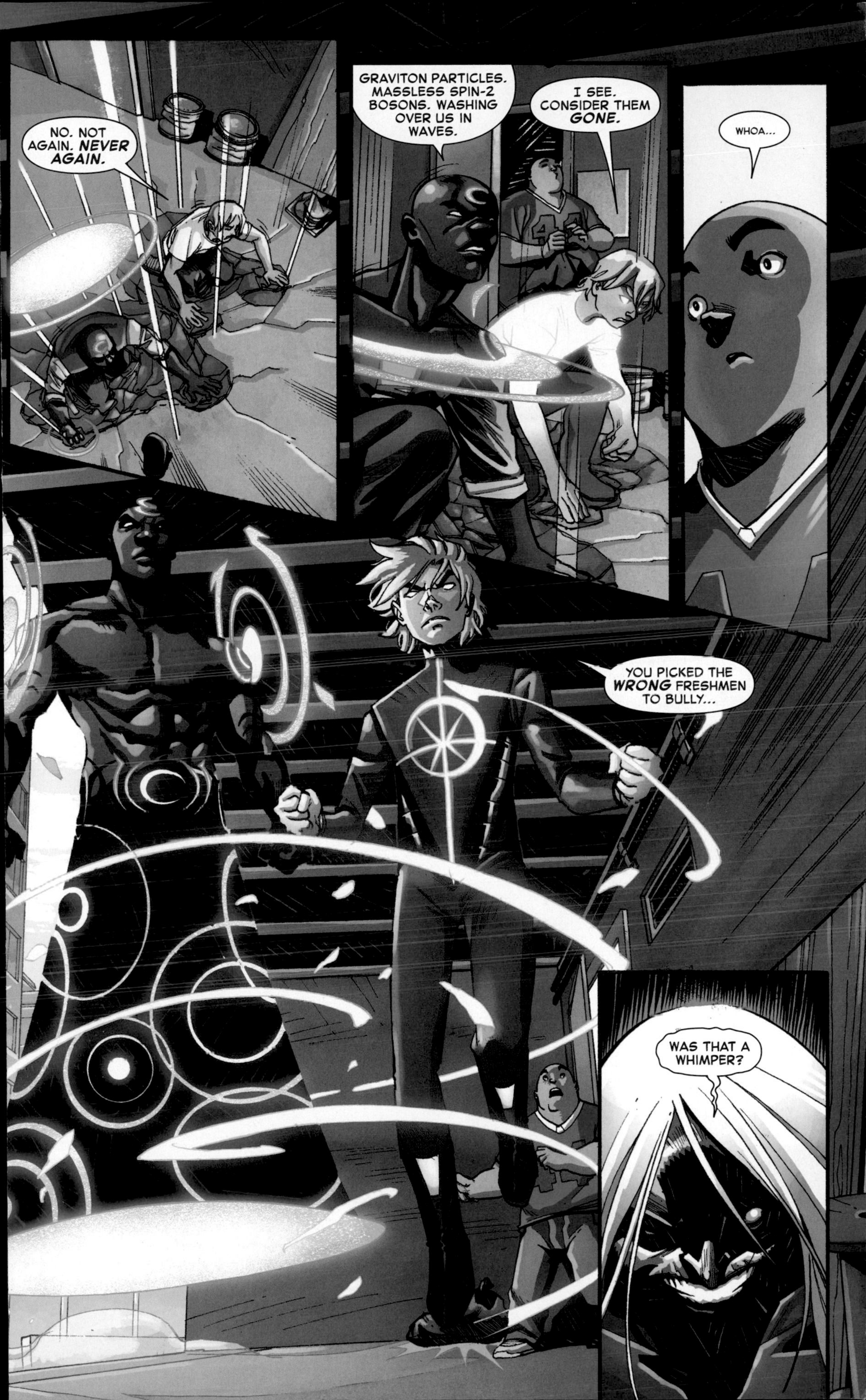
NO. NOT AGAIN. NEVER AGAIN.
GRAVITON PARTICLES. MASSLESS SPIN-2 BOSONS. WASHING OVER US IN WAVES.
I SEE. CONSIDER THEM GONE.
WHOA...
YOU PICKED THE WRONG FRESHMEN TO BULLY...
WAS THAT A WHIMPER?

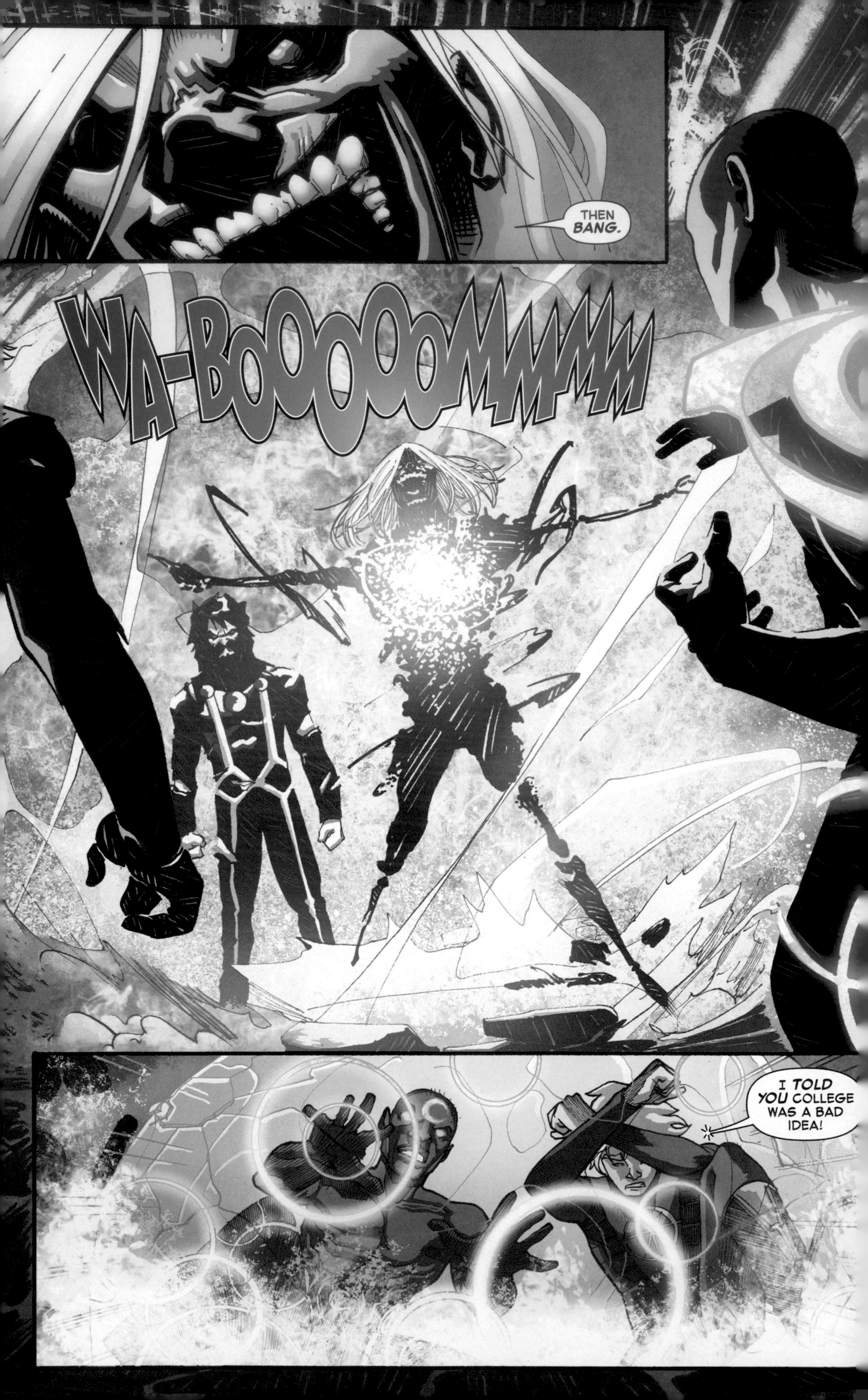
THEN BANG.
WA-BOOOOOMMMM
I TOLD YOU COLLEGE WAS A BAD IDEA!

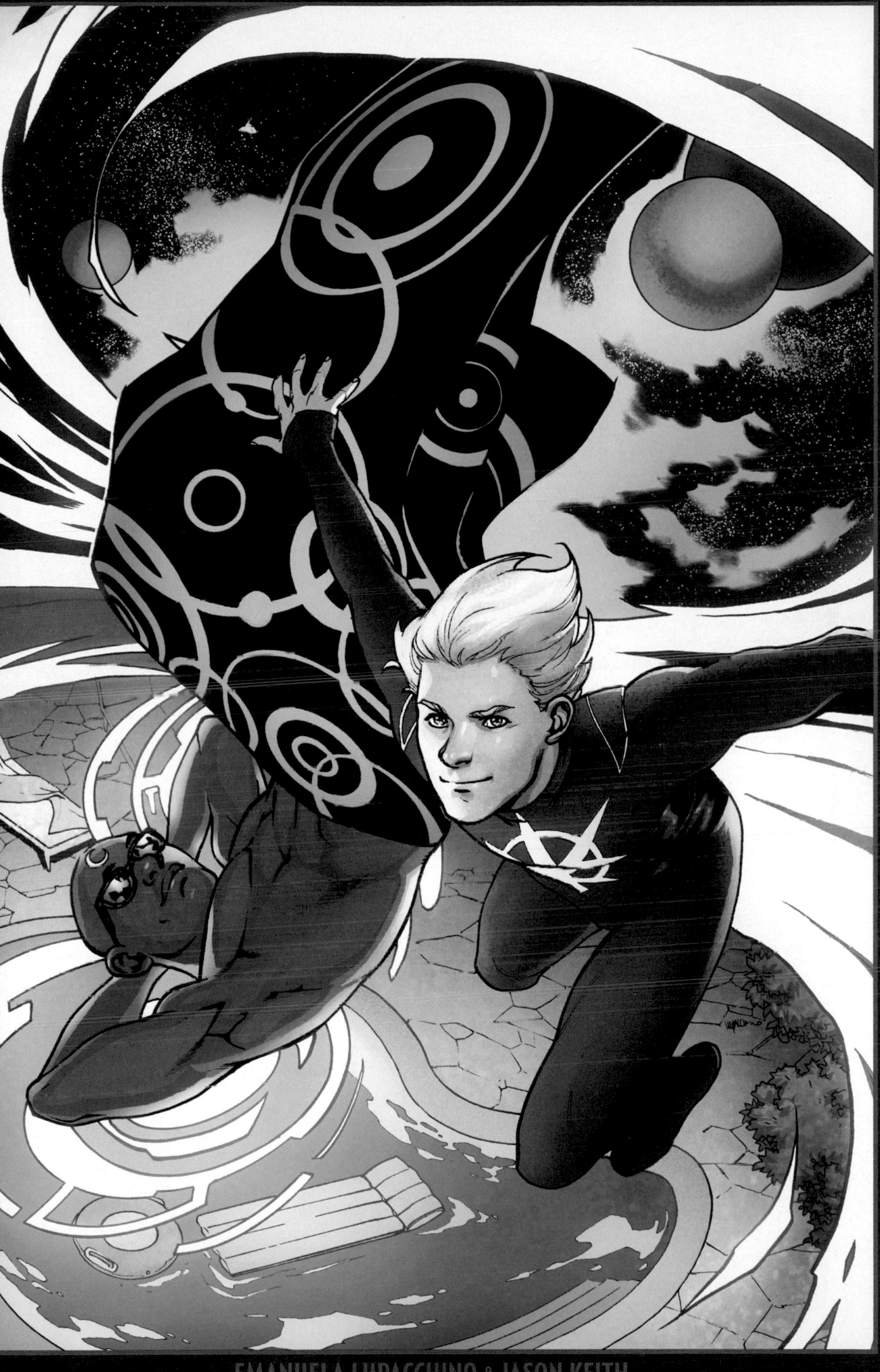

EMANUELA LUPACCHINO & JASON KEITH

1 VARIANT

CHAPTER 2: ORIENTATION

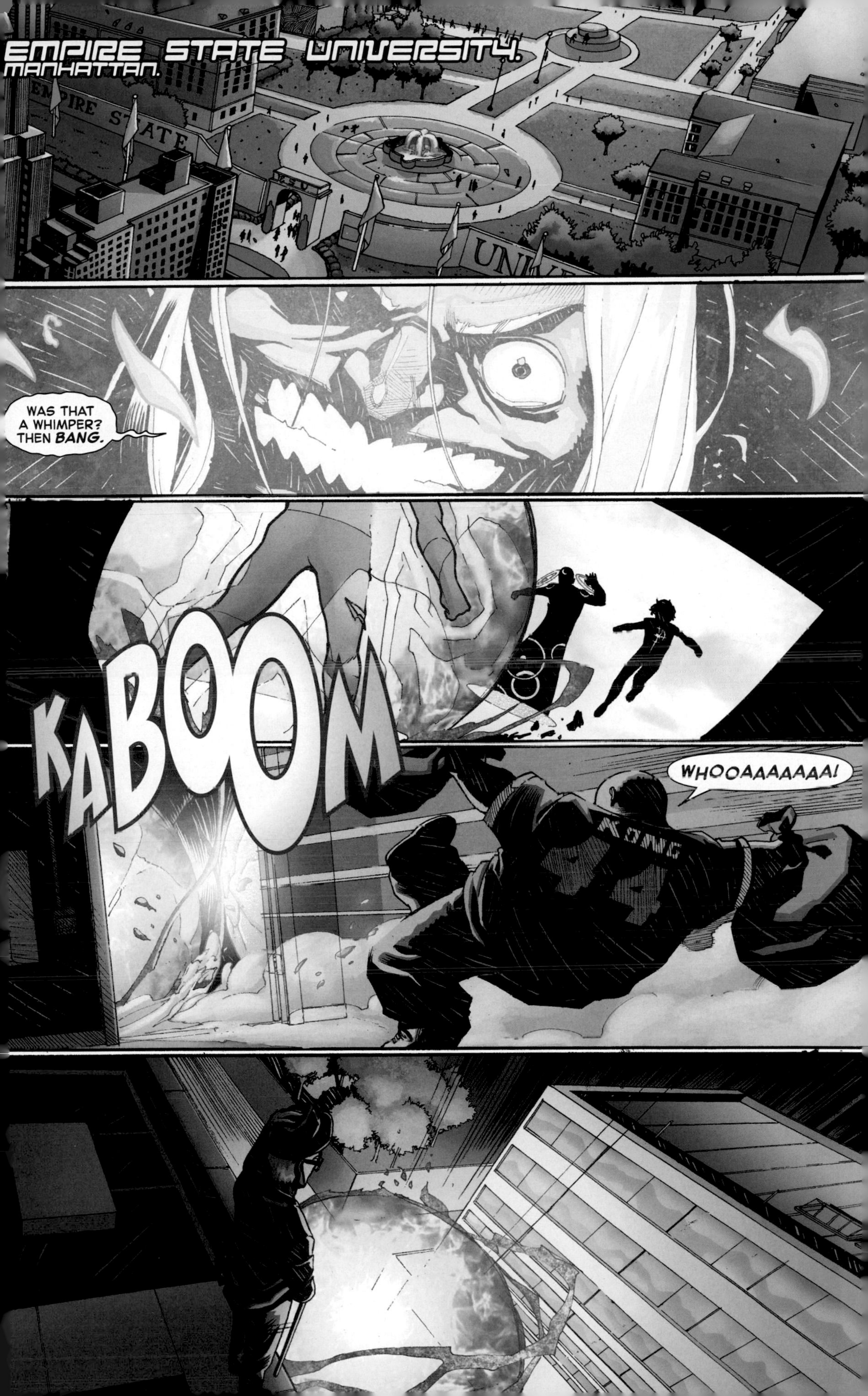
EMPIRE STATE UNIVERSITY.
MANHATTAN.
WAS THAT A WHIMPER? THEN BANG.
KABOOM
WHOOAAAAAAA!

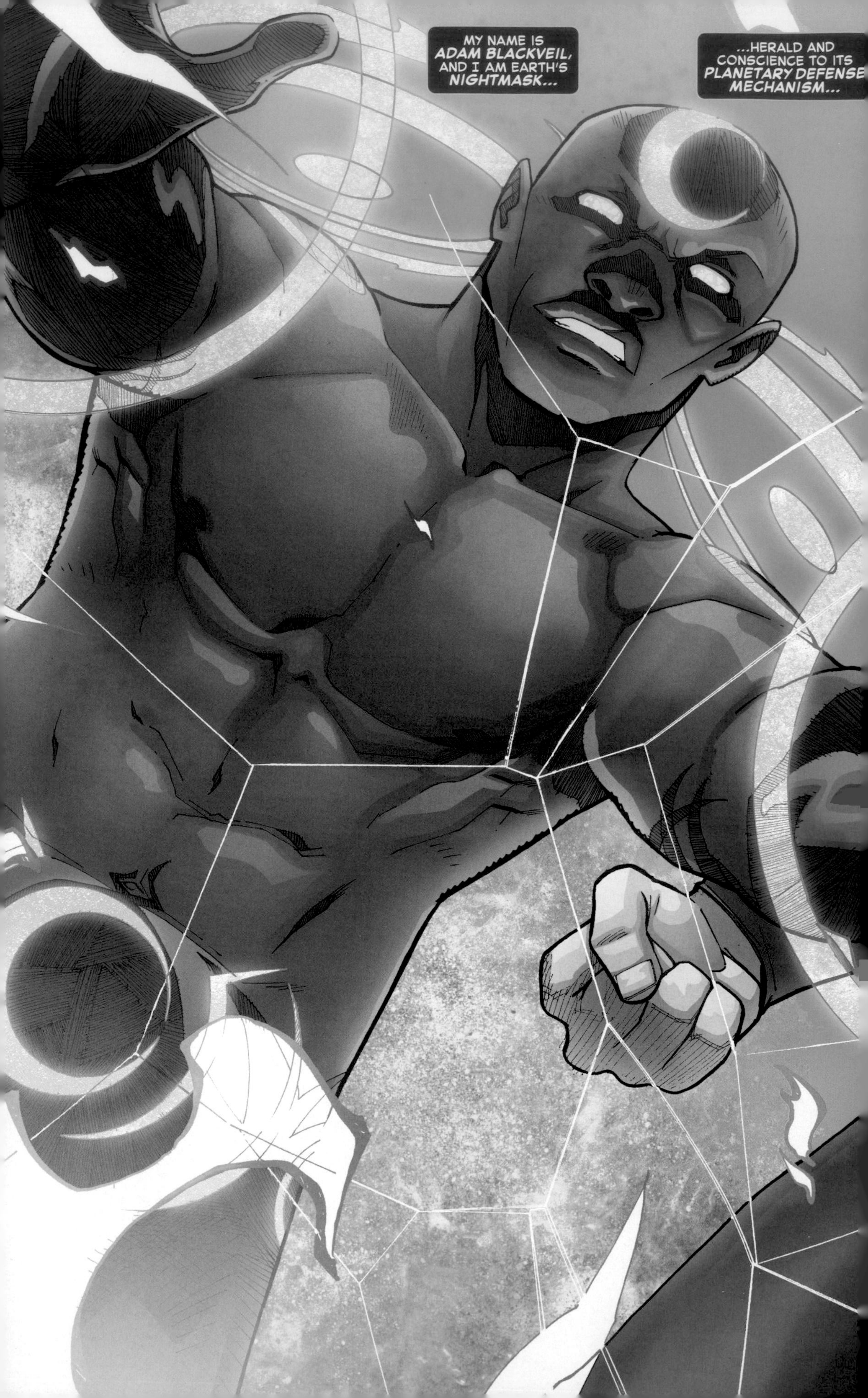
MY NAME IS *ADAM BLACKVEIL,* AND I AM EARTH'S *NIGHTMASK...*
...HERALD AND CONSCIENCE TO ITS *PLANETARY DEFENSE MECHANISM...*

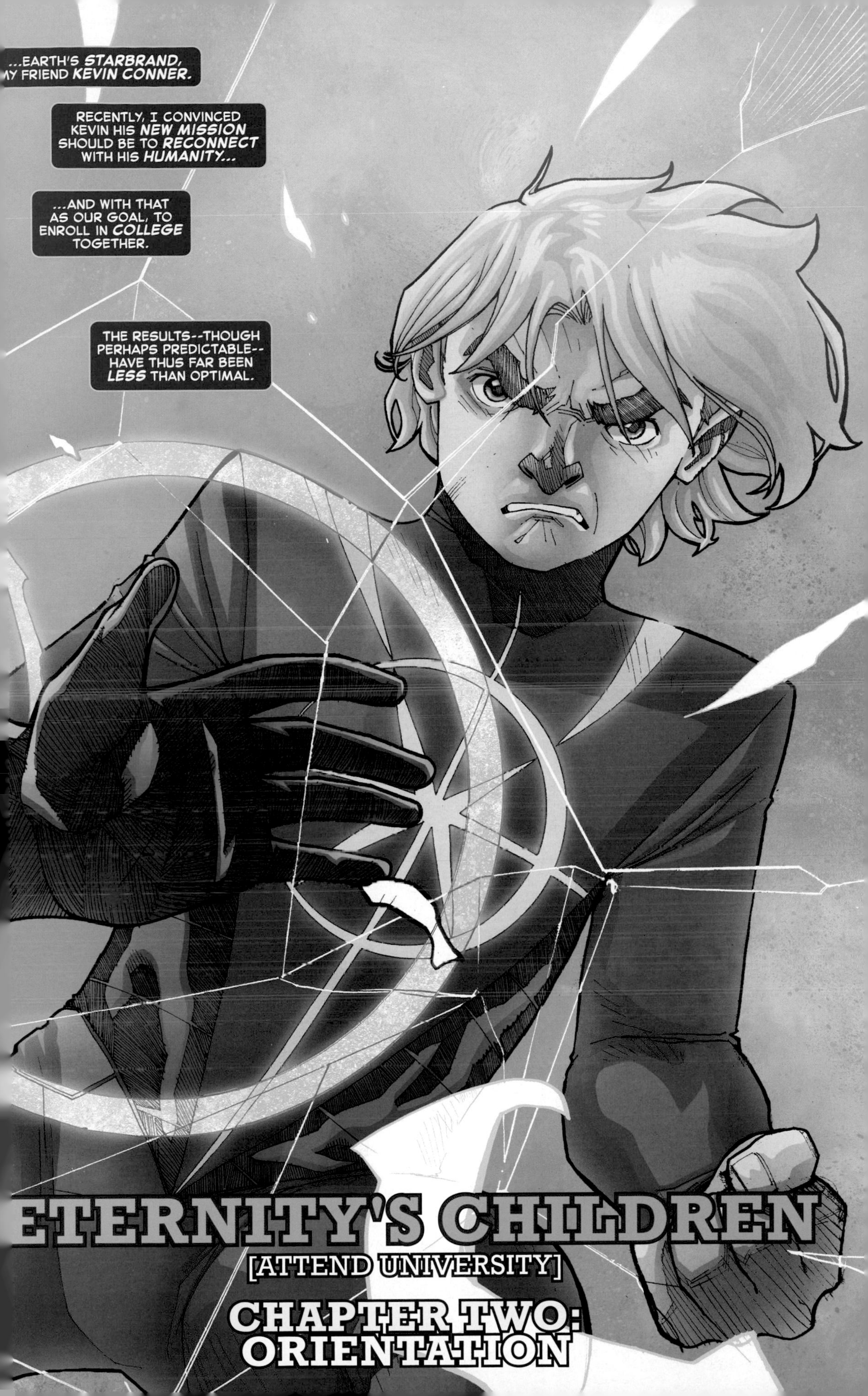
...EARTH'S STARBRAND, MY FRIEND KEVIN CONNER.
RECENTLY, I CONVINCED KEVIN HIS NEW MISSION SHOULD BE TO RECONNECT WITH HIS HUMANITY...
...AND WITH THAT AS OUR GOAL, TO ENROLL IN COLLEGE TOGETHER.
THE RESULTS--THOUGH PERHAPS PREDICTABLE--HAVE THUS FAR BEEN LESS THAN OPTIMAL.
ETERNITY'S CHILDREN
[ATTEND UNIVERSITY]
CHAPTER TWO: ORIENTATION

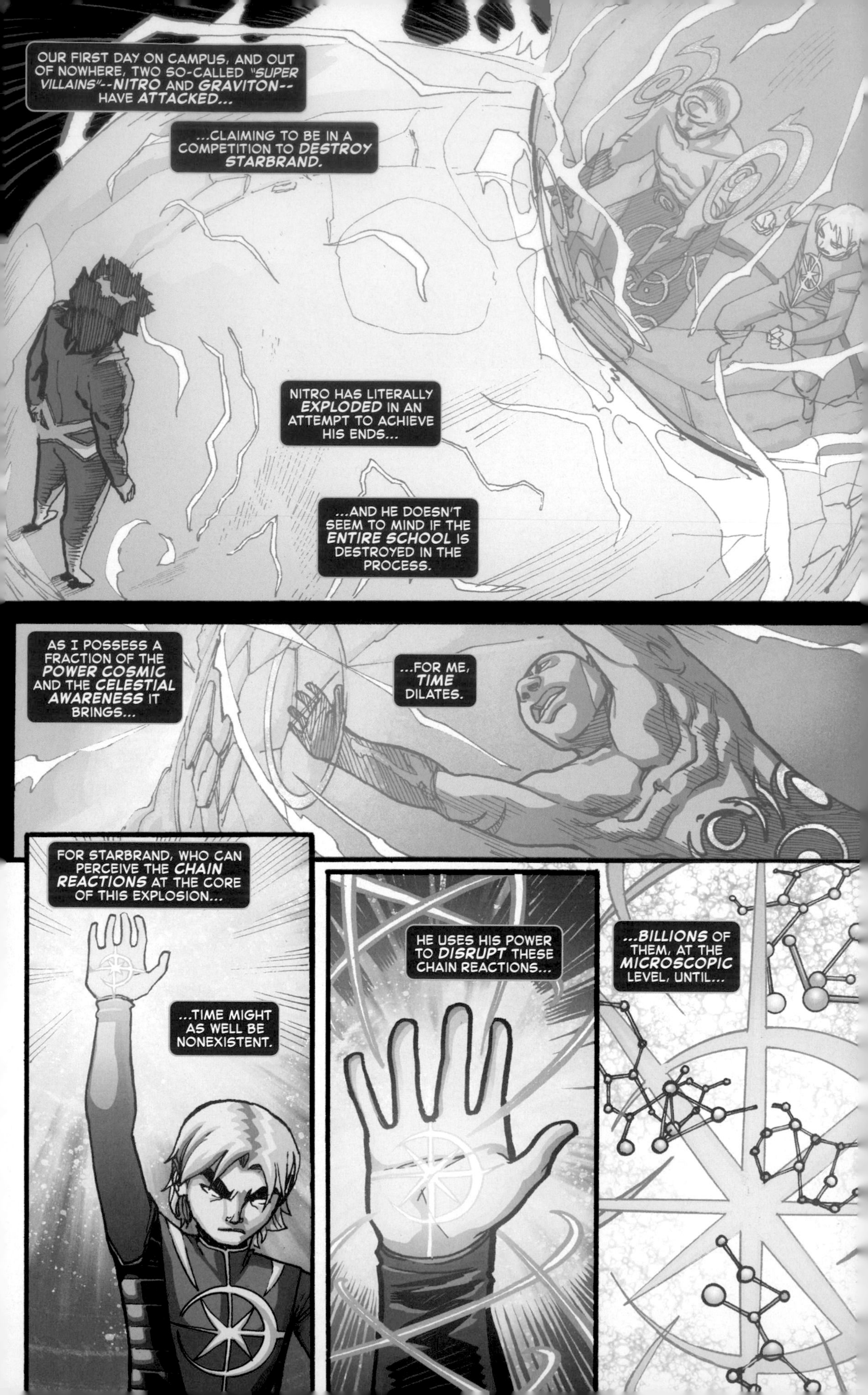
OUR FIRST DAY ON CAMPUS, AND OUT OF NOWHERE, TWO SO-CALLED "SUPER VILLAINS"--NITRO AND GRAVITON--HAVE ATTACKED...
...CLAIMING TO BE IN A COMPETITION TO DESTROY STARBRAND.
NITRO HAS LITERALLY EXPLODED IN AN ATTEMPT TO ACHIEVE HIS ENDS...
...AND HE DOESN'T SEEM TO MIND IF THE ENTIRE SCHOOL IS DESTROYED IN THE PROCESS.
AS I POSSESS A FRACTION OF THE POWER COSMIC AND THE CELESTIAL AWARENESS IT BRINGS...
...FOR ME, TIME DILATES.
FOR STARBRAND, WHO CAN PERCEIVE THE CHAIN REACTIONS AT THE CORE OF THIS EXPLOSION...
...TIME MIGHT AS WELL BE NONEXISTENT.
HE USES HIS POWER TO DISRUPT THESE CHAIN REACTIONS...
...BILLIONS OF THEM, AT THE MICROSCOPIC LEVEL, UNTIL...

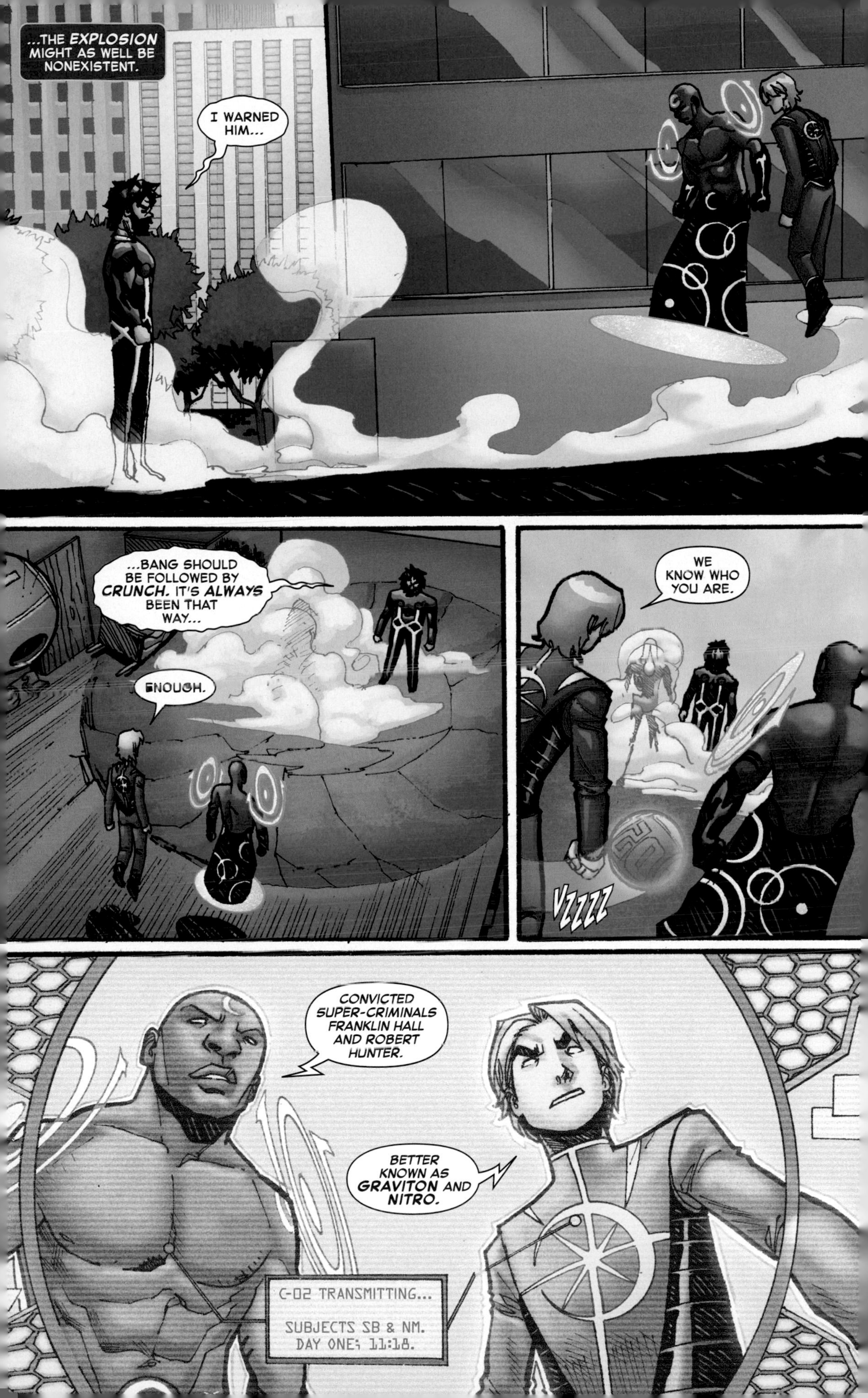
...THE EXPLOSION MIGHT AS WELL BE NONEXISTENT.
I WARNED HIM...
...BANG SHOULD BE FOLLOWED BY CRUNCH. IT'S ALWAYS BEEN THAT WAY...
ENOUGH.
WE KNOW WHO YOU ARE.
VZZZZ
CONVICTED SUPER-CRIMINALS FRANKLIN HALL AND ROBERT HUNTER.
BETTER KNOWN AS GRAVITON AND NITRO.
C-02 TRANSMITTING...
SUBJECTS SB & NM.
DAY ONE; 11:18.

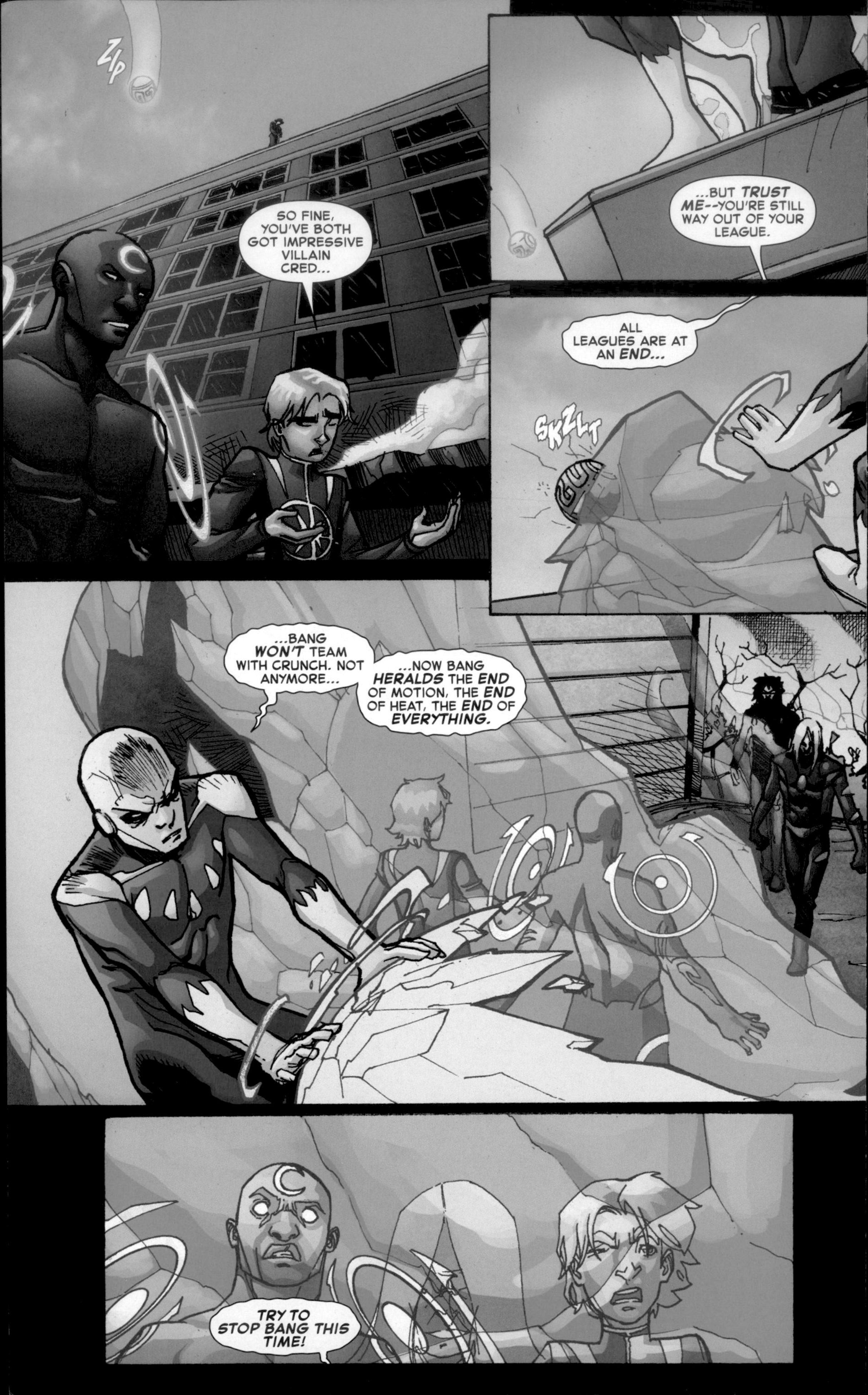
ZIP
SO FINE, YOU'VE BOTH GOT IMPRESSIVE VILLAIN CRED...
...BUT TRUST ME--YOU'RE STILL WAY OUT OF YOUR LEAGUE.
ALL LEAGUES ARE AT AN END...
SKZLT
...BANG WON'T TEAM WITH CRUNCH. NOT ANYMORE...
...NOW BANG HERALDS THE END OF MOTION, THE END OF HEAT, THE END OF EVERYTHING.
TRY TO STOP BANG THIS TIME!

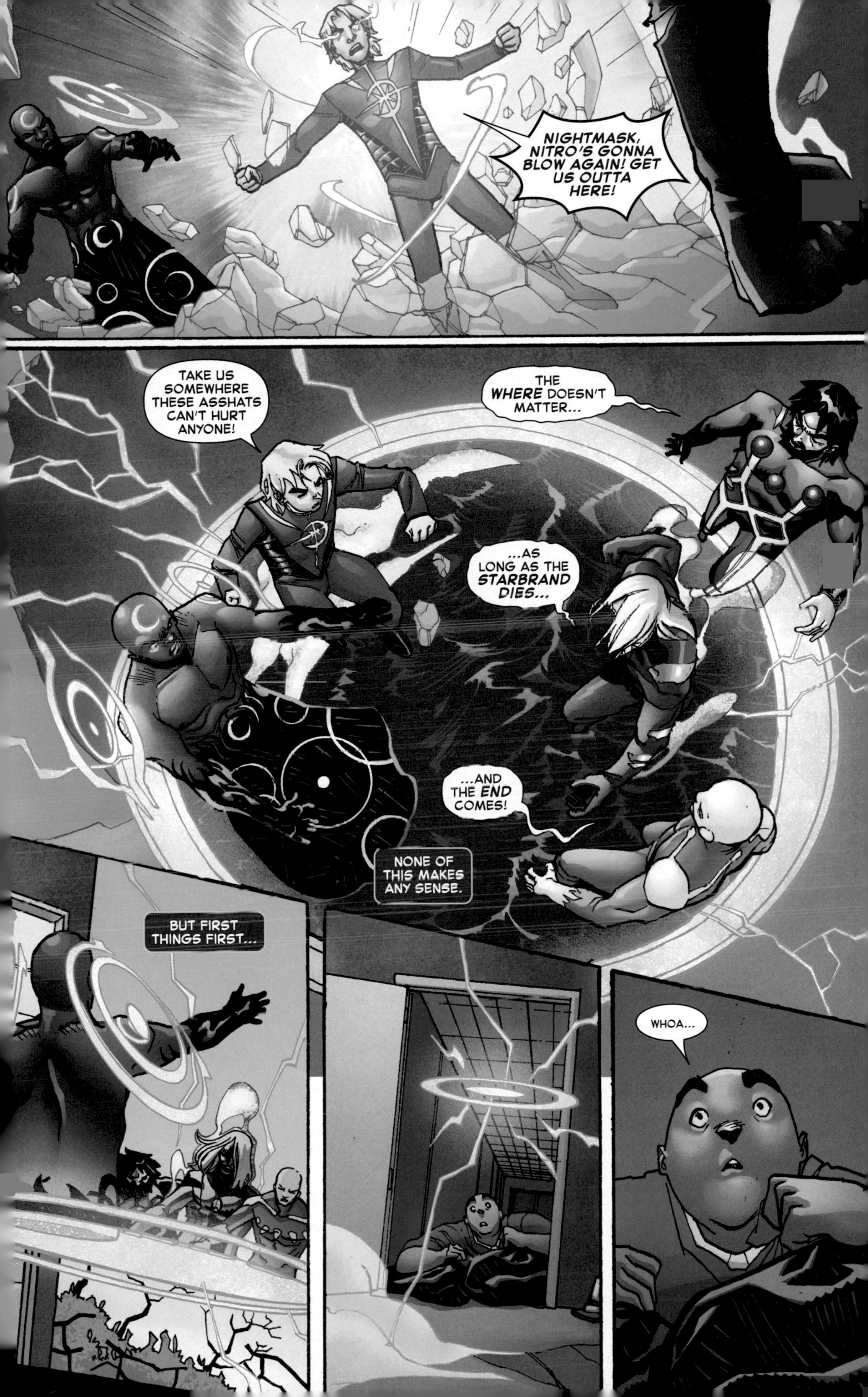
NIGHTMASK, NITRO'S GONNA BLOW AGAIN! GET US OUTTA HERE!
TAKE US SOMEWHERE THESE ASSHATS CAN'T HURT ANYONE!
THE WHERE DOESN'T MATTER...
...AS LONG AS THE STARBRAND DIES...
...AND THE END COMES!
NONE OF THIS MAKES ANY SENSE.
BUT FIRST THINGS FIRST...
WHOA...

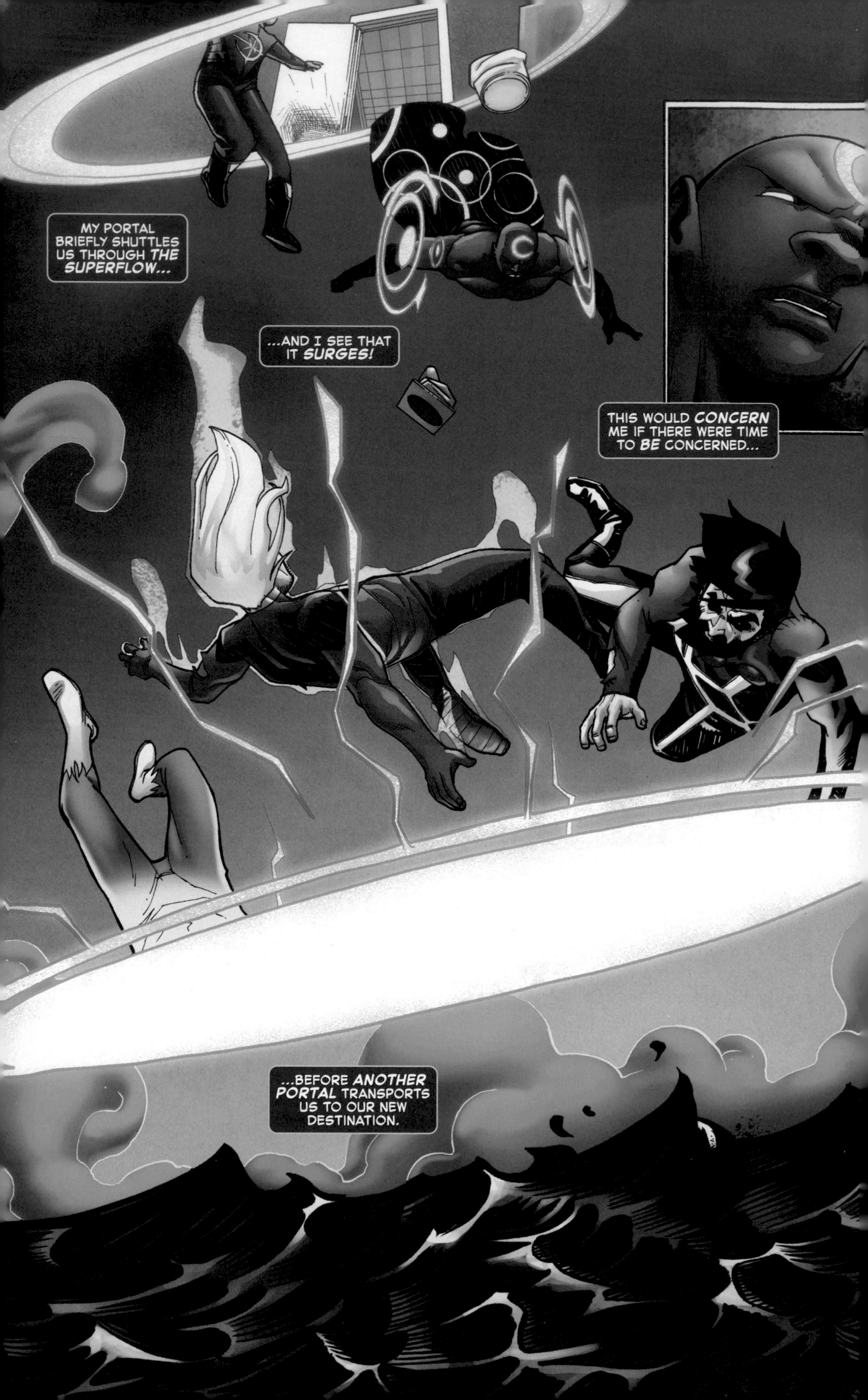
MY PORTAL BRIEFLY SHUTTLES US THROUGH THE SUPERFLOW...
...AND I SEE THAT IT SURGES!
THIS WOULD CONCERN ME IF THERE WERE TIME TO BE CONCERNED...
...BEFORE ANOTHER PORTAL TRANSPORTS US TO OUR NEW DESTINATION.

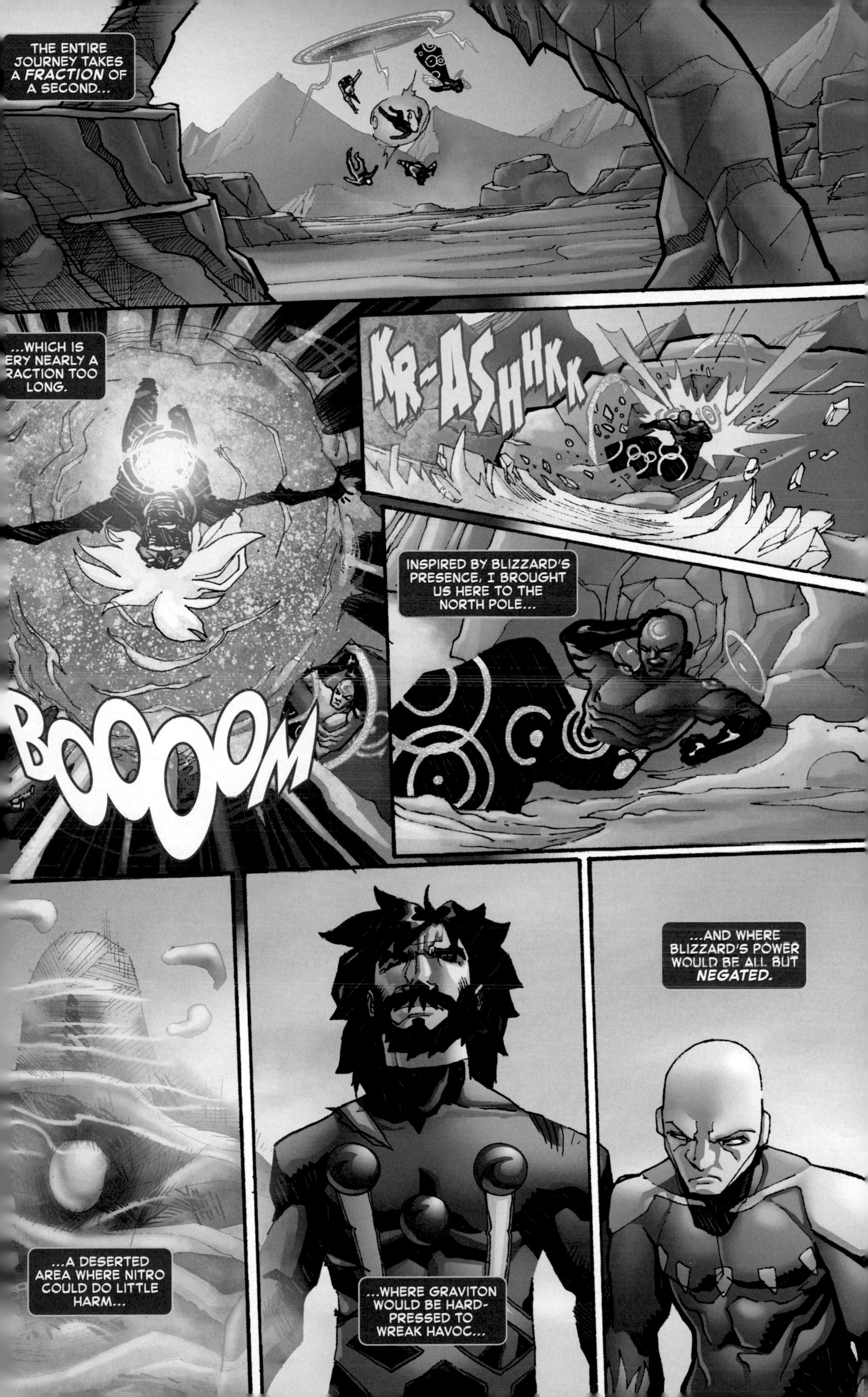

THE ENTIRE JOURNEY TAKES A *FRACTION* OF A SECOND...
...WHICH IS ERY NEARLY A RACTION TOO LONG.
KR-ASHHKK
BOOOOM
INSPIRED BY BLIZZARD'S PRESENCE, I BROUGHT US HERE TO THE NORTH POLE...
...A DESERTED AREA WHERE NITRO COULD DO LITTLE HARM...
...WHERE GRAVITON WOULD BE HARD-PRESSED TO WREAK HAVOC...
...AND WHERE BLIZZARD'S POWER WOULD BE ALL BUT *NEGATED.*

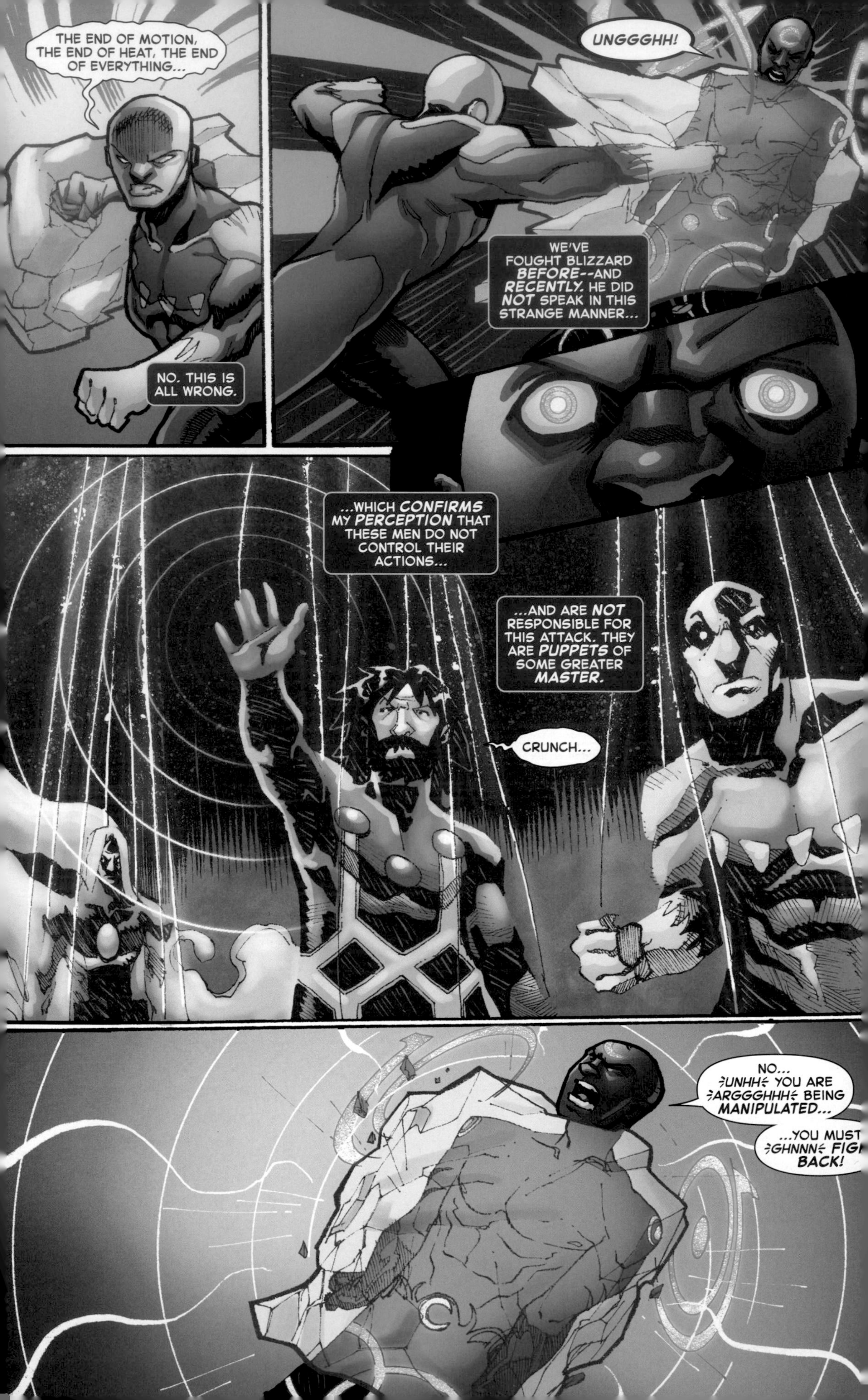
THE END OF MOTION, THE END OF HEAT, THE END OF EVERYTHING...
NO. THIS IS ALL WRONG.
UNGGGHH!
WE'VE FOUGHT BLIZZARD BEFORE--AND RECENTLY. HE DID NOT SPEAK IN THIS STRANGE MANNER...
...WHICH CONFIRMS MY PERCEPTION THAT THESE MEN DO NOT CONTROL THEIR ACTIONS...
...AND ARE NOT RESPONSIBLE FOR THIS ATTACK. THEY ARE PUPPETS OF SOME GREATER MASTER.
CRUNCH...
NO... UNHH YOU ARE ARGGGHHH BEING MANIPULATED...
...YOU MUST GHNNN FIG BACK!

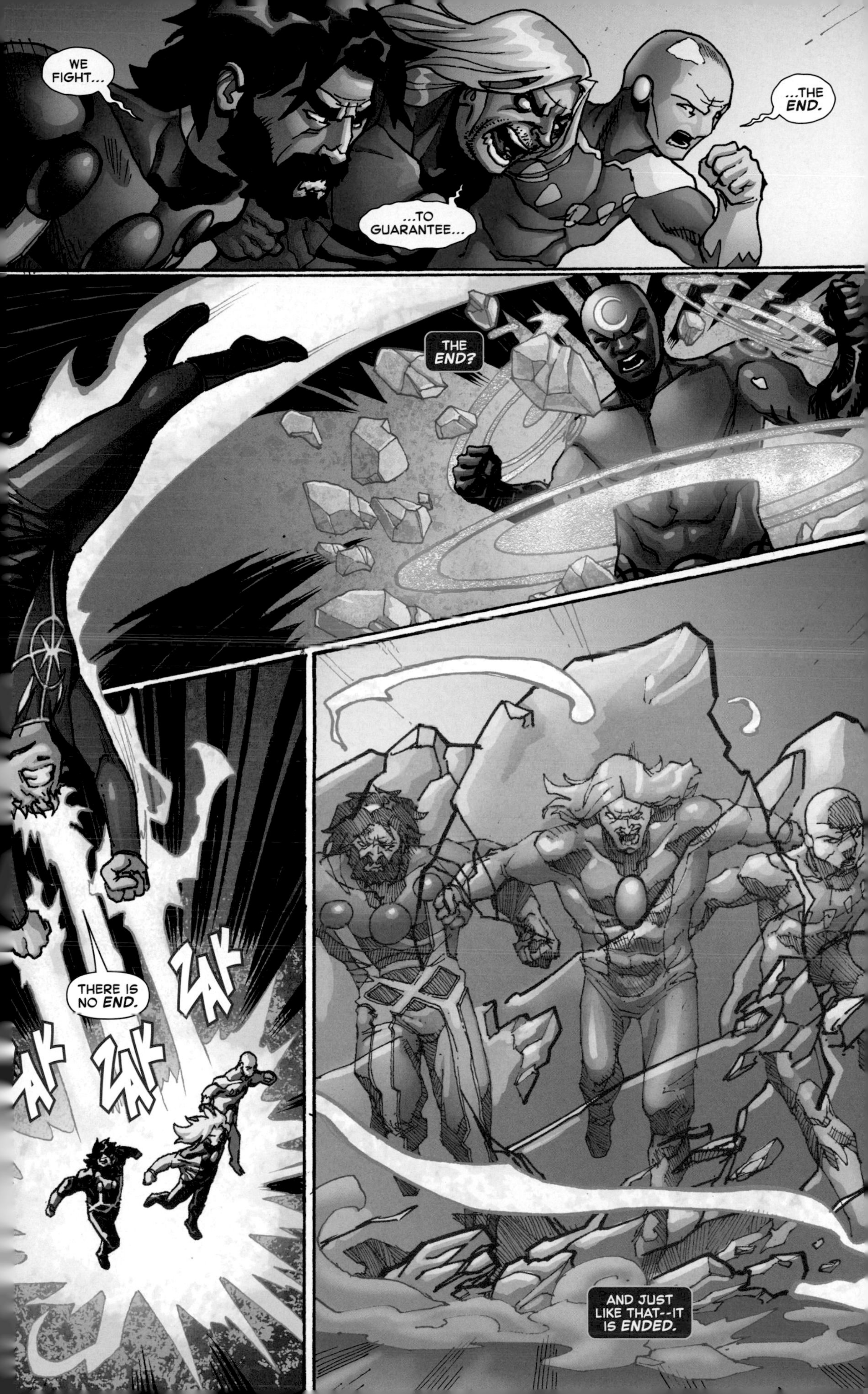
WE FIGHT...
...TO GUARANTEE...
...THE END.
THE END?
THERE IS NO END.
ZAK
ZAK
ZAK
AND JUST LIKE THAT--IT IS ENDED.

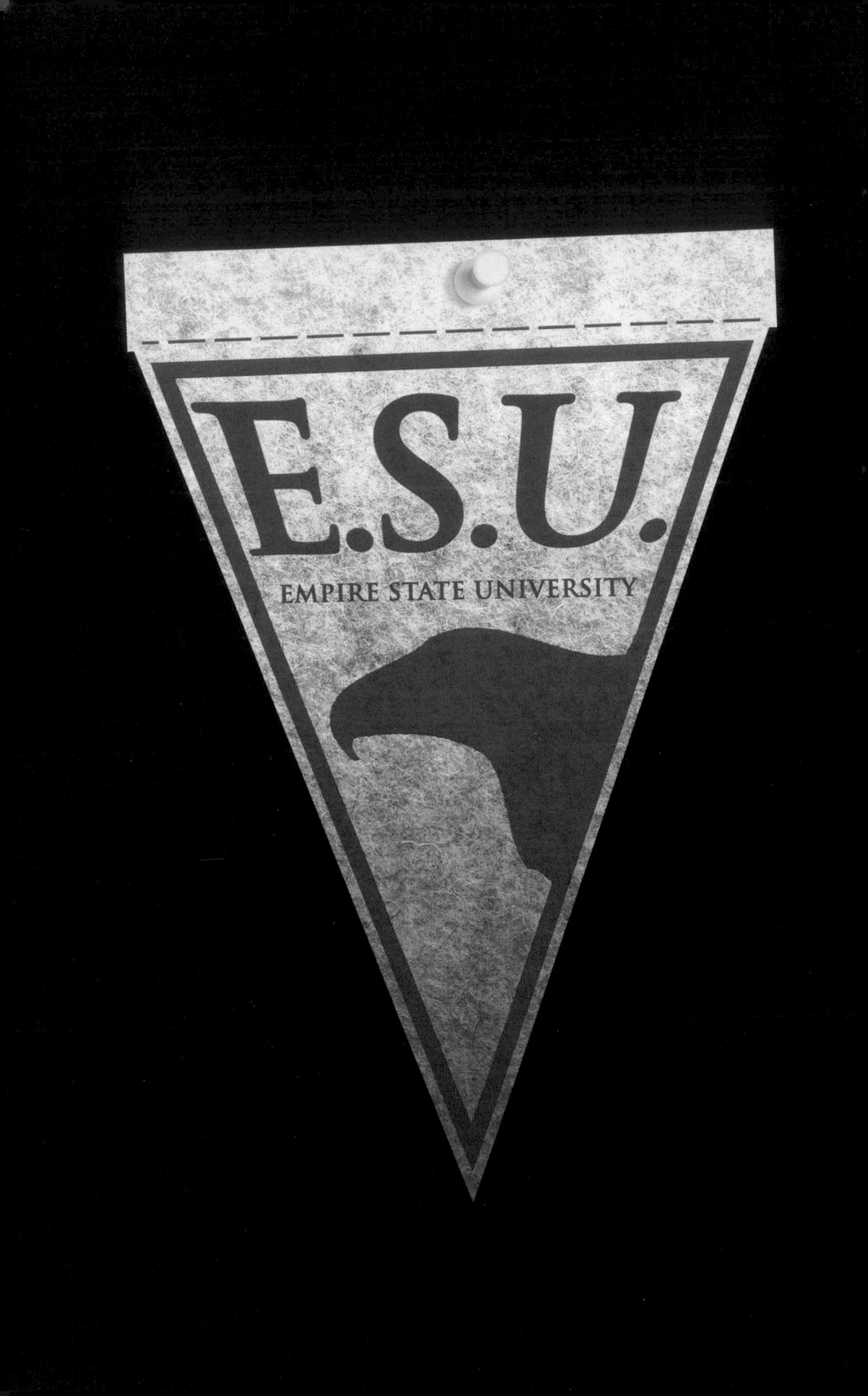
E.S.U.
EMPIRE STATE UNIVERSITY

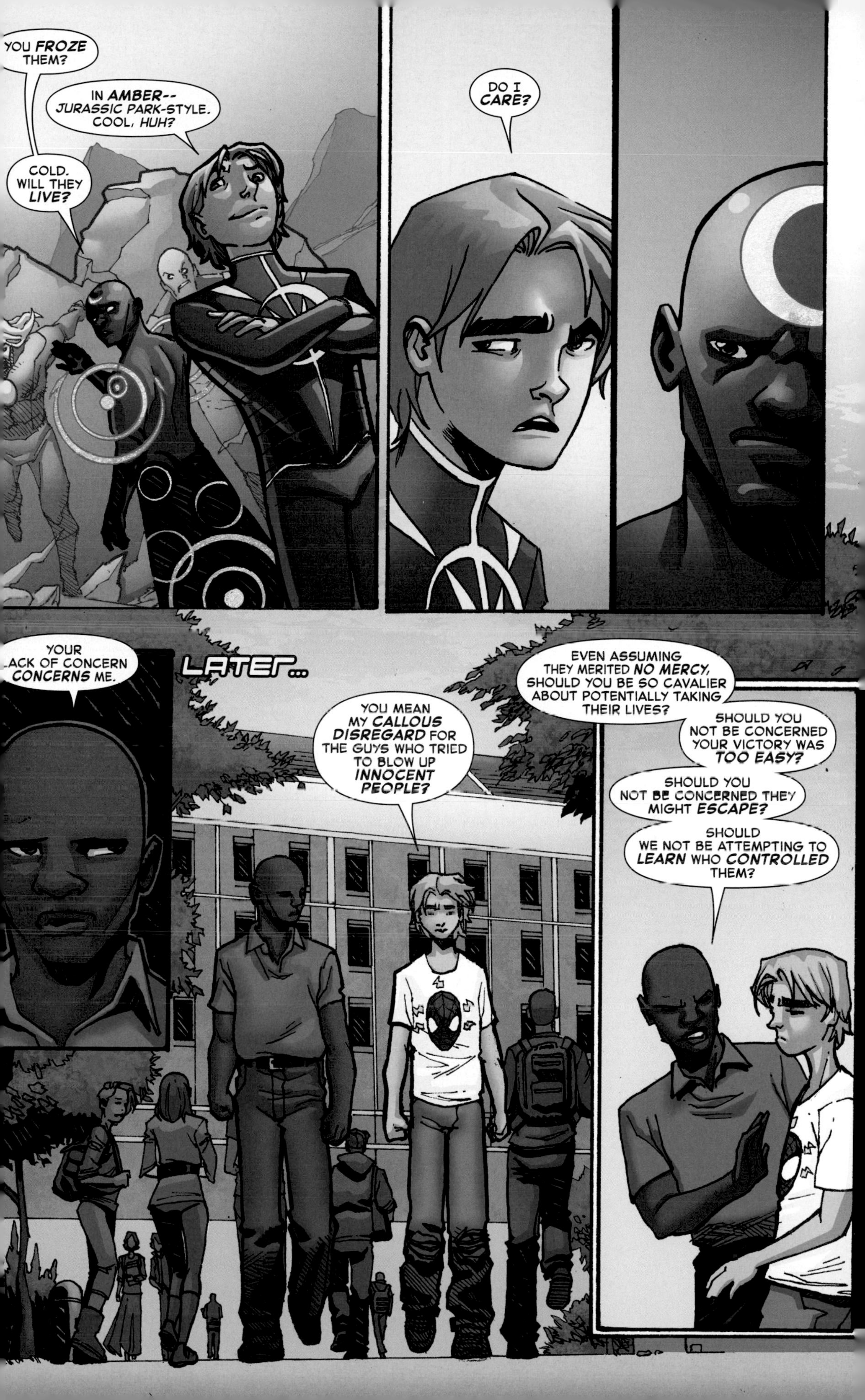

YOU FROZE THEM?
IN AMBER-- JURASSIC PARK-STYLE. COOL, HUH?
COLD. WILL THEY LIVE?
DO I CARE?
YOUR LACK OF CONCERN CONCERNS ME.
LATER...
YOU MEAN MY CALLOUS DISREGARD FOR THE GUYS WHO TRIED TO BLOW UP INNOCENT PEOPLE?
EVEN ASSUMING THEY MERITED NO MERCY, SHOULD YOU BE SO CAVALIER ABOUT POTENTIALLY TAKING THEIR LIVES?
SHOULD YOU NOT BE CONCERNED YOUR VICTORY WAS TOO EASY?
SHOULD YOU NOT BE CONCERNED THEY MIGHT ESCAPE?
SHOULD WE NOT BE ATTEMPTING TO LEARN WHO CONTROLLED THEM?

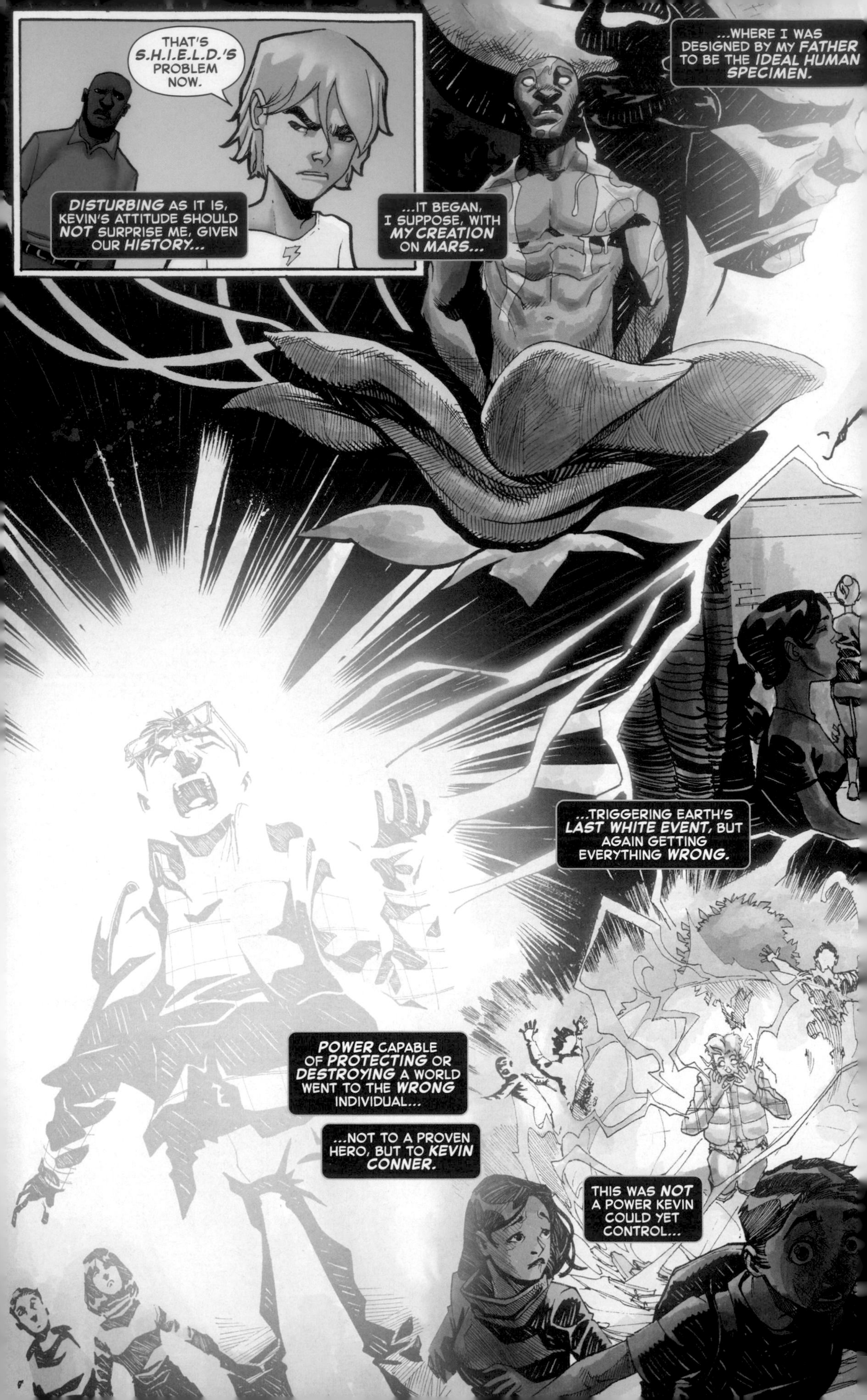

THAT'S S.H.I.E.L.D.'S PROBLEM NOW.
DISTURBING AS IT IS, KEVIN'S ATTITUDE SHOULD NOT SURPRISE ME, GIVEN OUR HISTORY...
...IT BEGAN, I SUPPOSE, WITH MY CREATION ON MARS...
...WHERE I WAS DESIGNED BY MY FATHER TO BE THE IDEAL HUMAN SPECIMEN.
...TRIGGERING EARTH'S LAST WHITE EVENT, BUT AGAIN GETTING EVERYTHING WRONG.
POWER CAPABLE OF PROTECTING OR DESTROYING A WORLD WENT TO THE WRONG INDIVIDUAL...
...NOT TO A PROVEN HERO, BUT TO KEVIN CONNER.
THIS WAS NOT A POWER KEVIN COULD YET CONTROL...

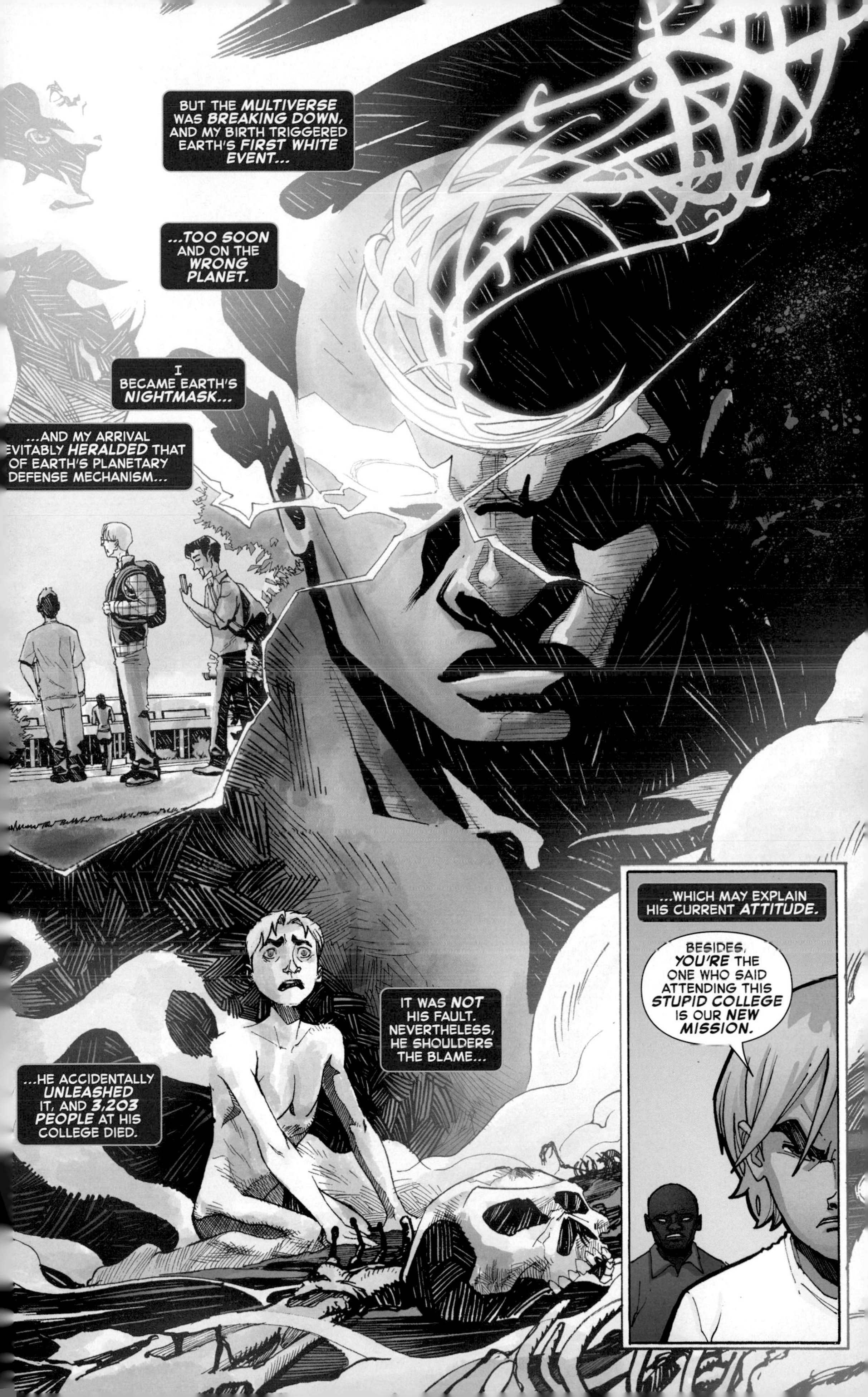
BUT THE MULTIVERSE WAS BREAKING DOWN, AND MY BIRTH TRIGGERED EARTH'S FIRST WHITE EVENT...
...TOO SOON AND ON THE WRONG PLANET.
I BECAME EARTH'S NIGHTMASK...
...AND MY ARRIVAL EVITABLY HERALDED THAT OF EARTH'S PLANETARY DEFENSE MECHANISM...
...HE ACCIDENTALLY UNLEASHED IT, AND 3,203 PEOPLE AT HIS COLLEGE DIED.
IT WAS NOT HIS FAULT. NEVERTHELESS, HE SHOULDERS THE BLAME...
...WHICH MAY EXPLAIN HIS CURRENT ATTITUDE.
BESIDES, YOU'RE THE ONE WHO SAID ATTENDING THIS STUPID COLLEGE IS OUR NEW MISSION.

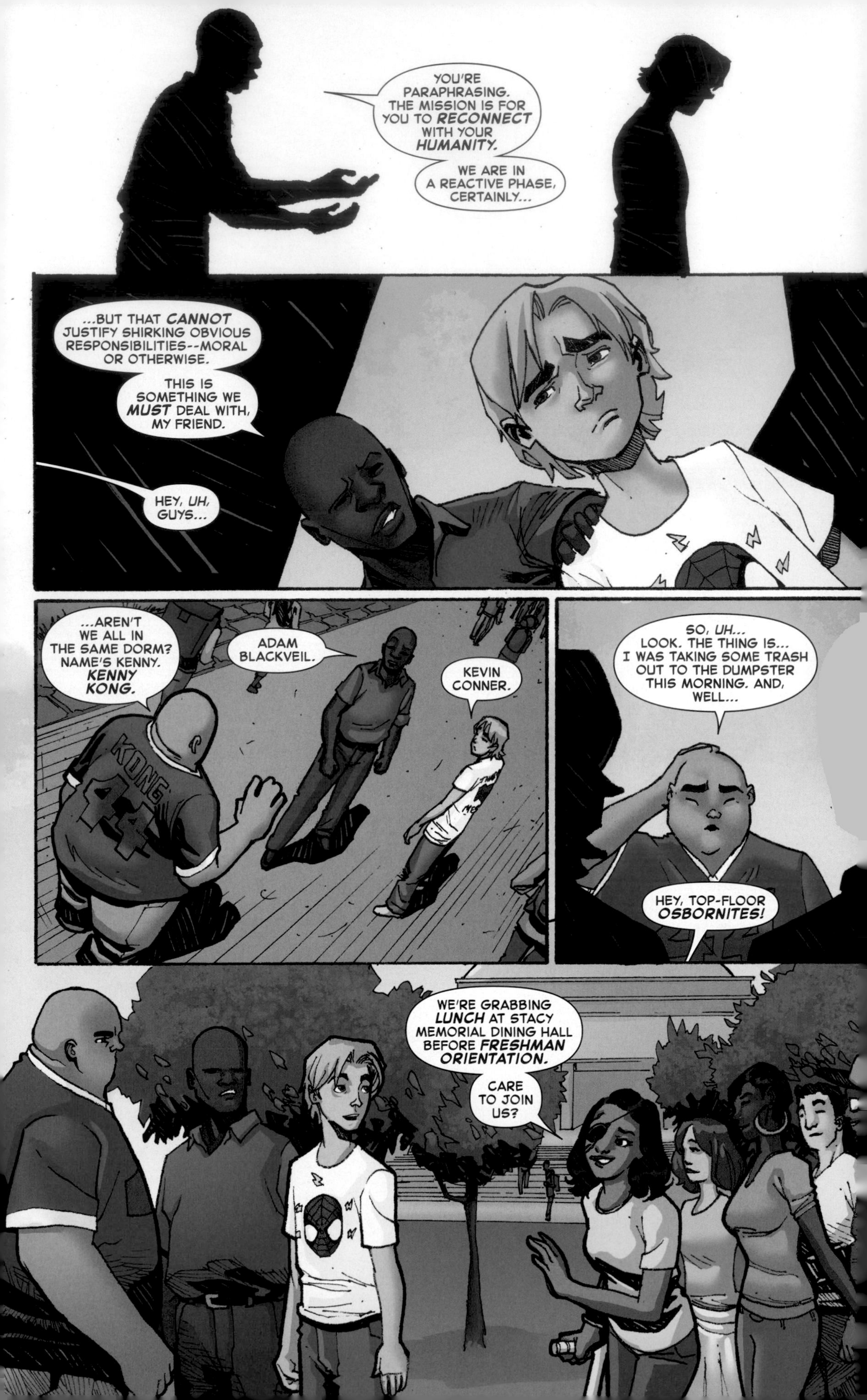

YOU'RE PARAPHRASING. THE MISSION IS FOR YOU TO RECONNECT WITH YOUR HUMANITY.
WE ARE IN A REACTIVE PHASE, CERTAINLY...
...BUT THAT CANNOT JUSTIFY SHIRKING OBVIOUS RESPONSIBILITIES--MORAL OR OTHERWISE.
THIS IS SOMETHING WE MUST DEAL WITH, MY FRIEND.
HEY, UH, GUYS...
...AREN'T WE ALL IN THE SAME DORM? NAME'S KENNY. KENNY KONG.
ADAM BLACKVEIL.
KEVIN CONNER.
KONG 44
SO, UH... LOOK. THE THING IS... I WAS TAKING SOME TRASH OUT TO THE DUMPSTER THIS MORNING. AND, WELL...
HEY, TOP-FLOOR OSBORNITES!
WE'RE GRABBING LUNCH AT STACY MEMORIAL DINING HALL BEFORE FRESHMAN ORIENTATION.
CARE TO JOIN US?

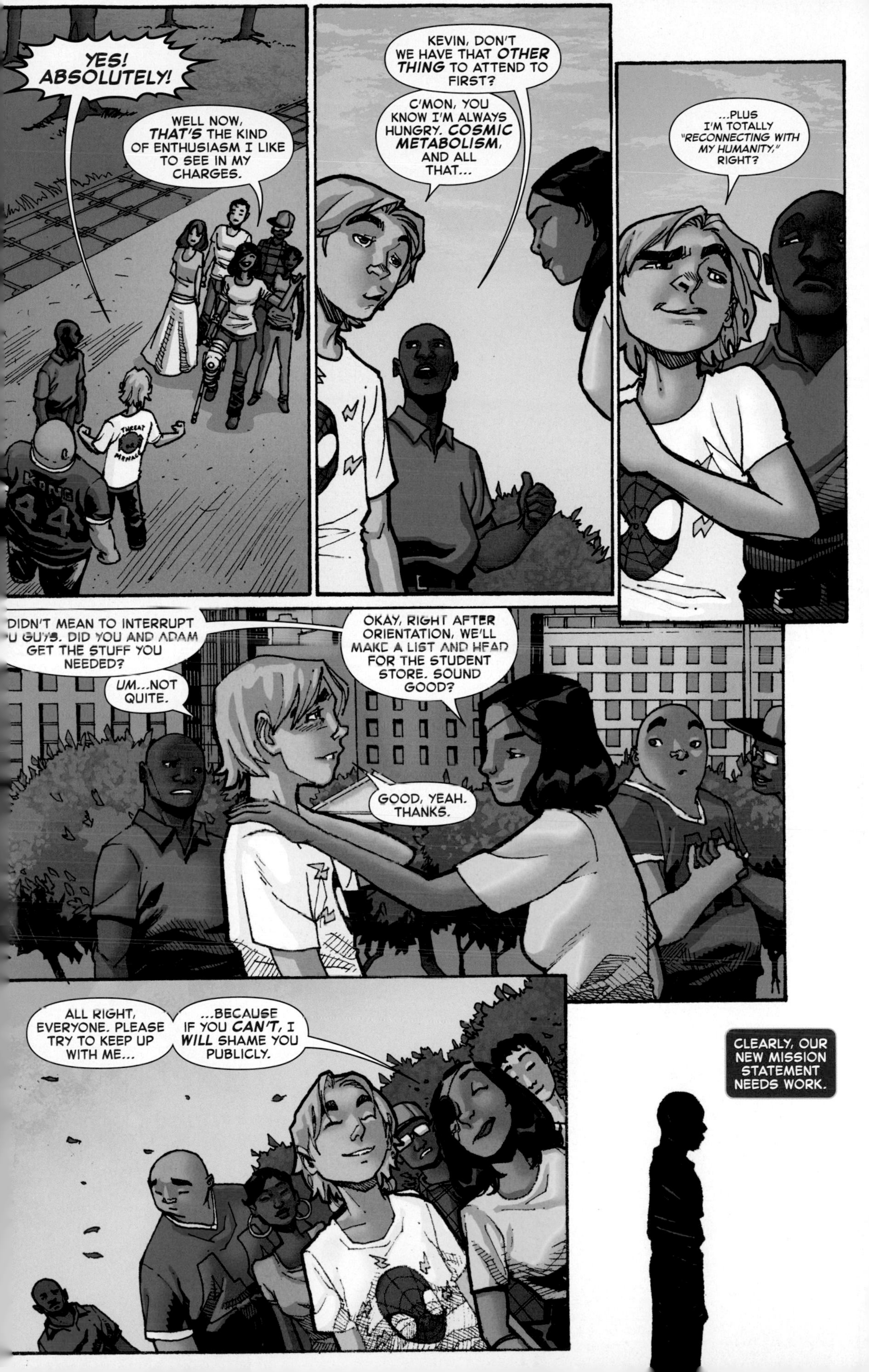
YES! ABSOLUTELY!
WELL NOW, THAT'S THE KIND OF ENTHUSIASM I LIKE TO SEE IN MY CHARGES.
KEVIN, DON'T WE HAVE THAT OTHER THING TO ATTEND TO FIRST?
C'MON, YOU KNOW I'M ALWAYS HUNGRY. COSMIC METABOLISM, AND ALL THAT...
...PLUS I'M TOTALLY "RECONNECTING WITH MY HUMANITY," RIGHT?
DIDN'T MEAN TO INTERRUPT U GUYS. DID YOU AND ADAM GET THE STUFF YOU NEEDED?
UM...NOT QUITE.
OKAY, RIGHT AFTER ORIENTATION, WE'LL MAKE A LIST AND HEAD FOR THE STUDENT STORE. SOUND GOOD?
GOOD, YEAH. THANKS.
ALL RIGHT, EVERYONE. PLEASE TRY TO KEEP UP WITH ME...
...BECAUSE IF YOU CAN'T, I WILL SHAME YOU PUBLICLY.
CLEARLY, OUR NEW MISSION STATEMENT NEEDS WORK.

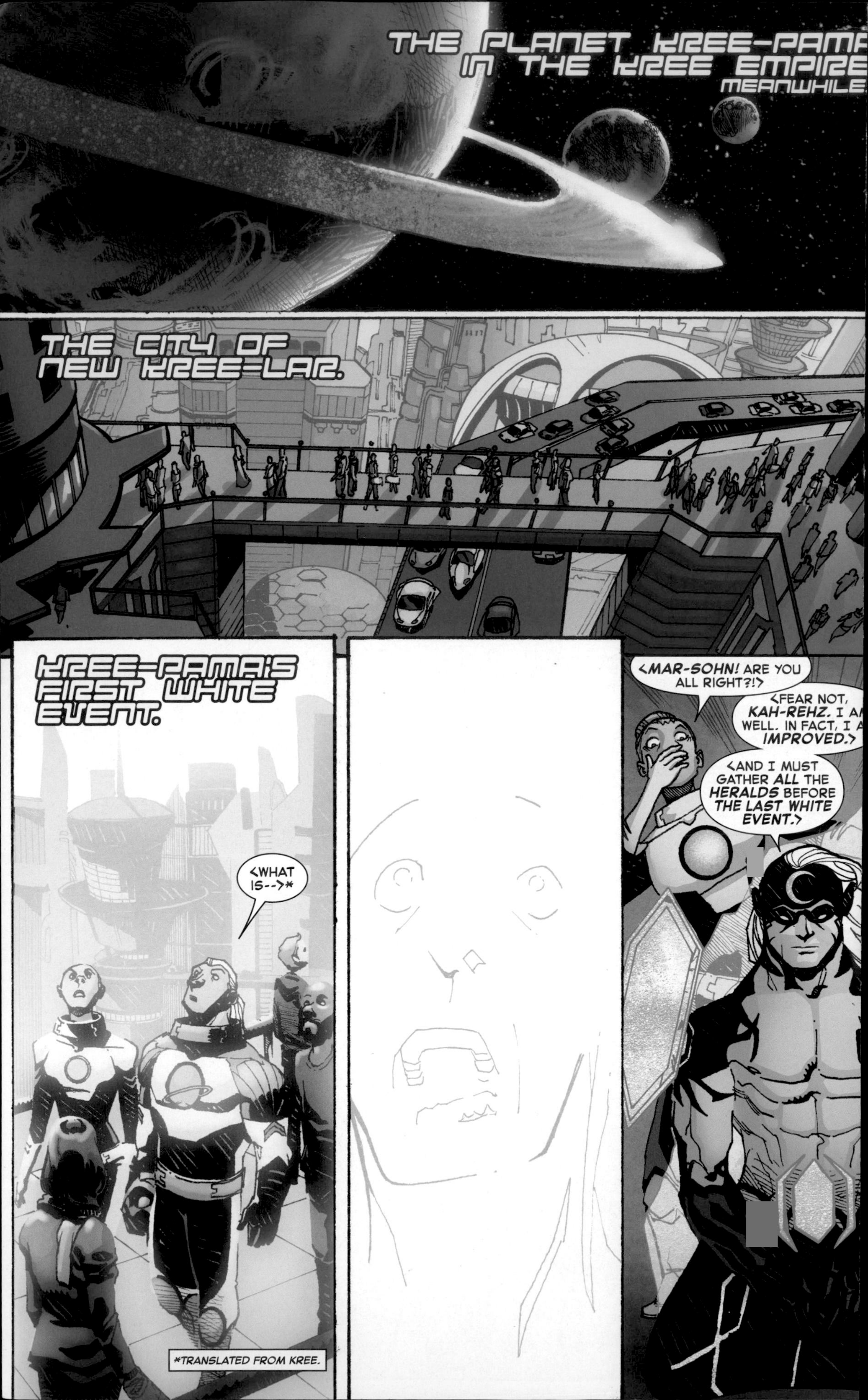

THE PLANET KREE-PAMA
IN THE KREE EMPIRE
MEANWHILE
THE CITY OF NEW KREE-LAR.
KREE-PAMA'S FIRST WHITE EVENT.
<WHAT IS-->*
*TRANSLATED FROM KREE.
<MAR-SOHN! ARE YOU ALL RIGHT?!>
<FEAR NOT, KAH-REHZ. I A WELL. IN FACT, I A IMPROVED.>
<AND I MUST GATHER ALL THE HERALDS BEFORE THE LAST WHITE EVENT.>

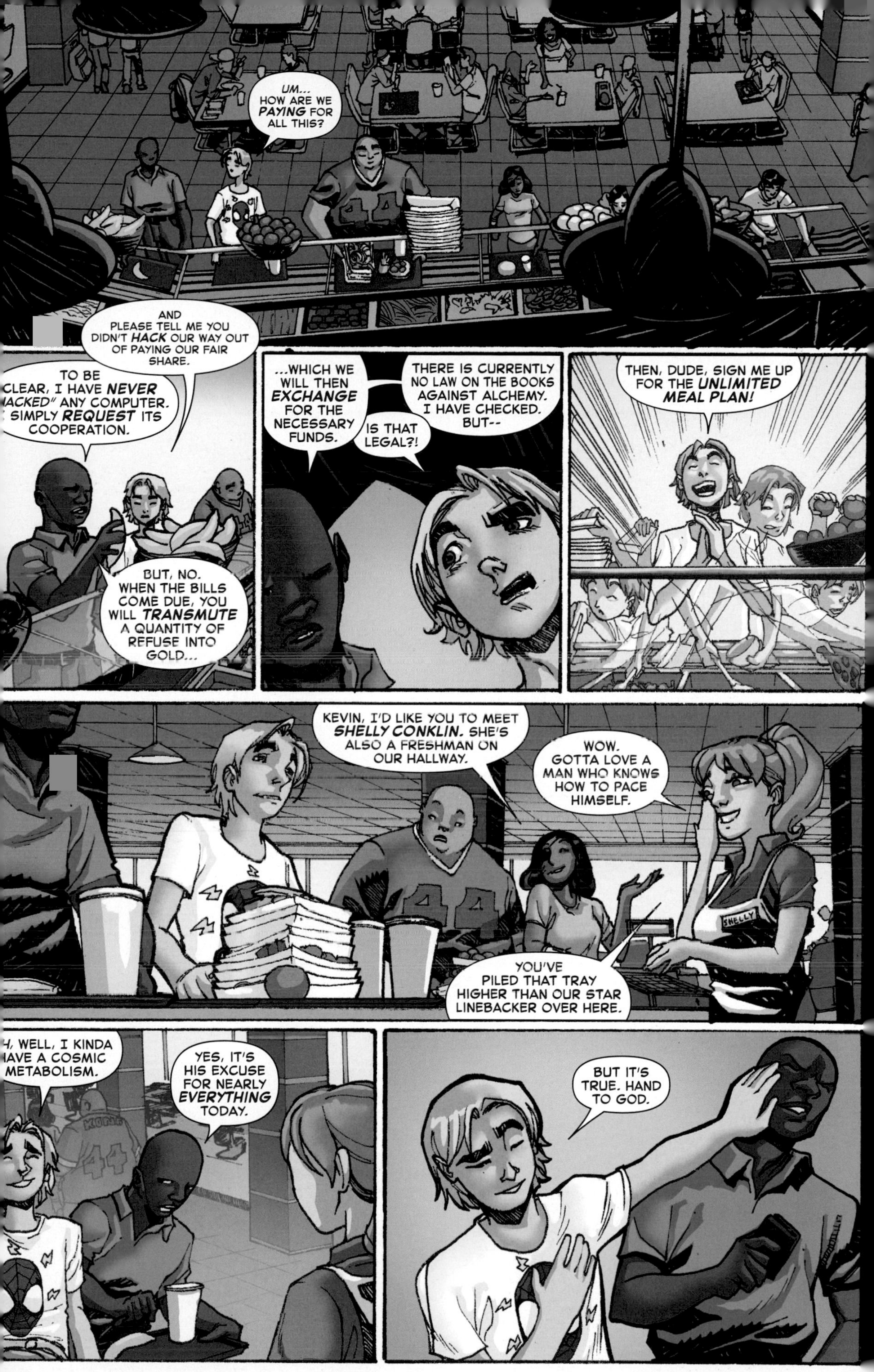
UM... HOW ARE WE PAYING FOR ALL THIS?
AND PLEASE TELL ME YOU DIDN'T HACK OUR WAY OUT OF PAYING OUR FAIR SHARE.
TO BE CLEAR, I HAVE NEVER "HACKED" ANY COMPUTER. I SIMPLY REQUEST ITS COOPERATION.
BUT, NO. WHEN THE BILLS COME DUE, YOU WILL TRANSMUTE A QUANTITY OF REFUSE INTO GOLD...
...WHICH WE WILL THEN EXCHANGE FOR THE NECESSARY FUNDS.
IS THAT LEGAL?!
THERE IS CURRENTLY NO LAW ON THE BOOKS AGAINST ALCHEMY. I HAVE CHECKED. BUT--
THEN, DUDE, SIGN ME UP FOR THE UNLIMITED MEAL PLAN!
KEVIN, I'D LIKE YOU TO MEET SHELLY CONKLIN. SHE'S ALSO A FRESHMAN ON OUR HALLWAY.
YOU'VE PILED THAT TRAY HIGHER THAN OUR STAR LINEBACKER OVER HERE.
WOW. GOTTA LOVE A MAN WHO KNOWS HOW TO PACE HIMSELF.
SHELLY
OH, WELL, I KINDA HAVE A COSMIC METABOLISM.
YES, IT'S HIS EXCUSE FOR NEARLY EVERYTHING TODAY.
BUT IT'S TRUE. HAND TO GOD.

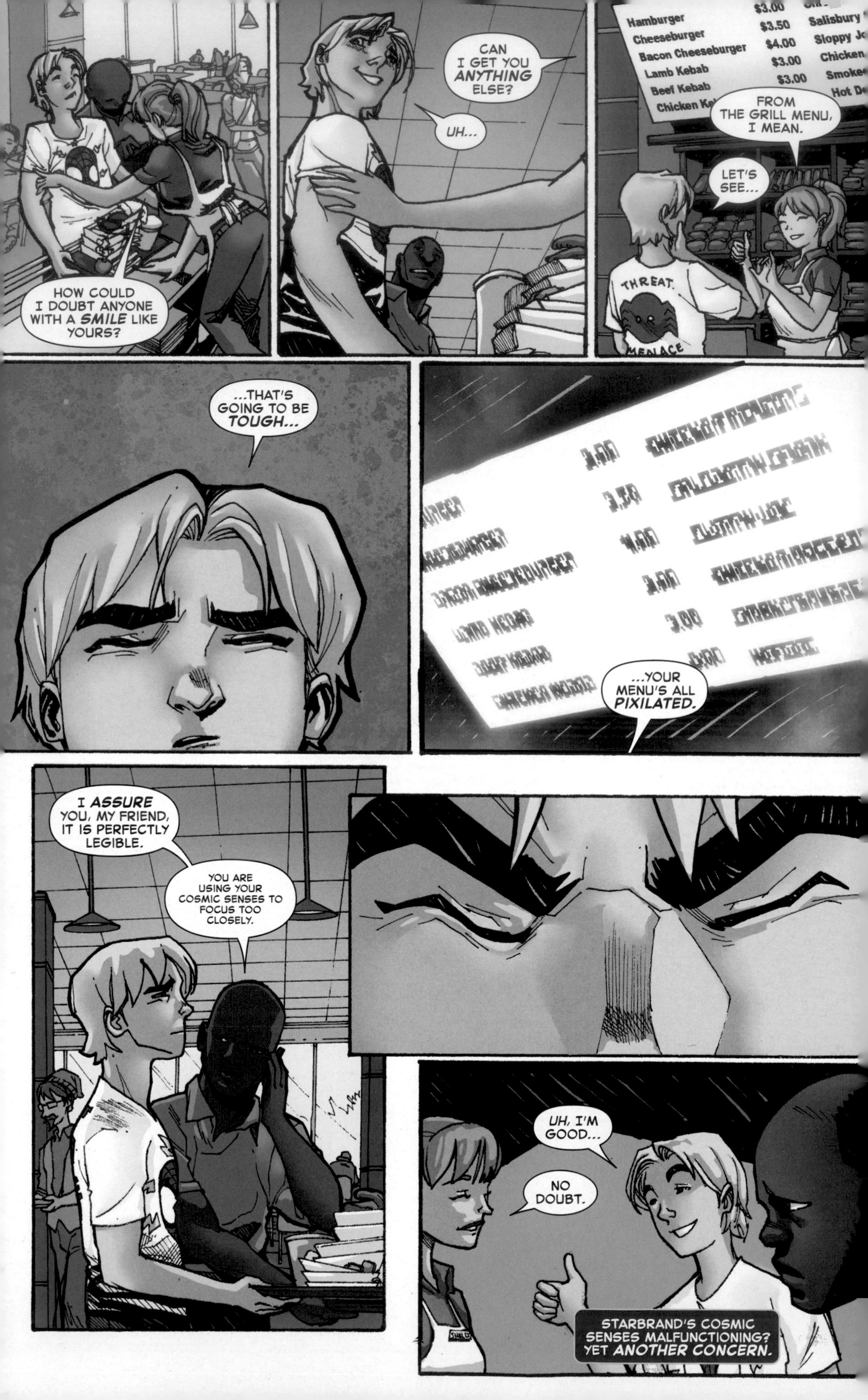
HOW COULD I DOUBT ANYONE WITH A *SMILE* LIKE YOURS?
CAN I GET YOU *ANYTHING* ELSE?
UH...
Hamburger
Cheeseburger
Bacon Cheeseburger
Lamb Kebab
Beef Kebab
$3.00
$3.50
$4.00
$3.00
$3.00
FROM THE GRILL MENU, I MEAN.
LET'S SEE...
THREAT
MENACE
...THAT'S GOING TO BE *TOUGH*...
...YOUR MENU'S ALL *PIXILATED.*
I *ASSURE* YOU, MY FRIEND, IT IS PERFECTLY LEGIBLE.
YOU ARE USING YOUR COSMIC SENSES TO FOCUS TOO CLOSELY.
UH, I'M GOOD...
NO DOUBT.
STARBRAND'S COSMIC SENSES MALFUNCTIONING? YET *ANOTHER CONCERN.*

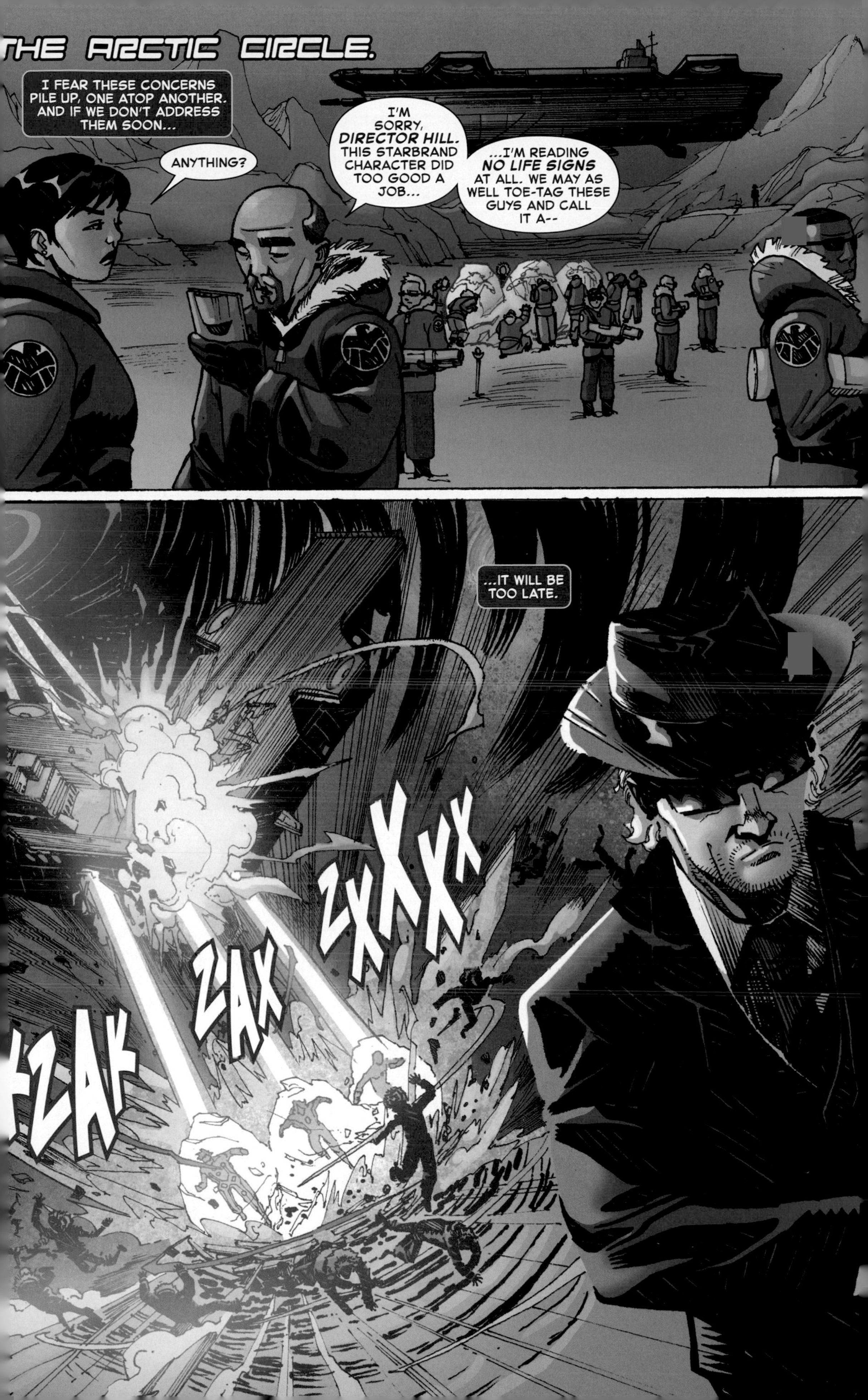
THE ARCTIC CIRCLE.
I FEAR THESE CONCERNS PILE UP, ONE ATOP ANOTHER. AND IF WE DON'T ADDRESS THEM SOON...
ANYTHING?
I'M SORRY, DIRECTOR HILL. THIS STARBRAND CHARACTER DID TOO GOOD A JOB...
...I'M READING NO LIFE SIGNS AT ALL. WE MAY AS WELL TOE-TAG THESE GUYS AND CALL IT A--
...IT WILL BE TOO LATE.
ZAK
ZAK
ZXXX

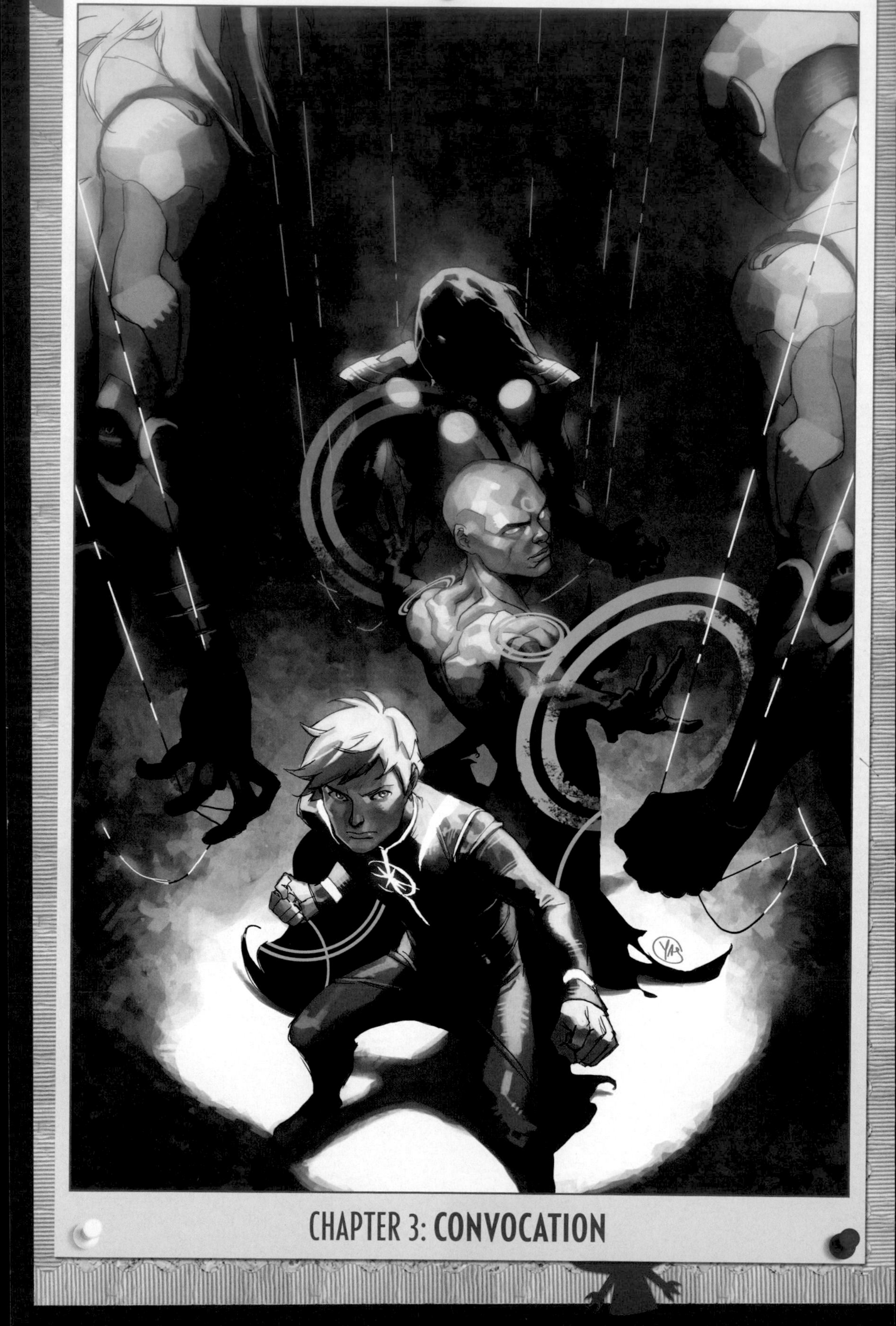

CHAPTER 3: CONVOCATION

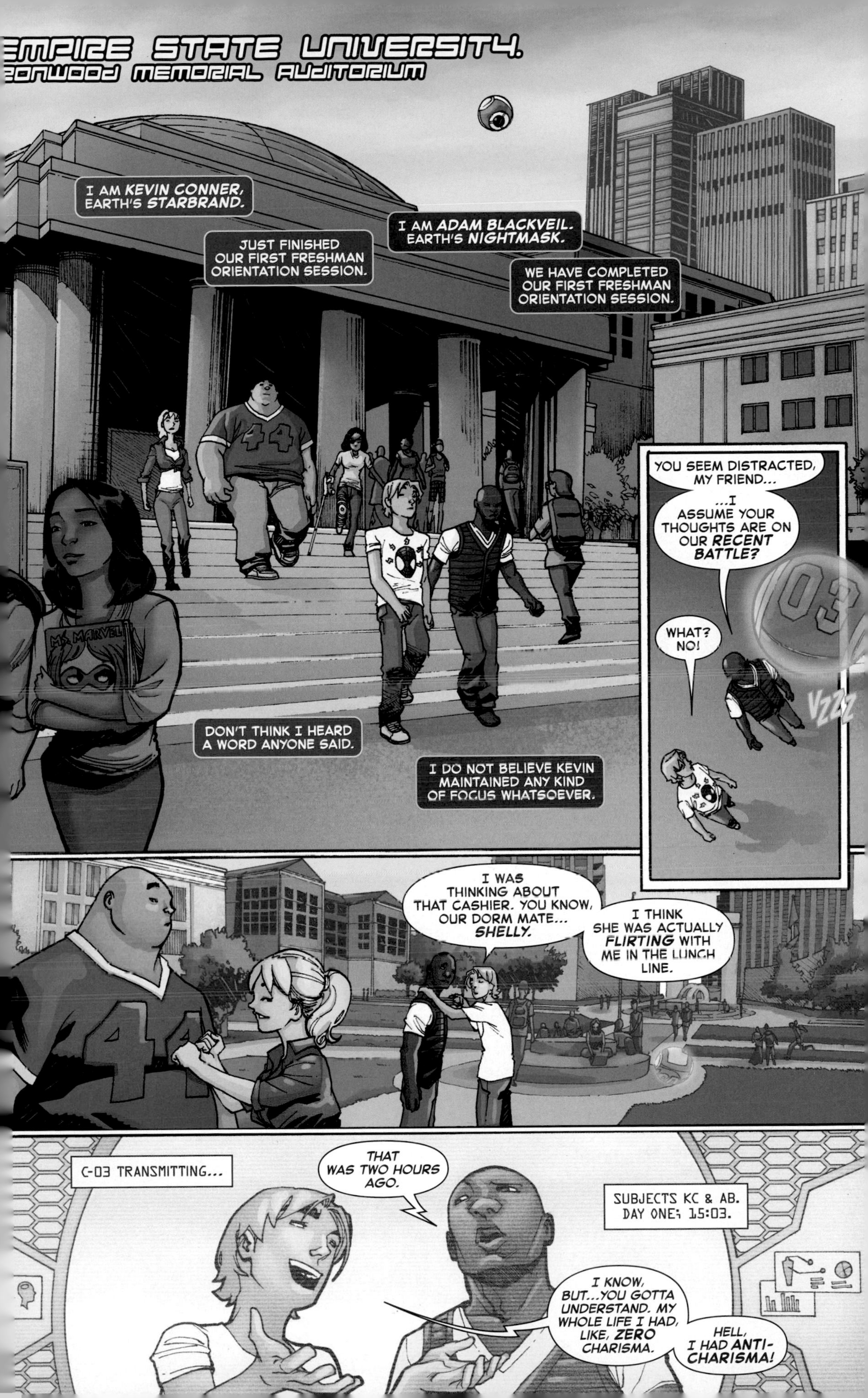
EMPIRE STATE UNIVERSITY.
ONWOOD MEMORIAL AUDITORIUM
I AM KEVIN CONNER, EARTH'S STARBRAND.
JUST FINISHED OUR FIRST FRESHMAN ORIENTATION SESSION.
I AM ADAM BLACKVEIL. EARTH'S NIGHTMASK.
WE HAVE COMPLETED OUR FIRST FRESHMAN ORIENTATION SESSION.
MS. MARVEL
DON'T THINK I HEARD A WORD ANYONE SAID.
I DO NOT BELIEVE KEVIN MAINTAINED ANY KIND OF FOCUS WHATSOEVER.
YOU SEEM DISTRACTED, MY FRIEND...
...I ASSUME YOUR THOUGHTS ARE ON OUR RECENT BATTLE?
WHAT? NO!
03
VZZZ
I WAS THINKING ABOUT THAT CASHIER. YOU KNOW, OUR DORM MATE... SHELLY.
I THINK SHE WAS ACTUALLY FLIRTING WITH ME IN THE LUNCH LINE.
C-03 TRANSMITTING...
THAT WAS TWO HOURS AGO.
SUBJECTS KC & AB. DAY ONE; 15:03.
I KNOW, BUT...YOU GOTTA UNDERSTAND. MY WHOLE LIFE I HAD, LIKE, ZERO CHARISMA.
HELL, I HAD ANTI-CHARISMA!

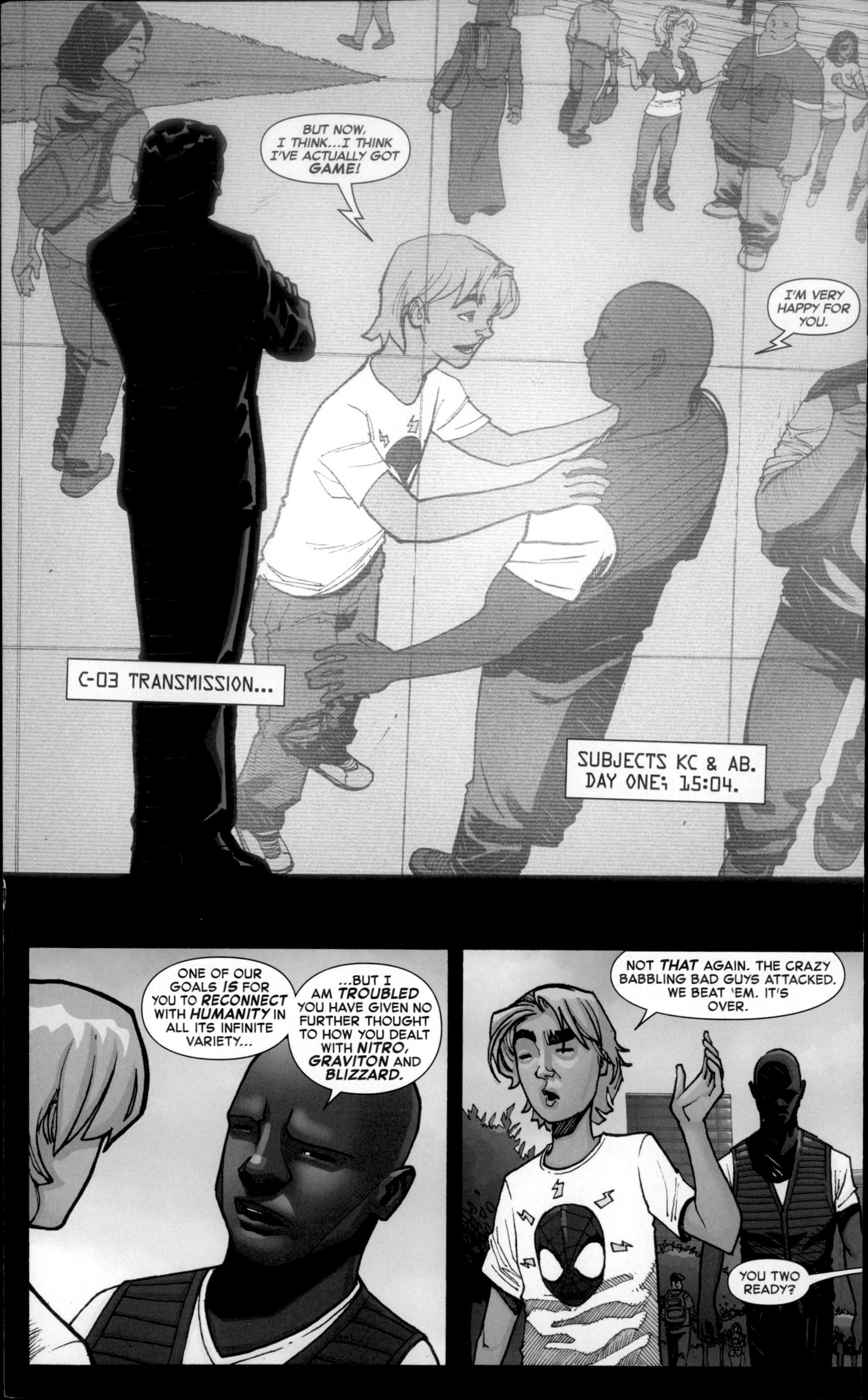
BUT NOW, I THINK...I THINK I'VE ACTUALLY GOT GAME!
I'M VERY HAPPY FOR YOU.
C-03 TRANSMISSION...
SUBJECTS KC & AB. DAY ONE; 15:04.
ONE OF OUR GOALS IS FOR YOU TO RECONNECT WITH HUMANITY IN ALL ITS INFINITE VARIETY...
...BUT I AM TROUBLED YOU HAVE GIVEN NO FURTHER THOUGHT TO HOW YOU DEALT WITH NITRO, GRAVITON AND BLIZZARD.
NOT THAT AGAIN. THE CRAZY BABBLING BAD GUYS ATTACKED. WE BEAT 'EM. IT'S OVER.
YOU TWO READY?

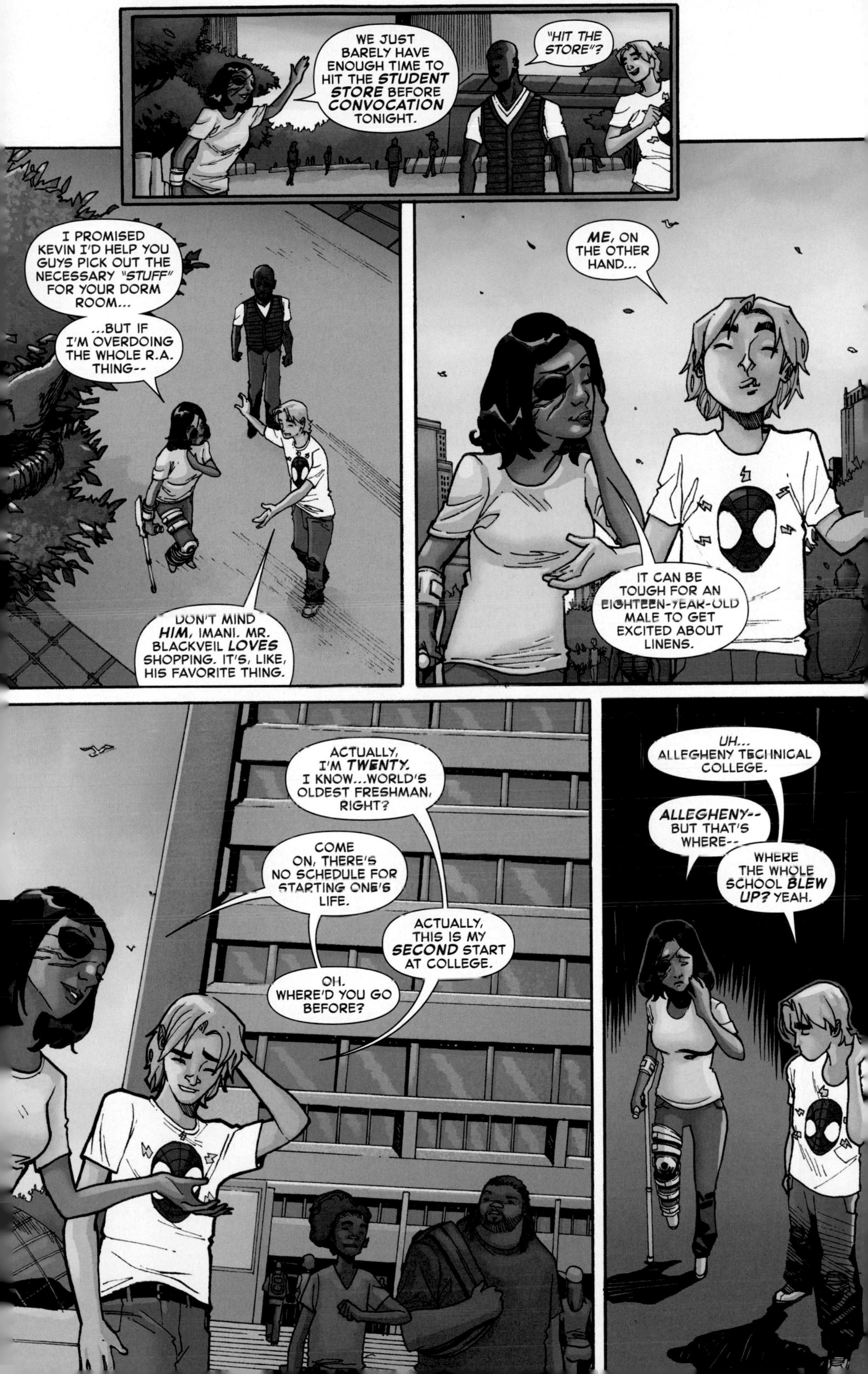

WE JUST BARELY HAVE ENOUGH TIME TO HIT THE **STUDENT STORE** BEFORE **CONVOCATION** TONIGHT.
"HIT THE STORE"?
I PROMISED KEVIN I'D HELP YOU GUYS PICK OUT THE NECESSARY *"STUFF"* FOR YOUR DORM ROOM...
...BUT IF I'M OVERDOING THE WHOLE R.A. THING--
DON'T MIND ***HIM***, IMANI. MR. BLACKVEIL ***LOVES*** SHOPPING. IT'S, LIKE, HIS FAVORITE THING.
ME, ON THE OTHER HAND...
IT CAN BE TOUGH FOR AN EIGHTEEN-YEAR-OLD MALE TO GET EXCITED ABOUT LINENS.
ACTUALLY, I'M ***TWENTY.*** I KNOW...WORLD'S OLDEST FRESHMAN, RIGHT?
COME ON, THERE'S NO SCHEDULE FOR STARTING ONE'S LIFE.
ACTUALLY, THIS IS MY ***SECOND*** START AT COLLEGE.
OH. WHERE'D YOU GO BEFORE?
UH... ALLEGHENY TECHNICAL COLLEGE.
ALLEGHENY-- BUT THAT'S WHERE--
WHERE THE WHOLE SCHOOL ***BLEW UP?*** YEAH.

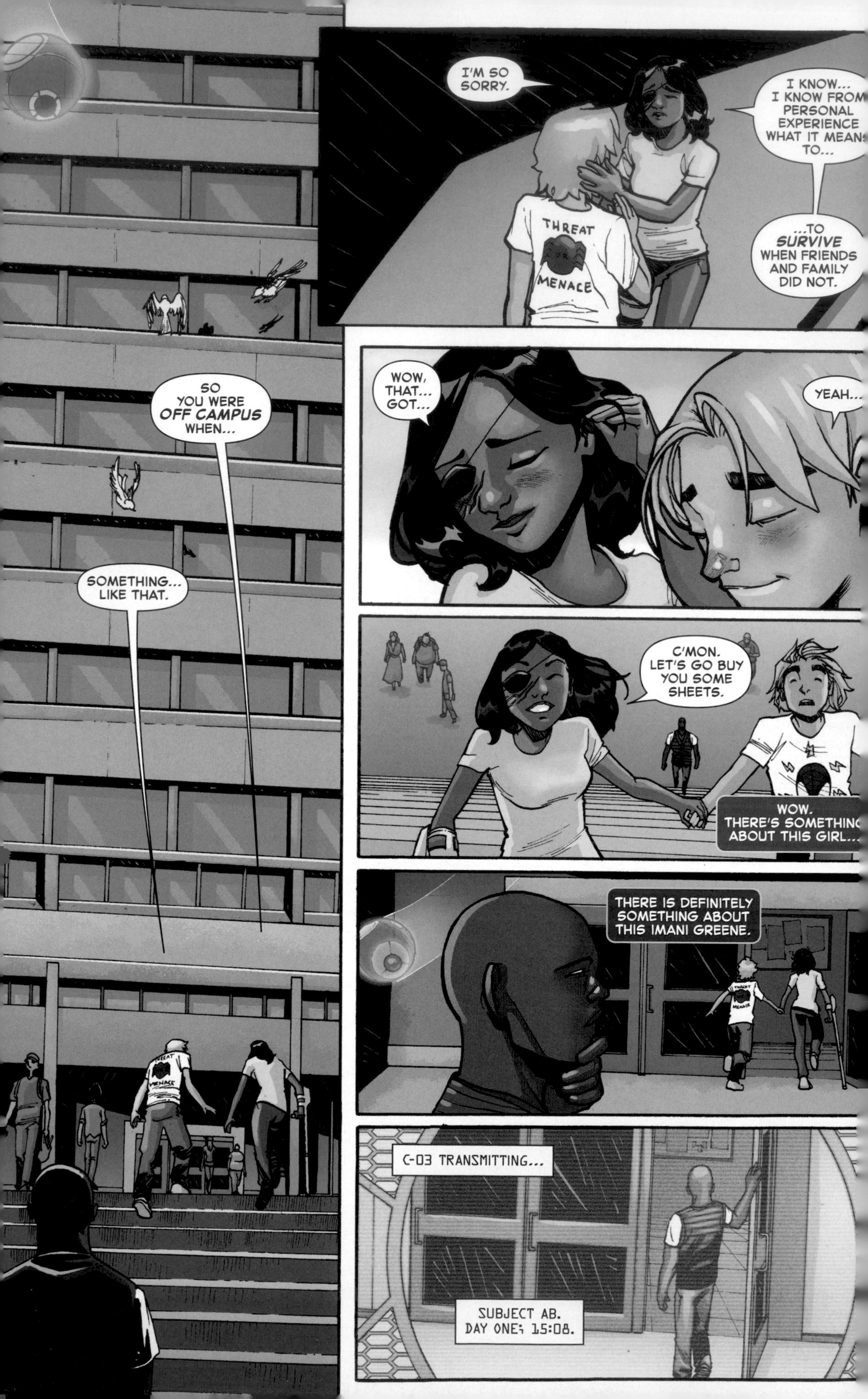
I'M SO SORRY.
I KNOW... I KNOW FROM PERSONAL EXPERIENCE WHAT IT MEANS TO...
...TO SURVIVE WHEN FRIENDS AND FAMILY DID NOT.
THREAT MENACE
SO YOU WERE OFF CAMPUS WHEN...
SOMETHING... LIKE THAT.
WOW, THAT... GOT...
YEAH...
C'MON. LET'S GO BUY YOU SOME SHEETS.
WOW. THERE'S SOMETHING ABOUT THIS GIRL...
THERE IS DEFINITELY SOMETHING ABOUT THIS IMANI GREENE.
C-03 TRANSMITTING...
SUBJECT AB. DAY ONE; 15:08.

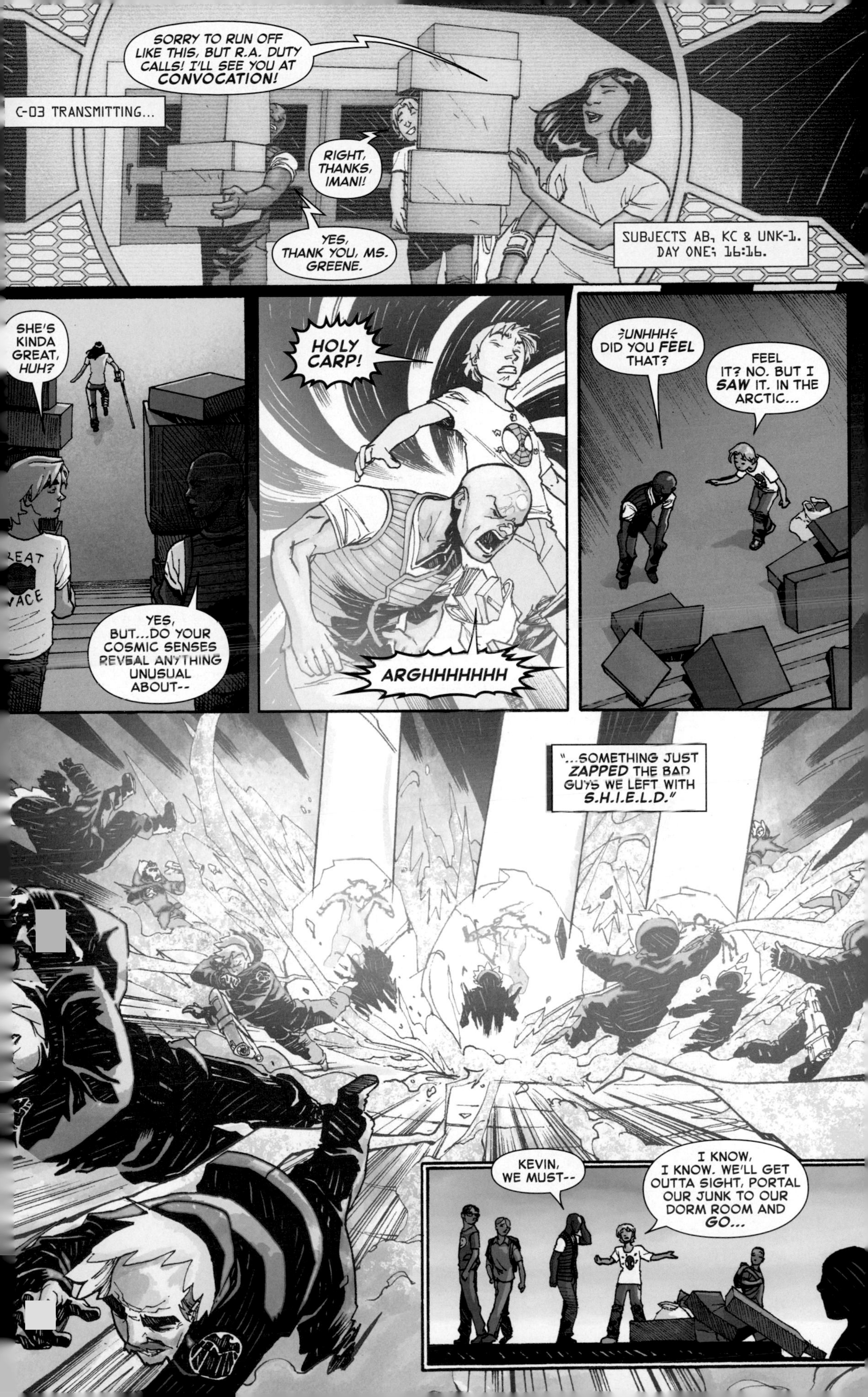
SORRY TO RUN OFF LIKE THIS, BUT R.A. DUTY CALLS! I'LL SEE YOU AT CONVOCATION!
C-03 TRANSMITTING...
RIGHT, THANKS, IMANI!
YES, THANK YOU, MS. GREENE.
SUBJECTS AB, KC & UNK-1. DAY ONE; 16:16.
SHE'S KINDA GREAT, HUH?
YES, BUT...DO YOUR COSMIC SENSES REVEAL ANYTHING UNUSUAL ABOUT--
HOLY CARP!
ARGHHHHHHH
UNHHH DID YOU FEEL THAT?
FEEL IT? NO. BUT I SAW IT. IN THE ARCTIC...
"...SOMETHING JUST ZAPPED THE BAD GUYS WE LEFT WITH S.H.I.E.L.D."
KEVIN, WE MUST--
I KNOW, I KNOW. WE'LL GET OUTTA SIGHT, PORTAL OUR JUNK TO OUR DORM ROOM AND GO...

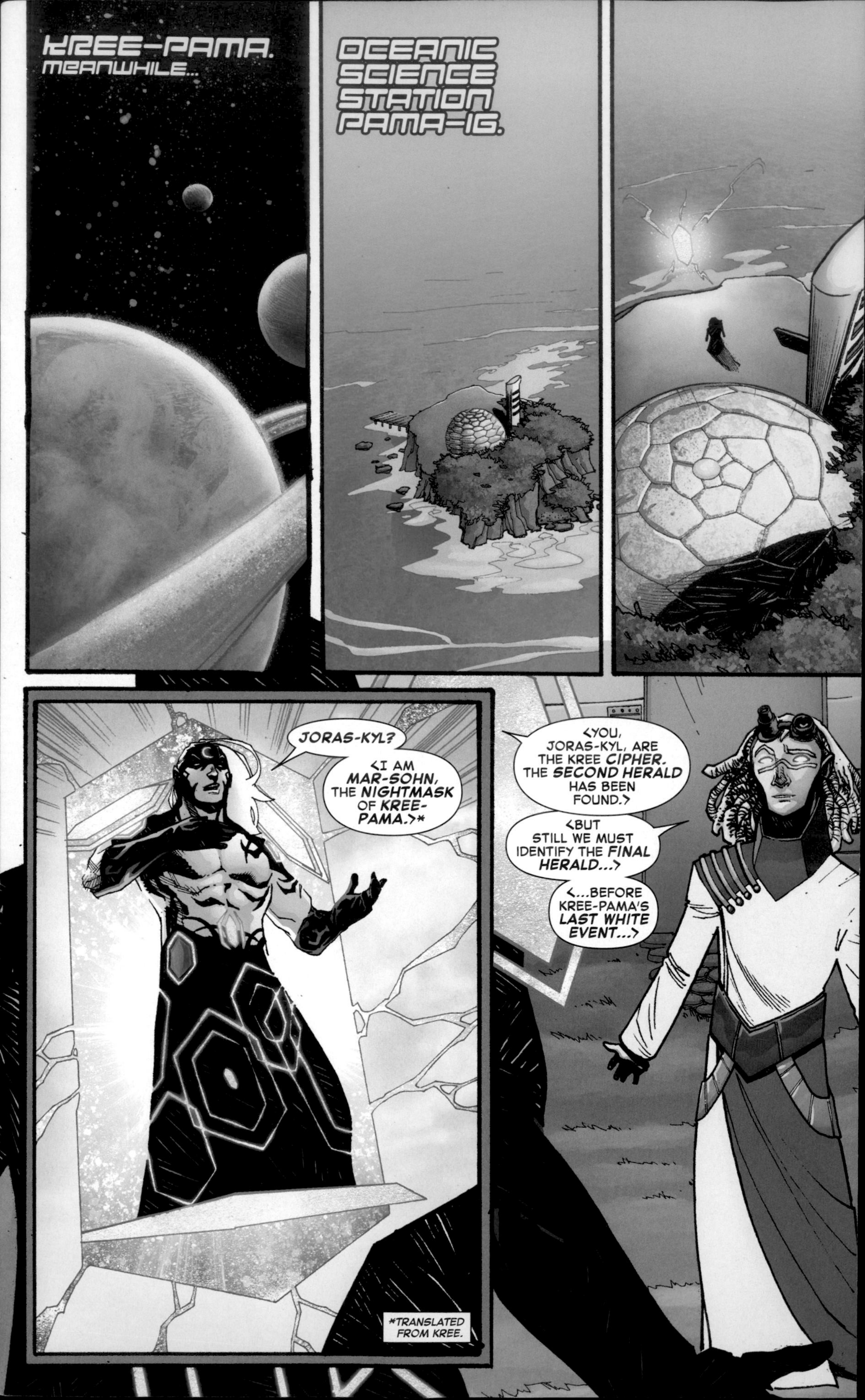

KREE-PAMA.
MEANWHILE...
OCEANIC SCIENCE STATION PAMA-16.
JORAS-KYL?
<I AM MAR-SOHN, THE NIGHTMASK OF KREE-PAMA.>*
<YOU, JORAS-KYL, ARE THE KREE CIPHER. THE SECOND HERALD HAS BEEN FOUND.>
<BUT STILL WE MUST IDENTIFY THE FINAL HERALD...>
<...BEFORE KREE-PAMA'S LAST WHITE EVENT...>
*TRANSLATED FROM KREE.

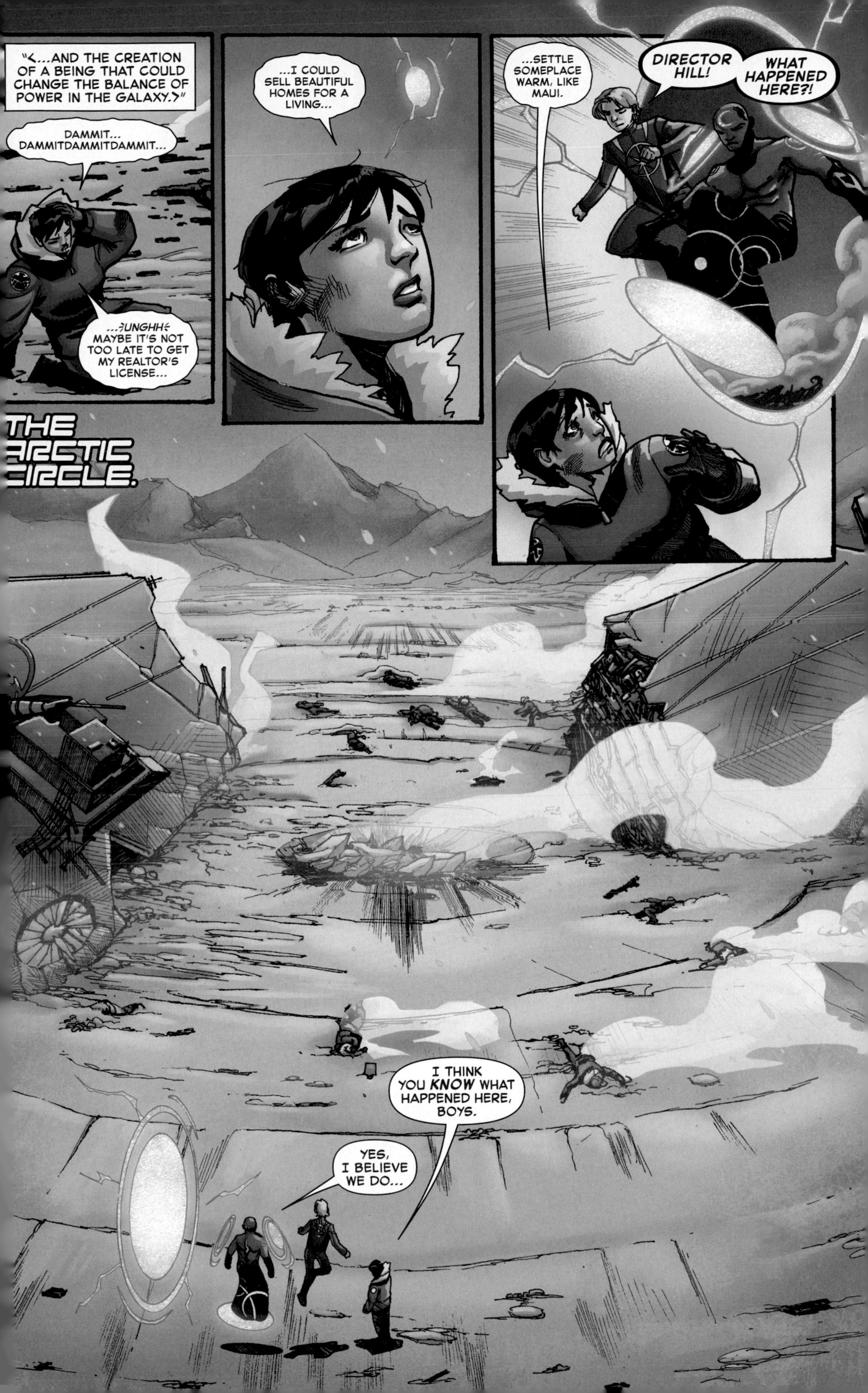
"<...AND THE CREATION OF A BEING THAT COULD CHANGE THE BALANCE OF POWER IN THE GALAXY.>"
DAMMIT... DAMMITDAMMITDAMMIT...
...UNGHH... MAYBE IT'S NOT TOO LATE TO GET MY REALTOR'S LICENSE...
...I COULD SELL BEAUTIFUL HOMES FOR A LIVING...
...SETTLE SOMEPLACE WARM, LIKE MAUI.
DIRECTOR HILL!
WHAT HAPPENED HERE?!
THE ARCTIC CIRCLE.
I THINK YOU KNOW WHAT HAPPENED HERE, BOYS.
YES, I BELIEVE WE DO...

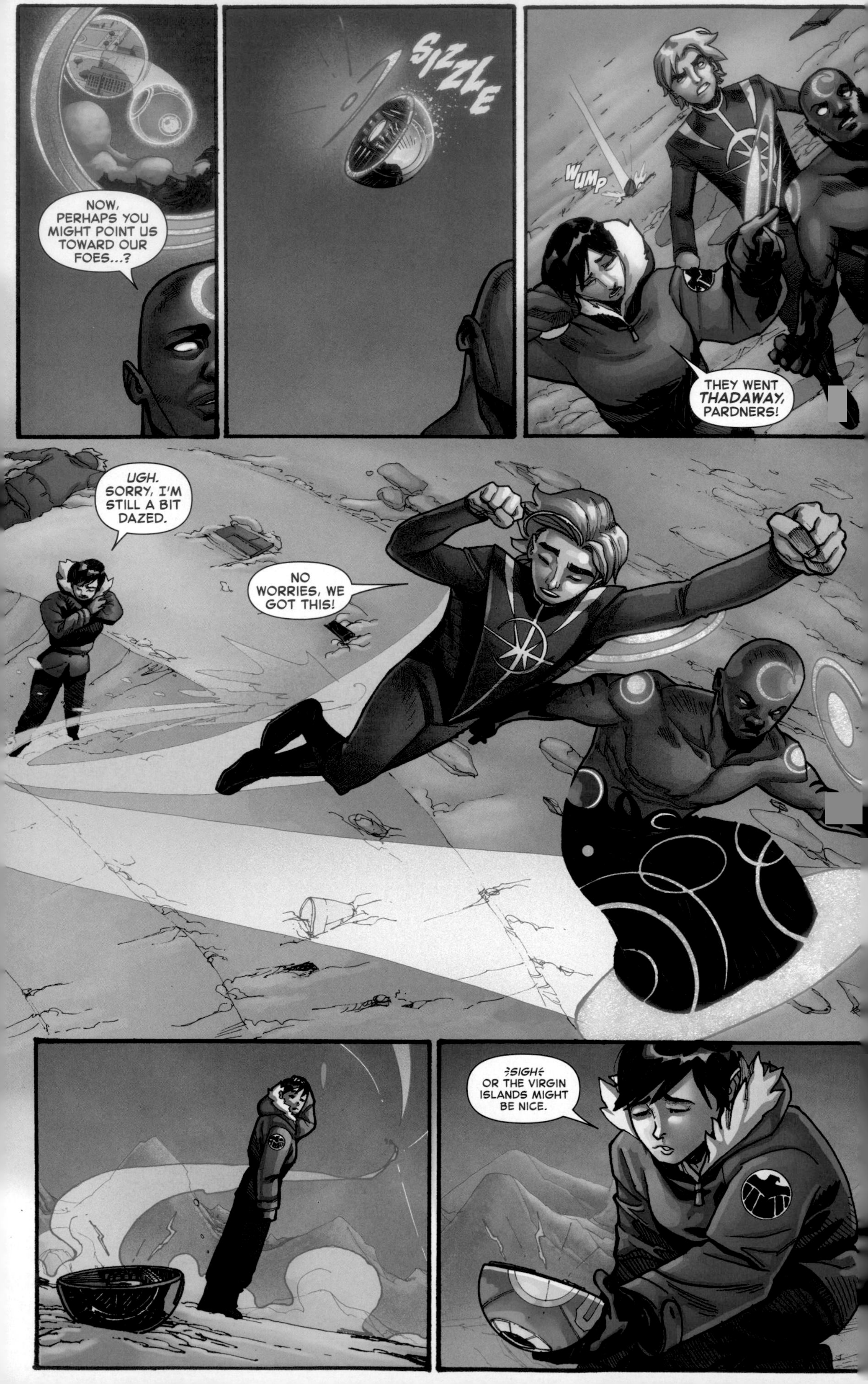
NOW, PERHAPS YOU MIGHT POINT US TOWARD OUR FOES...?
SIZZLE
WUMP
THEY WENT THADAWAY, PARDNERS!
UGH. SORRY, I'M STILL A BIT DAZED.
NO WORRIES, WE GOT THIS!
SIGH
OR THE VIRGIN ISLANDS MIGHT BE NICE.

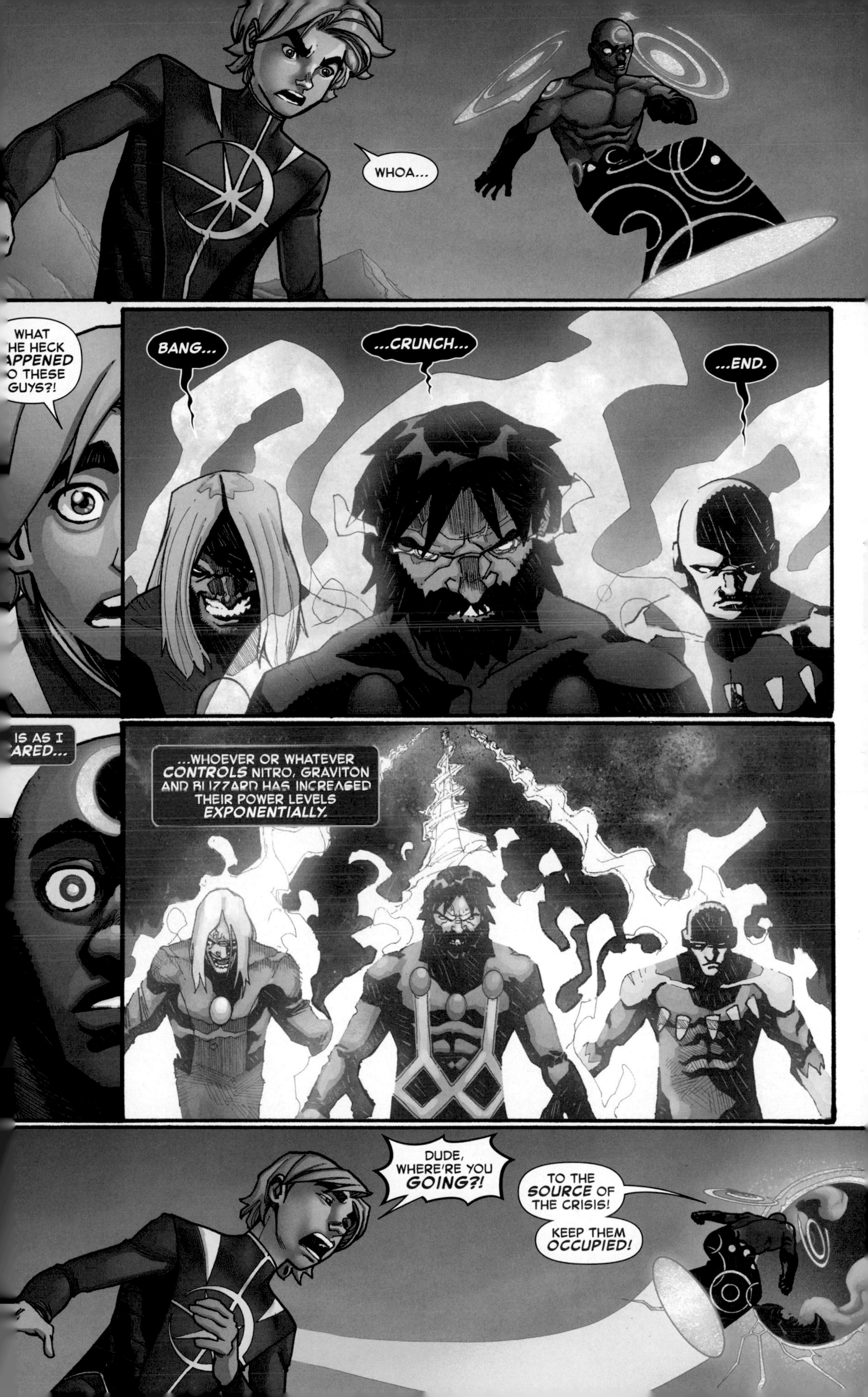
WHOA...
WHAT HE HECK APPENED O THESE GUYS?!
BANG...
...CRUNCH...
...END.
IS AS I ARED...
...WHOEVER OR WHATEVER CONTROLS NITRO, GRAVITON AND BLIZZARD HAS INCREASED THEIR POWER LEVELS EXPONENTIALLY.
DUDE, WHERE'RE YOU GOING?!
TO THE SOURCE OF THE CRISIS!
KEEP THEM OCCUPIED!

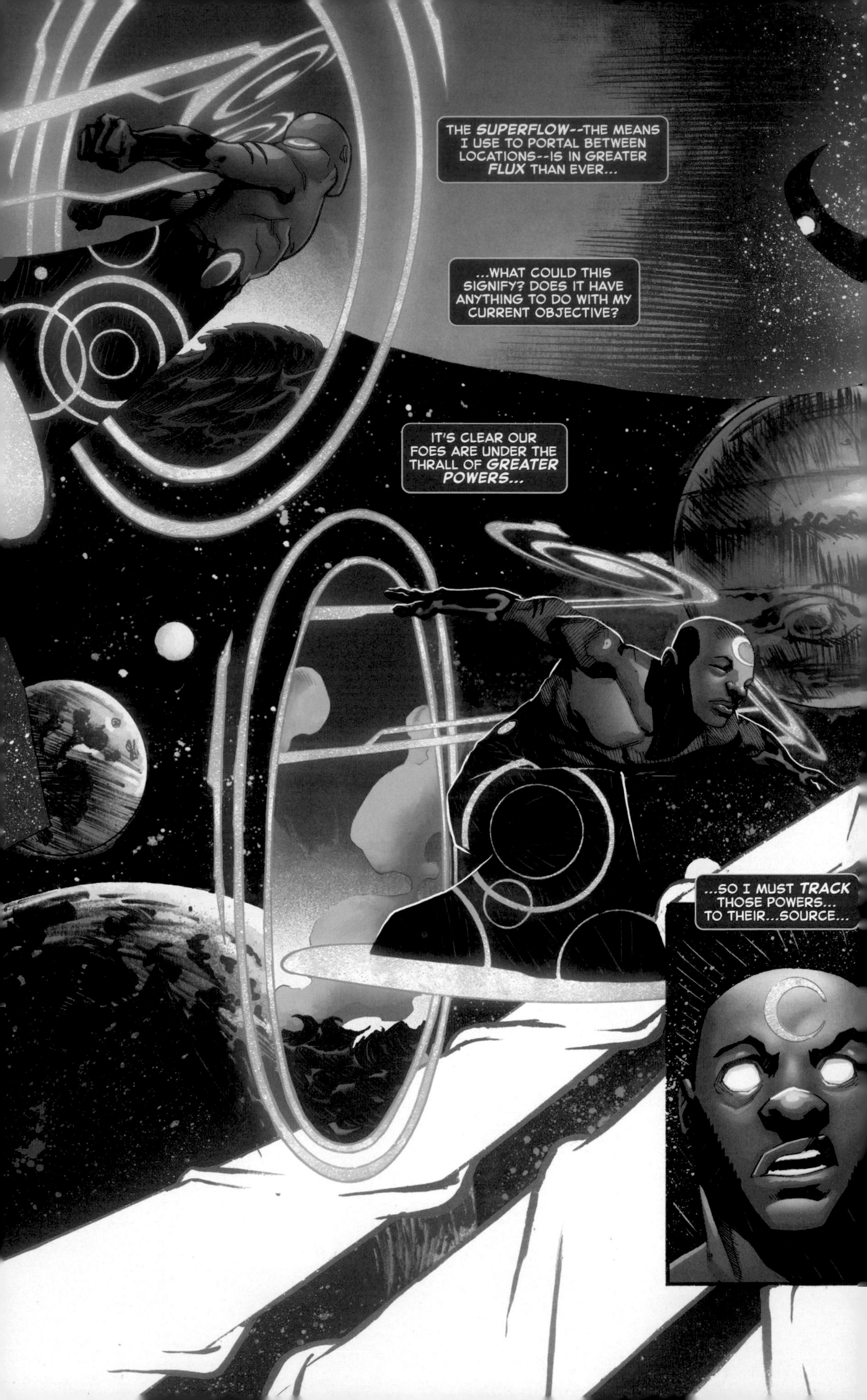
THE SUPERFLOW--THE MEANS I USE TO PORTAL BETWEEN LOCATIONS--IS IN GREATER FLUX THAN EVER...
...WHAT COULD THIS SIGNIFY? DOES IT HAVE ANYTHING TO DO WITH MY CURRENT OBJECTIVE?
IT'S CLEAR OUR FOES ARE UNDER THE THRALL OF GREATER POWERS...
...SO I MUST TRACK THOSE POWERS... TO THEIR...SOURCE...

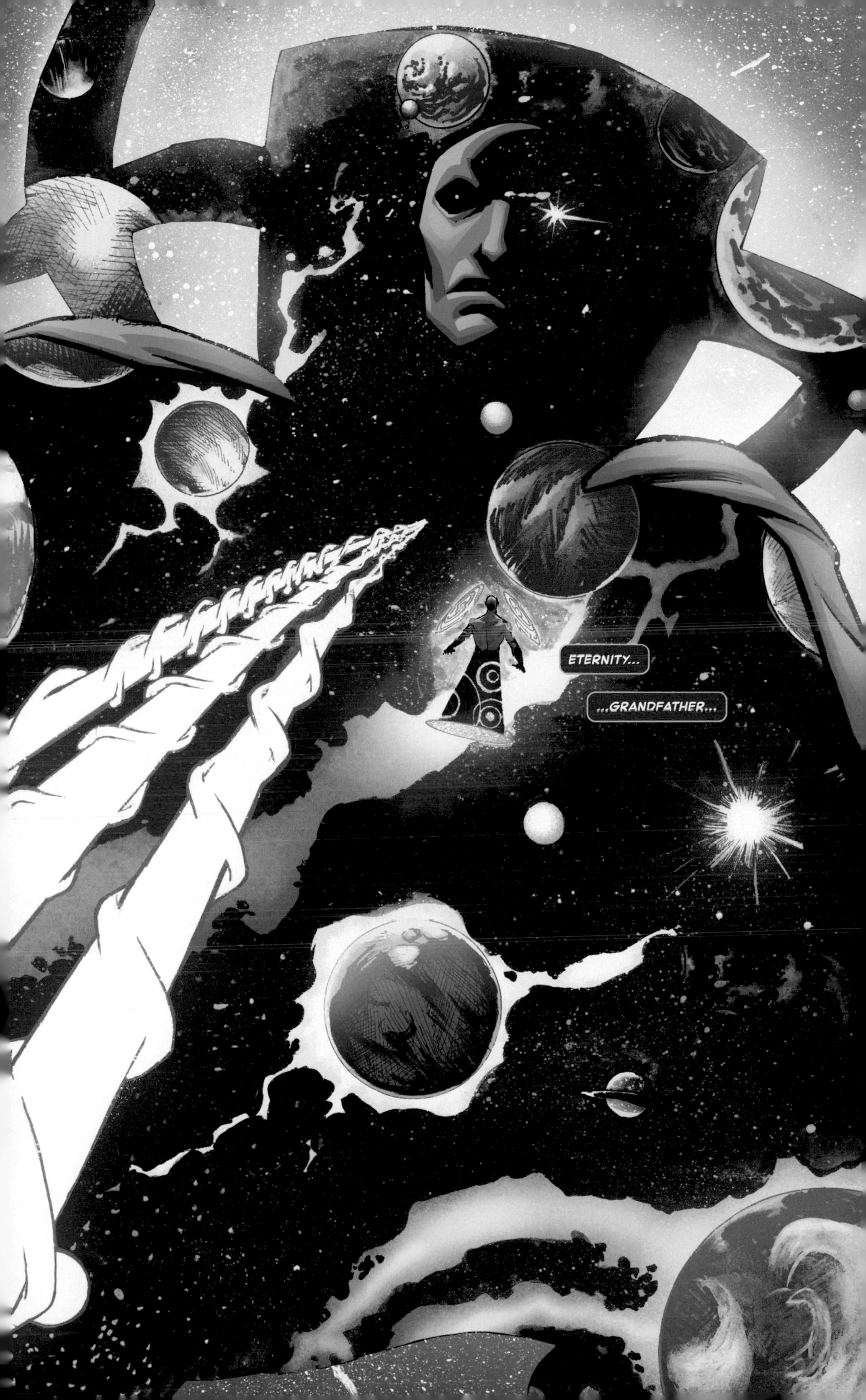
ETERNITY...
...GRANDFATHER...

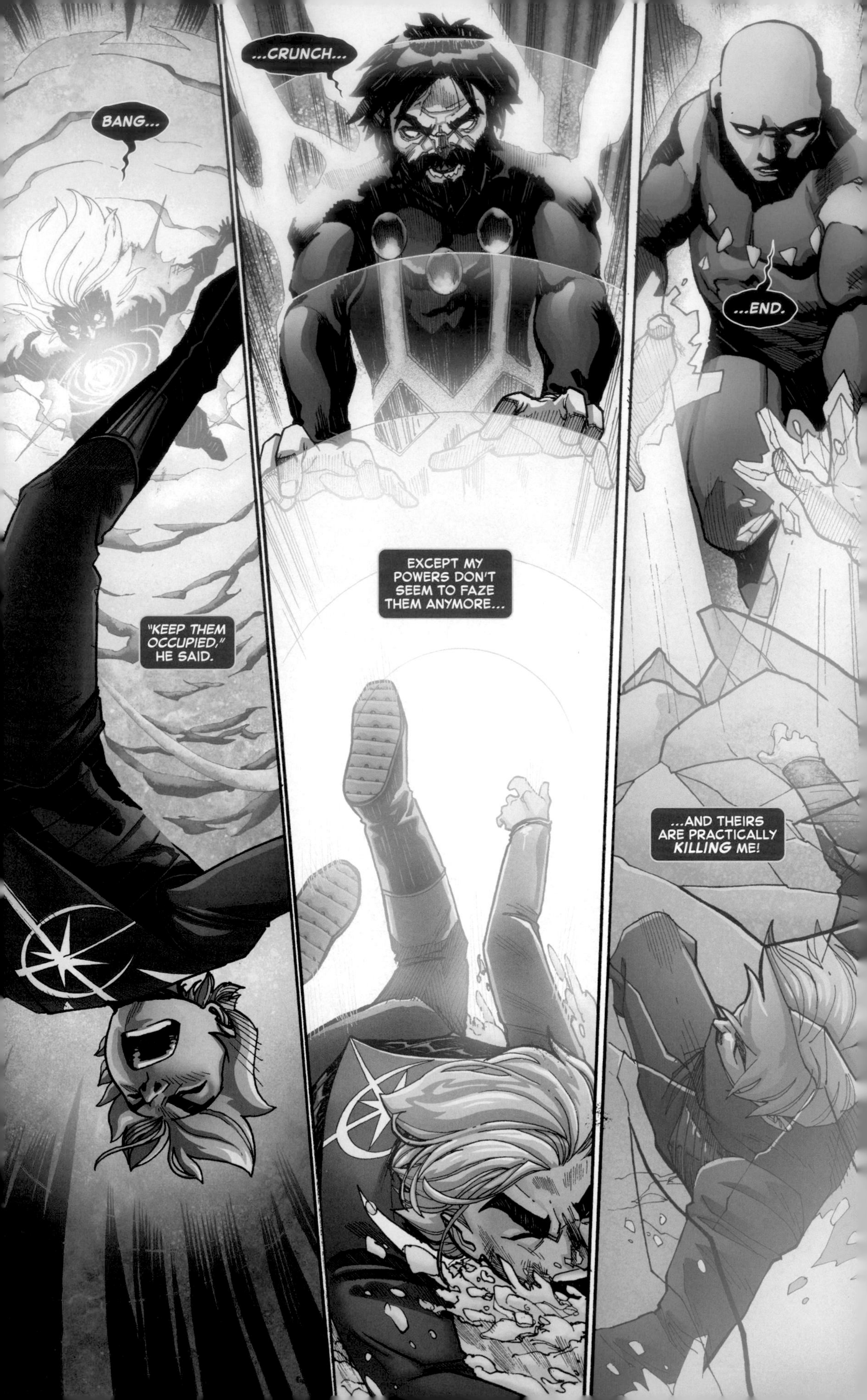
BANG...
...CRUNCH...
...END.
"KEEP THEM OCCUPIED," HE SAID.
EXCEPT MY POWERS DON'T SEEM TO FAZE THEM ANYMORE...
...AND THEIRS ARE PRACTICALLY KILLING ME!

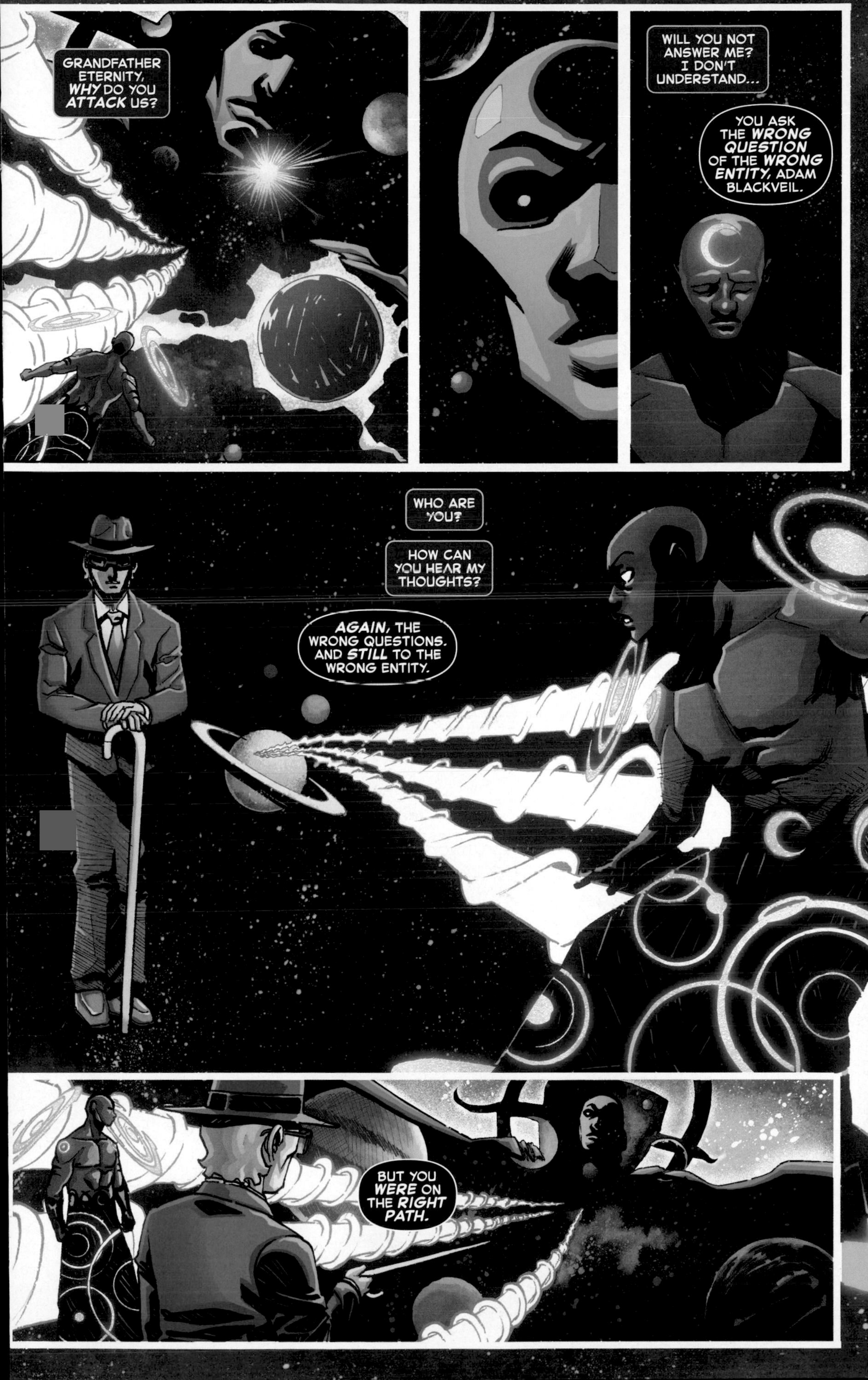
GRANDFATHER ETERNITY, WHY DO YOU ATTACK US?
WILL YOU NOT ANSWER ME? I DON'T UNDERSTAND...
YOU ASK THE WRONG QUESTION OF THE WRONG ENTITY, ADAM BLACKVEIL.
WHO ARE YOU?
HOW CAN YOU HEAR MY THOUGHTS?
AGAIN, THE WRONG QUESTIONS. AND STILL TO THE WRONG ENTITY.
BUT YOU WERE ON THE RIGHT PATH.

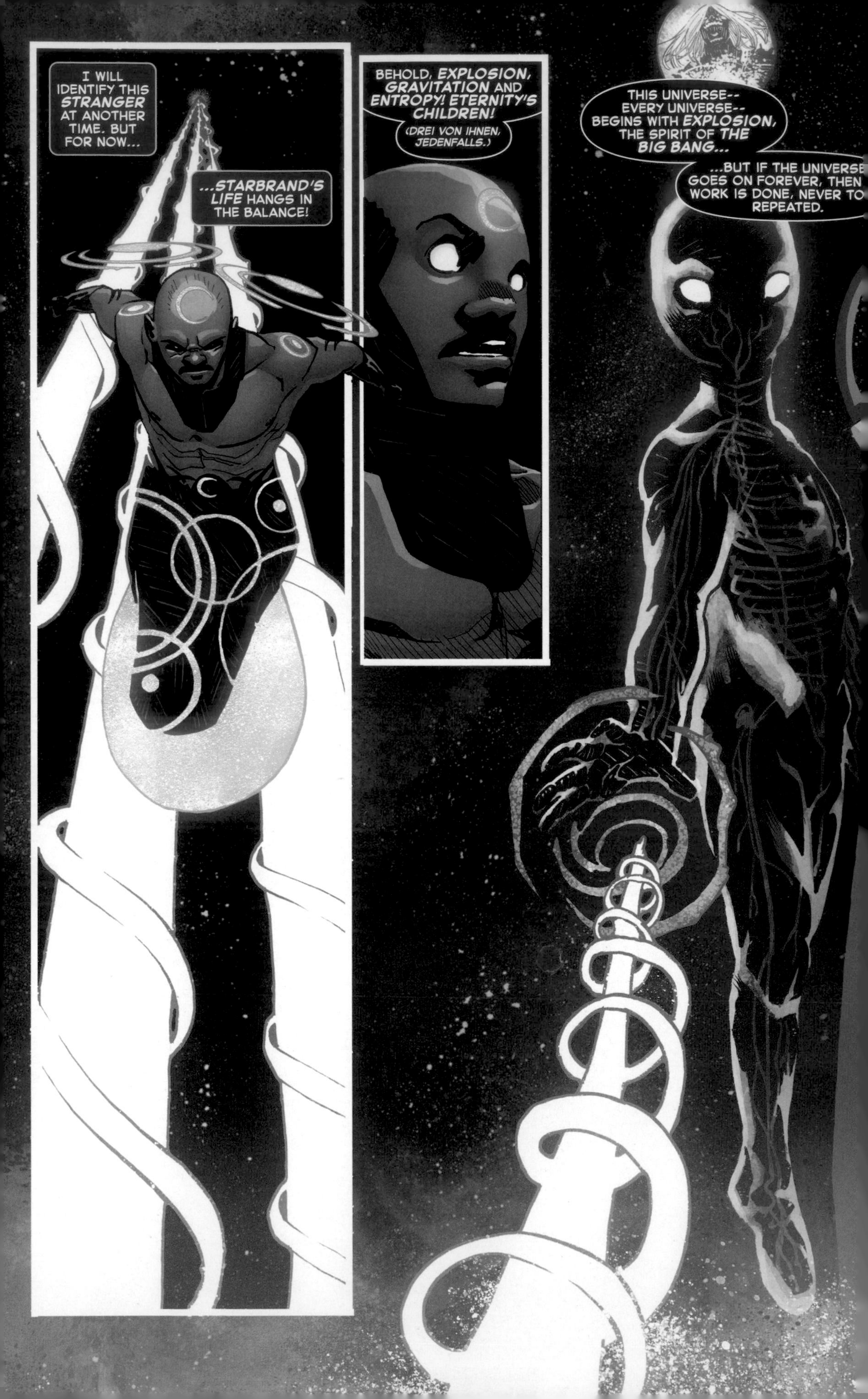
I WILL IDENTIFY THIS STRANGER AT ANOTHER TIME. BUT FOR NOW...
...STARBRAND'S LIFE HANGS IN THE BALANCE!
BEHOLD, EXPLOSION, GRAVITATION AND ENTROPY! ETERNITY'S CHILDREN!
(DREI VON IHNEN, JEDENFALLS.)
THIS UNIVERSE-- EVERY UNIVERSE-- BEGINS WITH EXPLOSION, THE SPIRIT OF THE BIG BANG...
...BUT IF THE UNIVERSE GOES ON FOREVER, THEN WORK IS DONE, NEVER TO REPEATED.

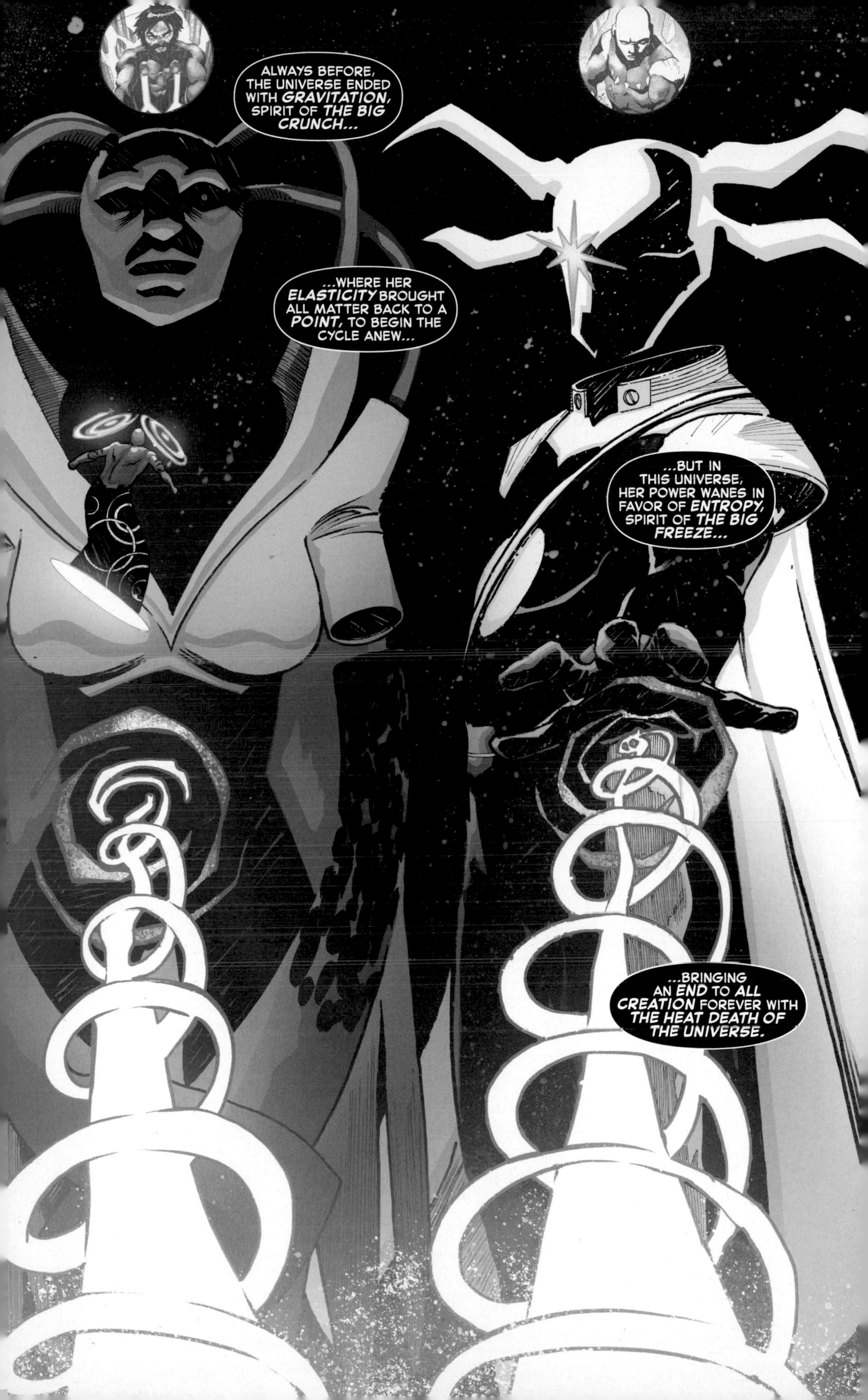
ALWAYS BEFORE, THE UNIVERSE ENDED WITH GRAVITATION, SPIRIT OF THE BIG CRUNCH...
...WHERE HER ELASTICITY BROUGHT ALL MATTER BACK TO A POINT, TO BEGIN THE CYCLE ANEW...
...BUT IN THIS UNIVERSE, HER POWER WANES IN FAVOR OF ENTROPY, SPIRIT OF THE BIG FREEZE...
...BRINGING AN END TO ALL CREATION FOREVER WITH THE HEAT DEATH OF THE UNIVERSE.

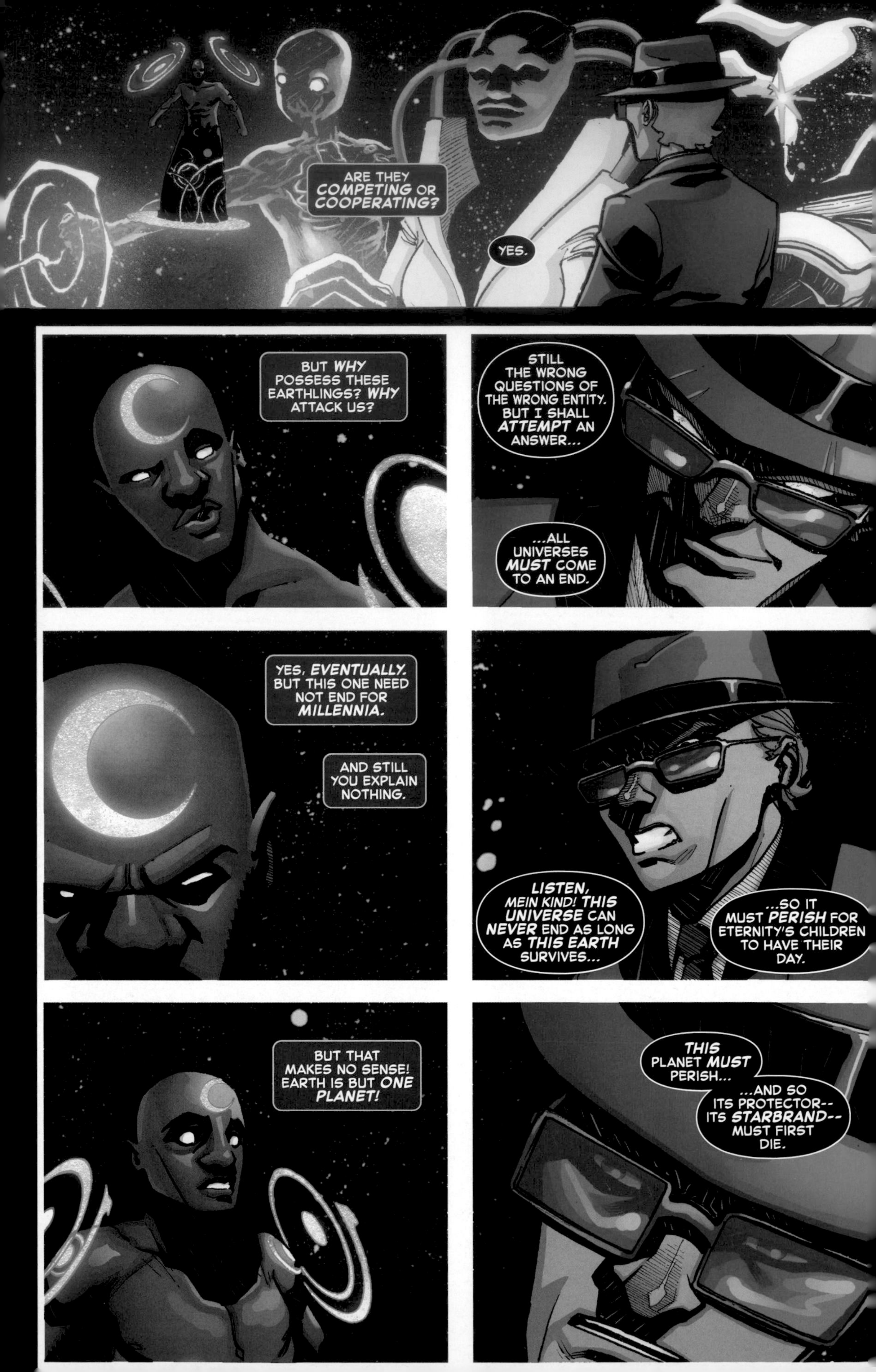
ARE THEY COMPETING OR COOPERATING?
YES.
BUT WHY POSSESS THESE EARTHLINGS? WHY ATTACK US?
STILL THE WRONG QUESTIONS OF THE WRONG ENTITY. BUT I SHALL ATTEMPT AN ANSWER...
...ALL UNIVERSES MUST COME TO AN END.
YES, EVENTUALLY. BUT THIS ONE NEED NOT END FOR MILLENNIA.
AND STILL YOU EXPLAIN NOTHING.
LISTEN, MEIN KIND! THIS UNIVERSE CAN NEVER END AS LONG AS THIS EARTH SURVIVES...
...SO IT MUST PERISH FOR ETERNITY'S CHILDREN TO HAVE THEIR DAY.
BUT THAT MAKES NO SENSE! EARTH IS BUT ONE PLANET!
THIS PLANET MUST PERISH...
...AND SO ITS PROTECTOR-- ITS STARBRAND-- MUST FIRST DIE.

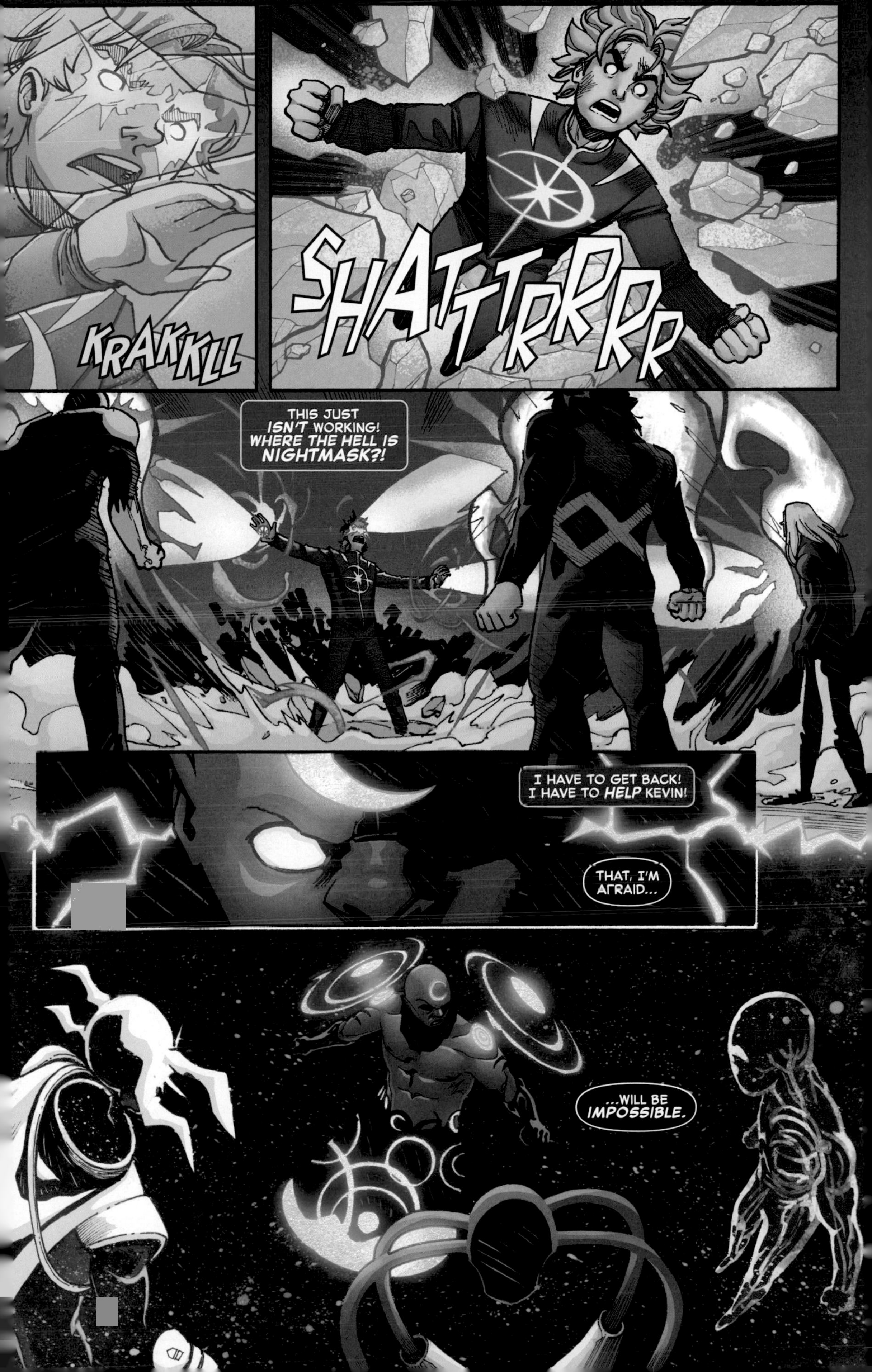
KRAKKLL
SHATTTRRRRR
THIS JUST ISN'T WORKING! WHERE THE HELL IS NIGHTMASK?!
I HAVE TO GET BACK! I HAVE TO HELP KEVIN!
THAT, I'M AFRAID...
...WILL BE IMPOSSIBLE.

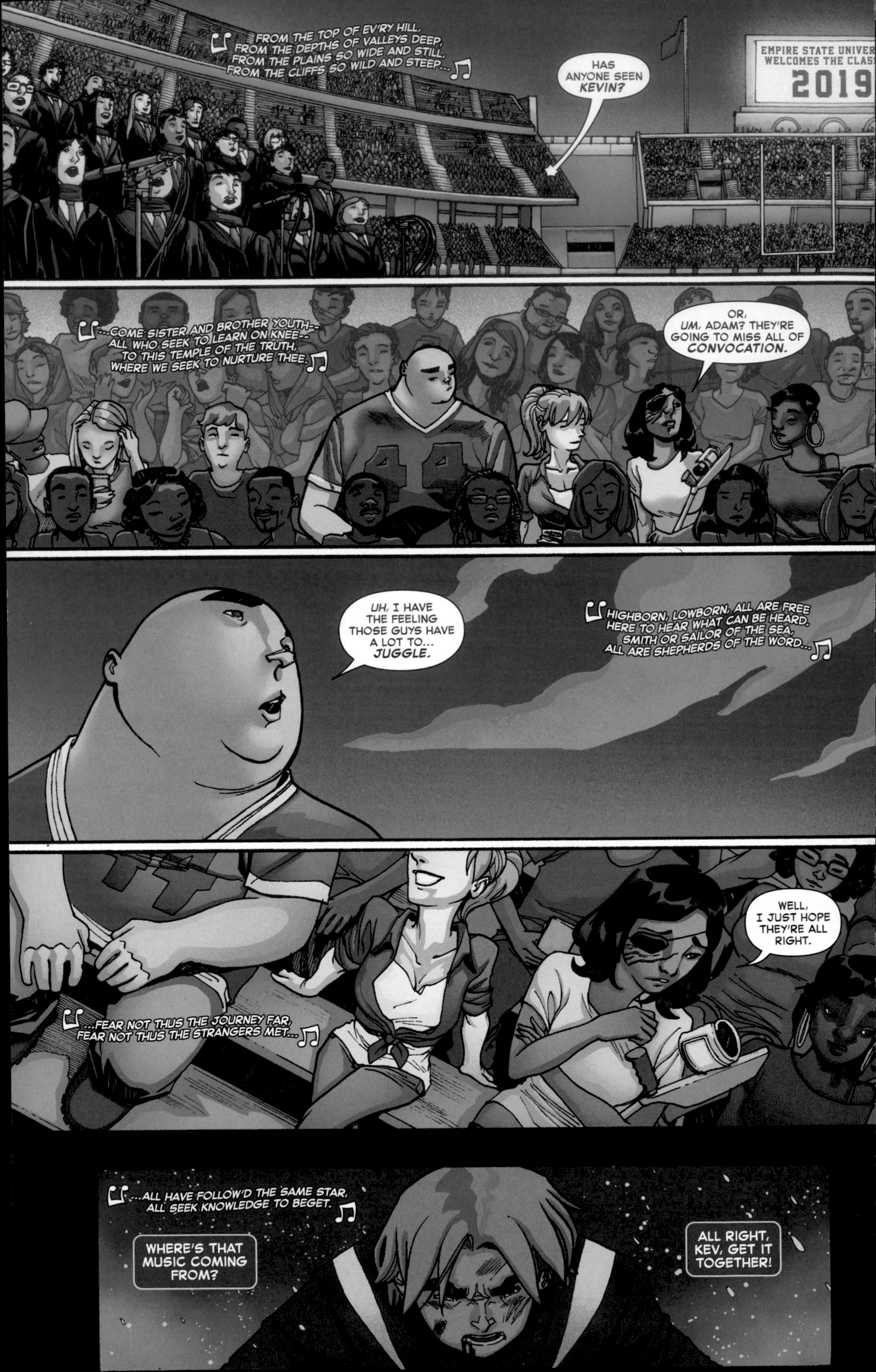
FROM THE TOP OF EV'RY HILL, FROM THE DEPTHS OF VALLEYS DEEP, FROM THE PLAINS SO WIDE AND STILL, FROM THE CLIFFS SO WILD AND STEEP...
HAS ANYONE SEEN KEVIN?
EMPIRE STATE UNIVER WELCOMES THE CLASS 2019
...COME SISTER AND BROTHER YOUTH-- ALL WHO SEEK TO LEARN ON KNEE-- TO THIS TEMPLE OF THE TRUTH, WHERE WE SEEK TO NURTURE THEE.
OR, UM, ADAM? THEY'RE GOING TO MISS ALL OF CONVOCATION.
UH, I HAVE THE FEELING THOSE GUYS HAVE A LOT TO... JUGGLE.
HIGHBORN, LOWBORN, ALL ARE FREE HERE TO HEAR WHAT CAN BE HEARD. SMITH OR SAILOR OF THE SEA, ALL ARE SHEPHERDS OF THE WORD...
WELL, I JUST HOPE THEY'RE ALL RIGHT.
...FEAR NOT THUS THE JOURNEY FAR, FEAR NOT THUS THE STRANGERS MET...
...ALL HAVE FOLLOW'D THE SAME STAR, ALL SEEK KNOWLEDGE TO BEGET.
WHERE'S THAT MUSIC COMING FROM?
ALL RIGHT, KEV, GET IT TOGETHER!

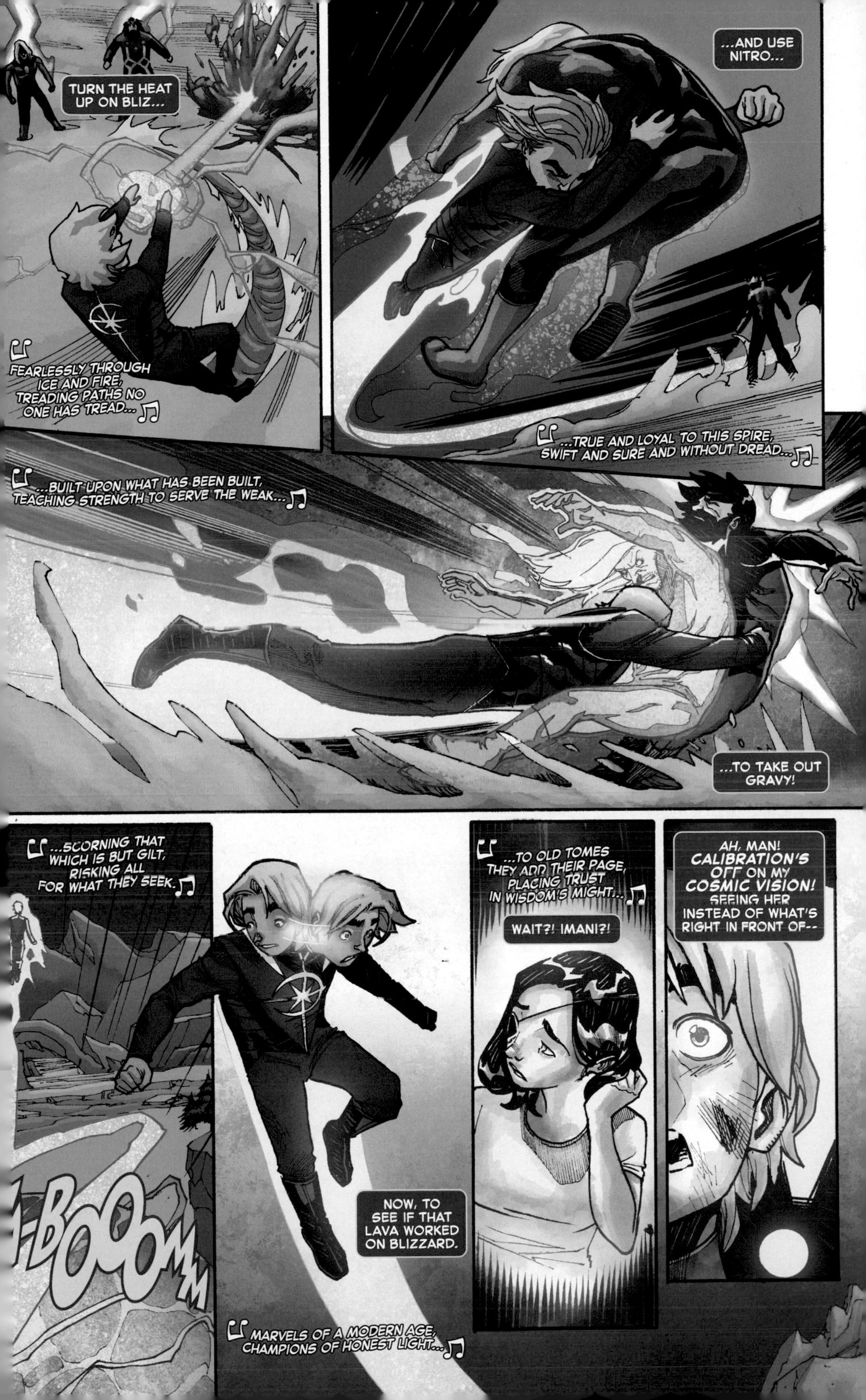
TURN THE HEAT UP ON BLIZ...
FEARLESSLY THROUGH ICE AND FIRE, TREADING PATHS NO ONE HAS TREAD... ♫
...AND USE NITRO...
...TRUE AND LOYAL TO THIS SPIRE, SWIFT AND SURE AND WITHOUT DREAD... ♫
...BUILT UPON WHAT HAS BEEN BUILT, TEACHING STRENGTH TO SERVE THE WEAK... ♫
...TO TAKE OUT GRAVY!
...SCORNING THAT WHICH IS BUT GILT, RISKING ALL FOR WHAT THEY SEEK. ♫
BOOOOMMM
NOW, TO SEE IF THAT LAVA WORKED ON BLIZZARD.
MARVELS OF A MODERN AGE, CHAMPIONS OF HONEST LIGHT... ♫
...TO OLD TOMES THEY ADD THEIR PAGE, PLACING TRUST IN WISDOM'S MIGHT... ♫
WAIT?! IMANI?!
AH, MAN! CALIBRATION'S OFF ON MY COSMIC VISION! SEEING HER INSTEAD OF WHAT'S RIGHT IN FRONT OF--

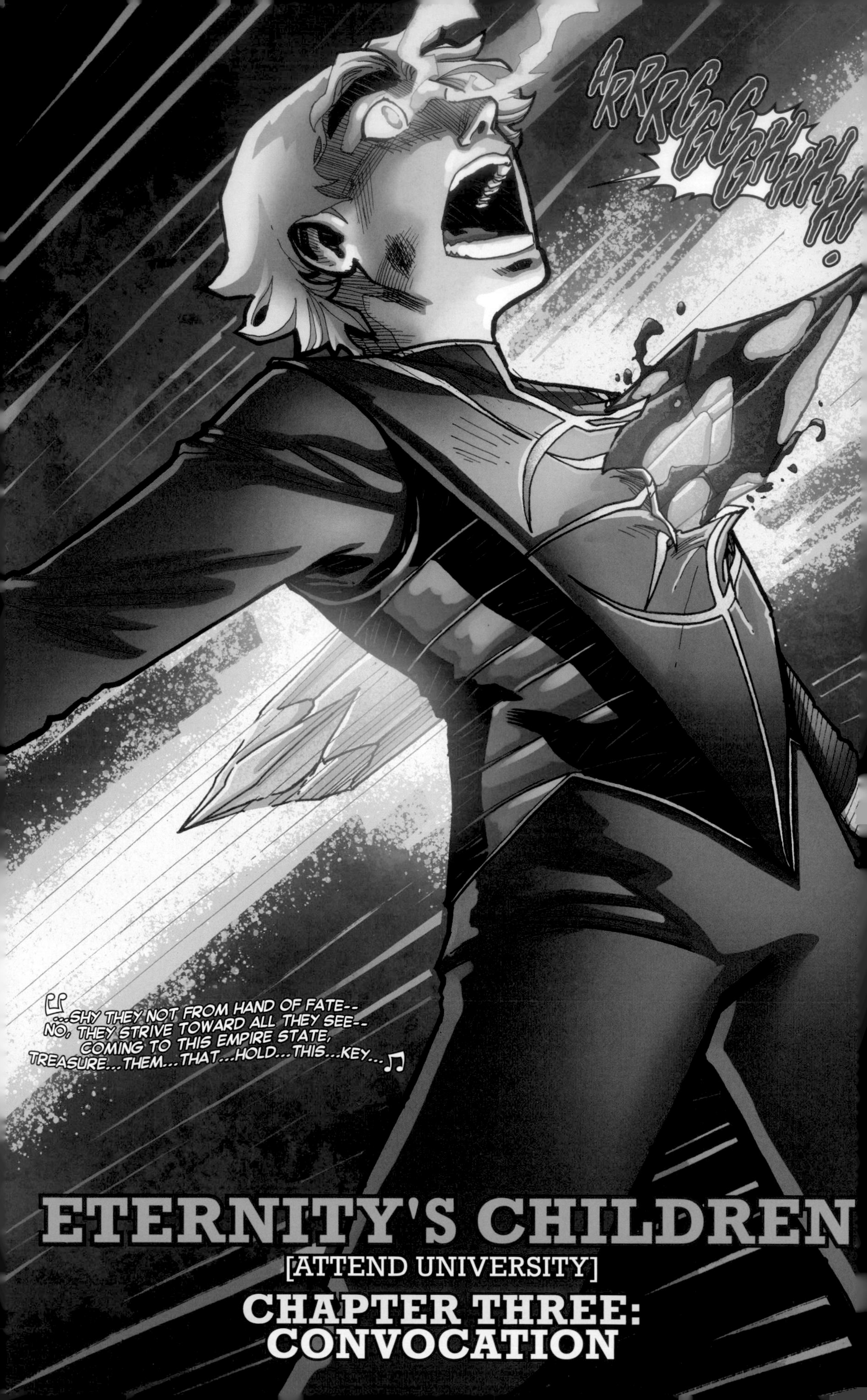
ARRGGGHHH!
...SHY THEY NOT FROM HAND OF FATE-- NO, THEY STRIVE TOWARD ALL THEY SEE-- COMING TO THIS EMPIRE STATE, TREASURE...THEM...THAT...HOLD...THIS...KEY...
ETERNITY'S CHILDREN
[ATTEND UNIVERSITY]
CHAPTER THREE: CONVOCATION

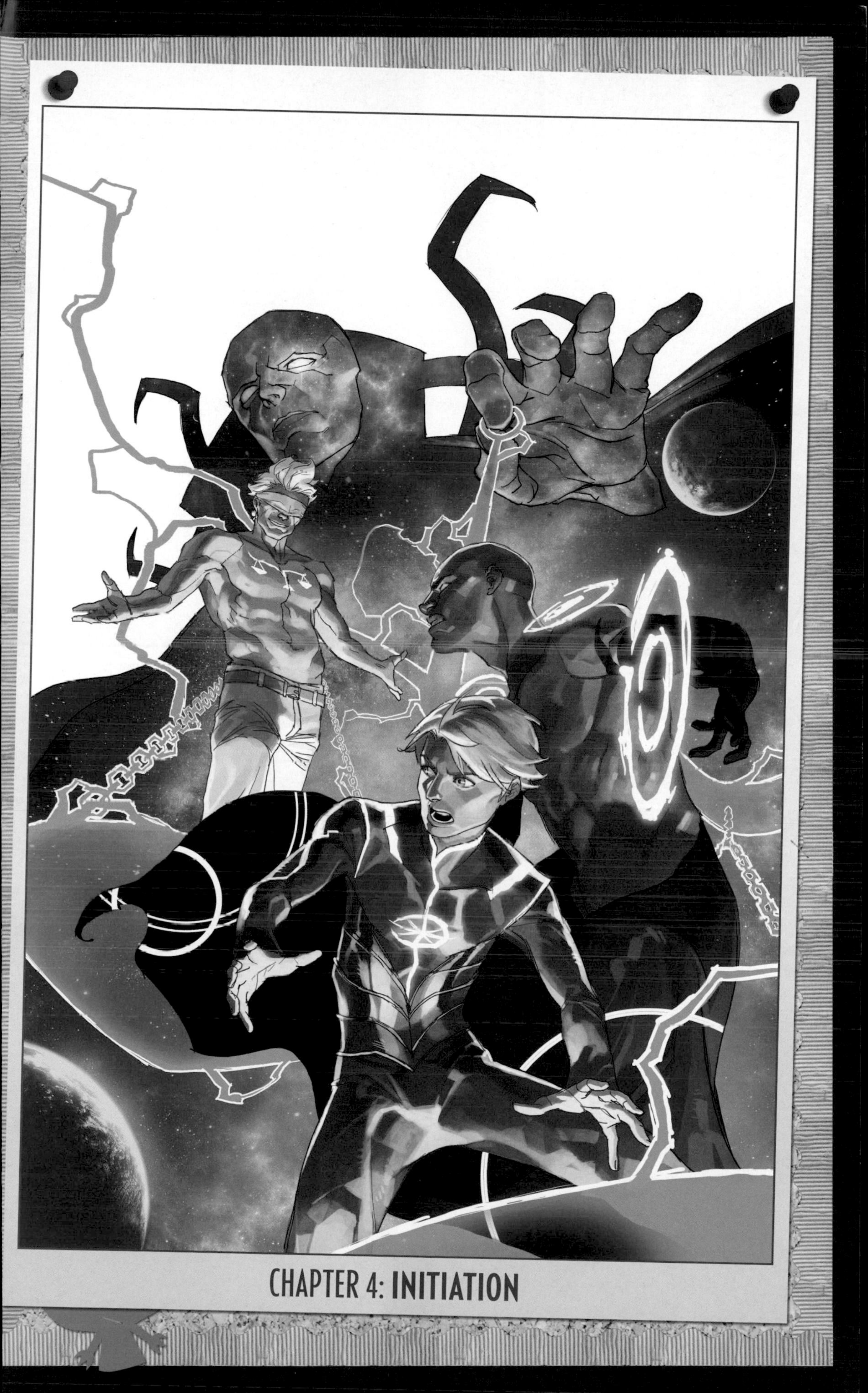

CHAPTER 4: INITIATION

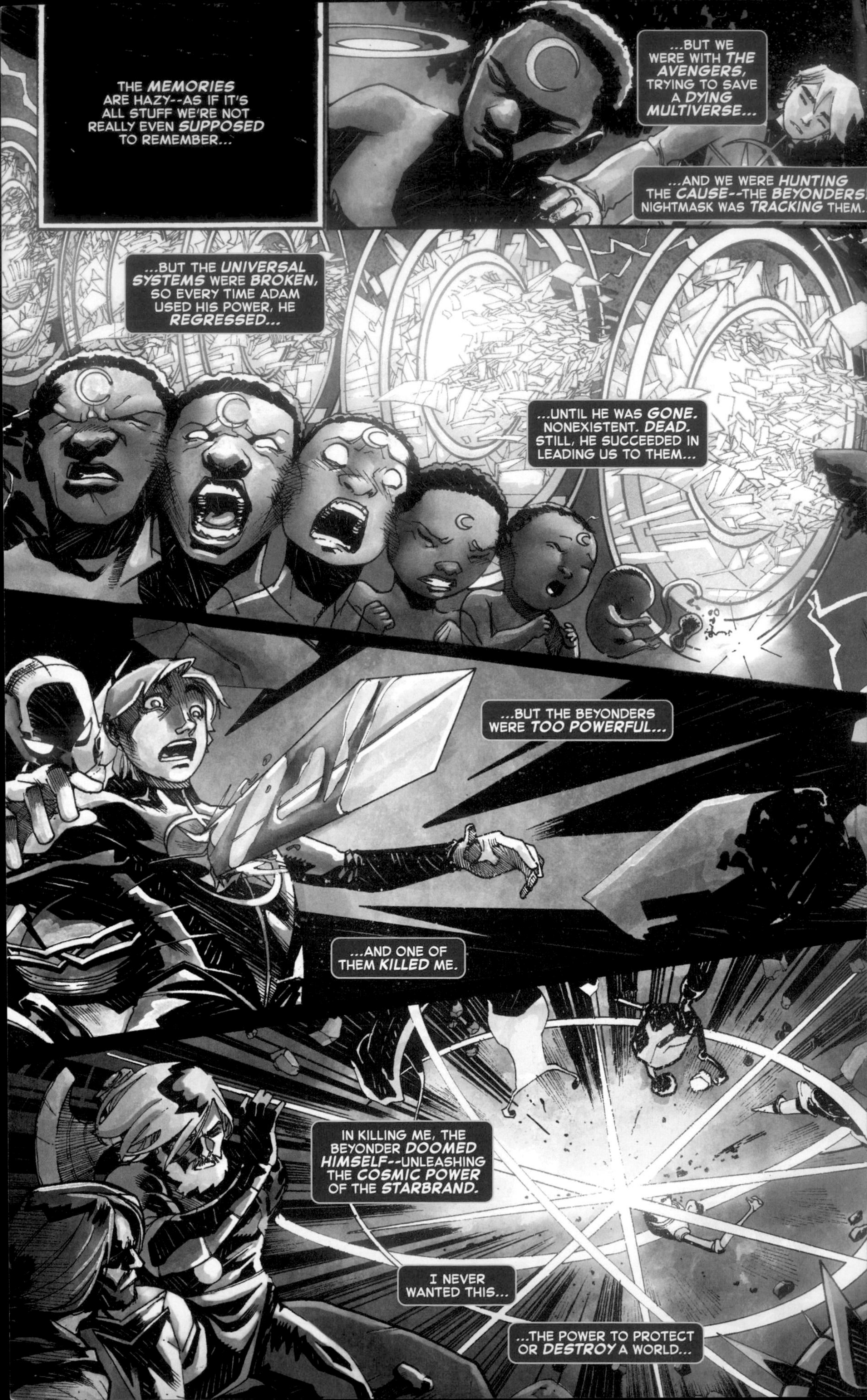
THE MEMORIES ARE HAZY--AS IF IT'S ALL STUFF WE'RE NOT REALLY EVEN SUPPOSED TO REMEMBER...
...BUT WE WERE WITH THE AVENGERS, TRYING TO SAVE A DYING MULTIVERSE...
...AND WE WERE HUNTING THE CAUSE--THE BEYONDERS. NIGHTMASK WAS TRACKING THEM.
...BUT THE UNIVERSAL SYSTEMS WERE BROKEN, SO EVERY TIME ADAM USED HIS POWER, HE REGRESSED...
...UNTIL HE WAS GONE. NONEXISTENT. DEAD. STILL, HE SUCCEEDED IN LEADING US TO THEM...
...BUT THE BEYONDERS WERE TOO POWERFUL...
...AND ONE OF THEM KILLED ME.
IN KILLING ME, THE BEYONDER DOOMED HIMSELF--UNLEASHING THE COSMIC POWER OF THE STARBRAND.
I NEVER WANTED THIS...
...THE POWER TO PROTECT OR DESTROY A WORLD...

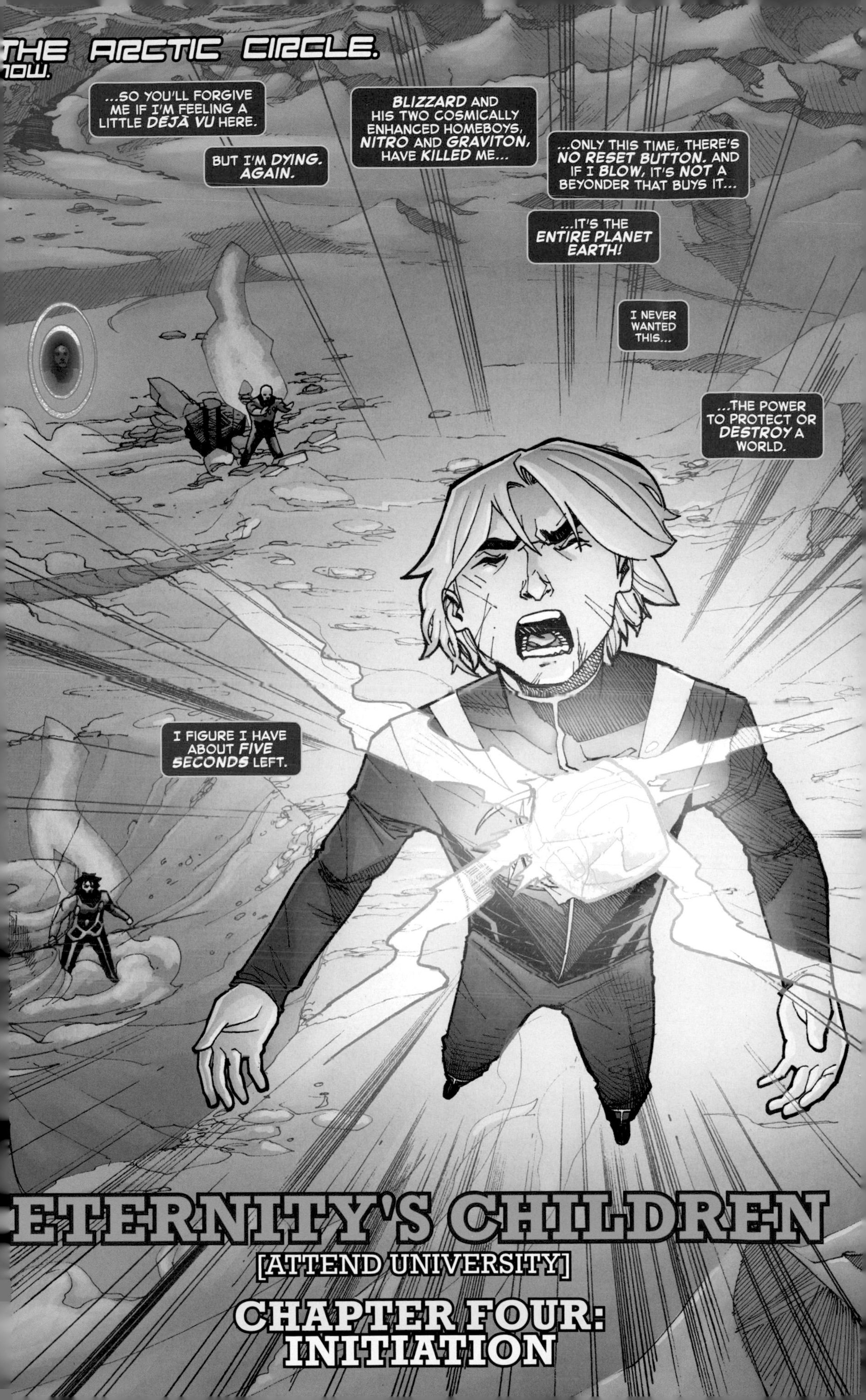

THE ARCTIC CIRCLE.
NOW.
...SO YOU'LL FORGIVE ME IF I'M FEELING A LITTLE DÉJÀ VU HERE.
BUT I'M DYING. AGAIN.
BLIZZARD AND HIS TWO COSMICALLY ENHANCED HOMEBOYS, NITRO AND GRAVITON, HAVE KILLED ME...
...ONLY THIS TIME, THERE'S NO RESET BUTTON. AND IF I BLOW, IT'S NOT A BEYONDER THAT BUYS IT...
...IT'S THE ENTIRE PLANET EARTH!
I NEVER WANTED THIS...
...THE POWER TO PROTECT OR DESTROY A WORLD.
I FIGURE I HAVE ABOUT FIVE SECONDS LEFT.
ETERNITY'S CHILDREN
[ATTEND UNIVERSITY]
CHAPTER FOUR: INITIATION

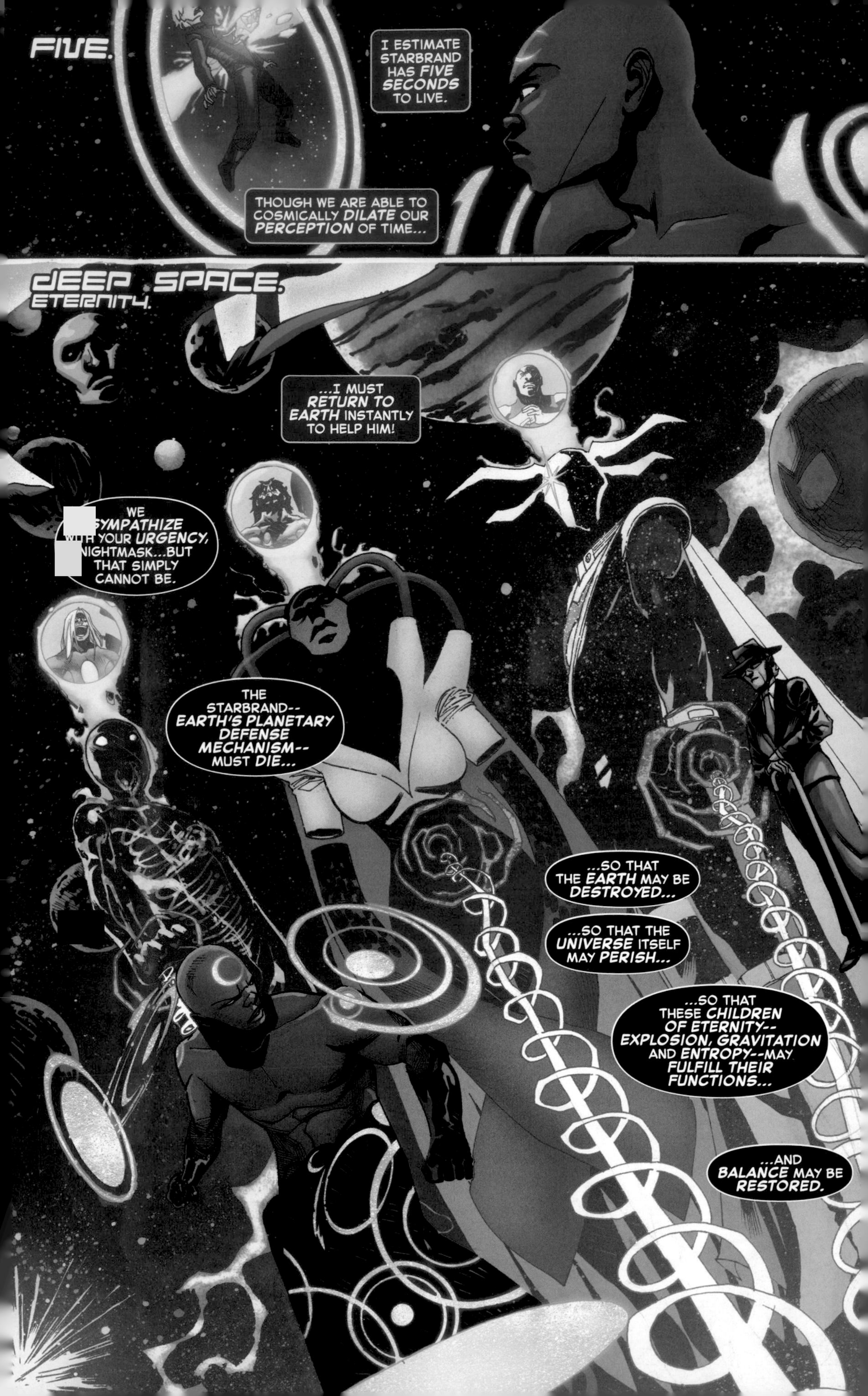
FIVE.
I ESTIMATE STARBRAND HAS FIVE SECONDS TO LIVE.
THOUGH WE ARE ABLE TO COSMICALLY DILATE OUR PERCEPTION OF TIME...
DEEP SPACE. ETERNITY.
...I MUST RETURN TO EARTH INSTANTLY TO HELP HIM!
WE SYMPATHIZE WITH YOUR URGENCY, NIGHTMASK...BUT THAT SIMPLY CANNOT BE.
THE STARBRAND-- EARTH'S PLANETARY DEFENSE MECHANISM-- MUST DIE...
...SO THAT THE EARTH MAY BE DESTROYED...
...SO THAT THE UNIVERSE ITSELF MAY PERISH...
...SO THAT THESE CHILDREN OF ETERNITY-- EXPLOSION, GRAVITATION AND ENTROPY--MAY FULFILL THEIR FUNCTIONS...
...AND BALANCE MAY BE RESTORED.

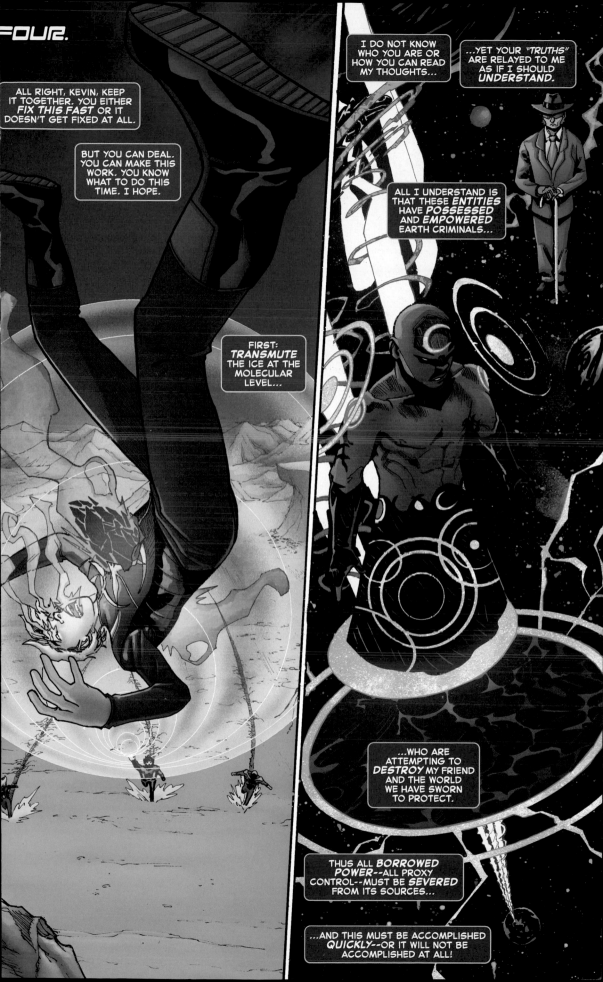

FOUR

ALL RIGHT, KEVIN, KEEP IT TOGETHER. YOU EITHER *FIX THIS FAST* OR IT DOESN'T GET FIXED AT ALL.

BUT YOU CAN DEAL. YOU CAN MAKE THIS WORK. YOU KNOW WHAT TO DO THIS TIME. I HOPE.

FIRST: *TRANSMUTE* THE ICE AT THE MOLECULAR LEVEL...

I DO NOT KNOW WHO YOU ARE OR HOW YOU CAN READ MY THOUGHTS...

...YET YOUR *"TRUTHS"* ARE RELAYED TO ME AS IF I SHOULD *UNDERSTAND.*

ALL I UNDERSTAND IS THAT THESE *ENTITIES* HAVE *POSSESSED* AND *EMPOWERED* EARTH CRIMINALS...

...WHO ARE ATTEMPTING TO *DESTROY* MY FRIEND AND THE WORLD WE HAVE SWORN TO PROTECT.

THUS ALL *BORROWED POWER*--ALL PROXY CONTROL--MUST BE *SEVERED* FROM ITS SOURCES...

...AND THIS MUST BE ACCOMPLISHED *QUICKLY*--OR IT WILL NOT BE ACCOMPLISHED AT ALL!

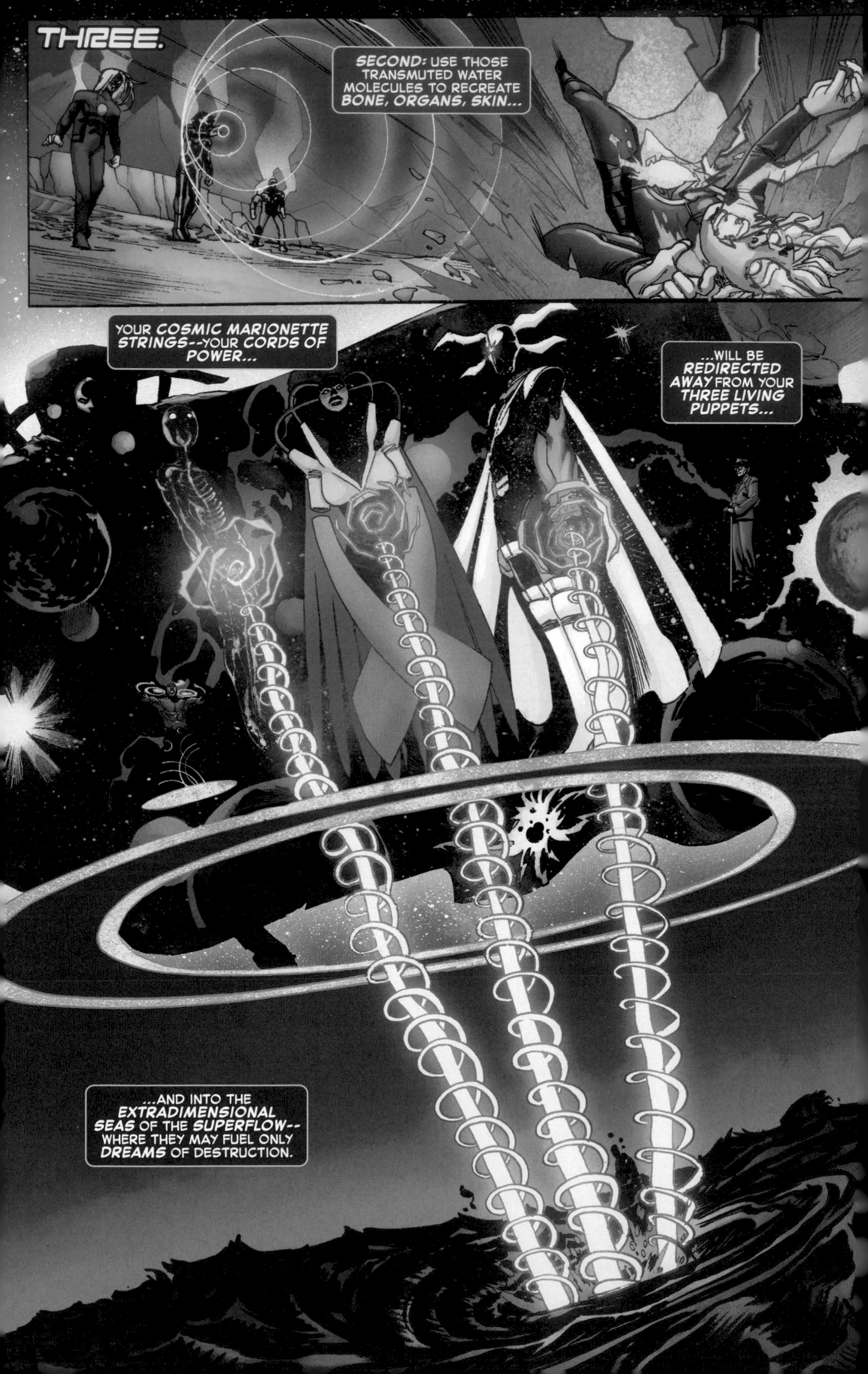
THREE.
SECOND: USE THOSE TRANSMUTED WATER MOLECULES TO RECREATE BONE, ORGANS, SKIN...
YOUR COSMIC MARIONETTE STRINGS--YOUR CORDS OF POWER...
...WILL BE REDIRECTED AWAY FROM YOUR THREE LIVING PUPPETS...
...AND INTO THE EXTRADIMENSIONAL SEAS OF THE SUPERFLOW--WHERE THEY MAY FUEL ONLY DREAMS OF DESTRUCTION.

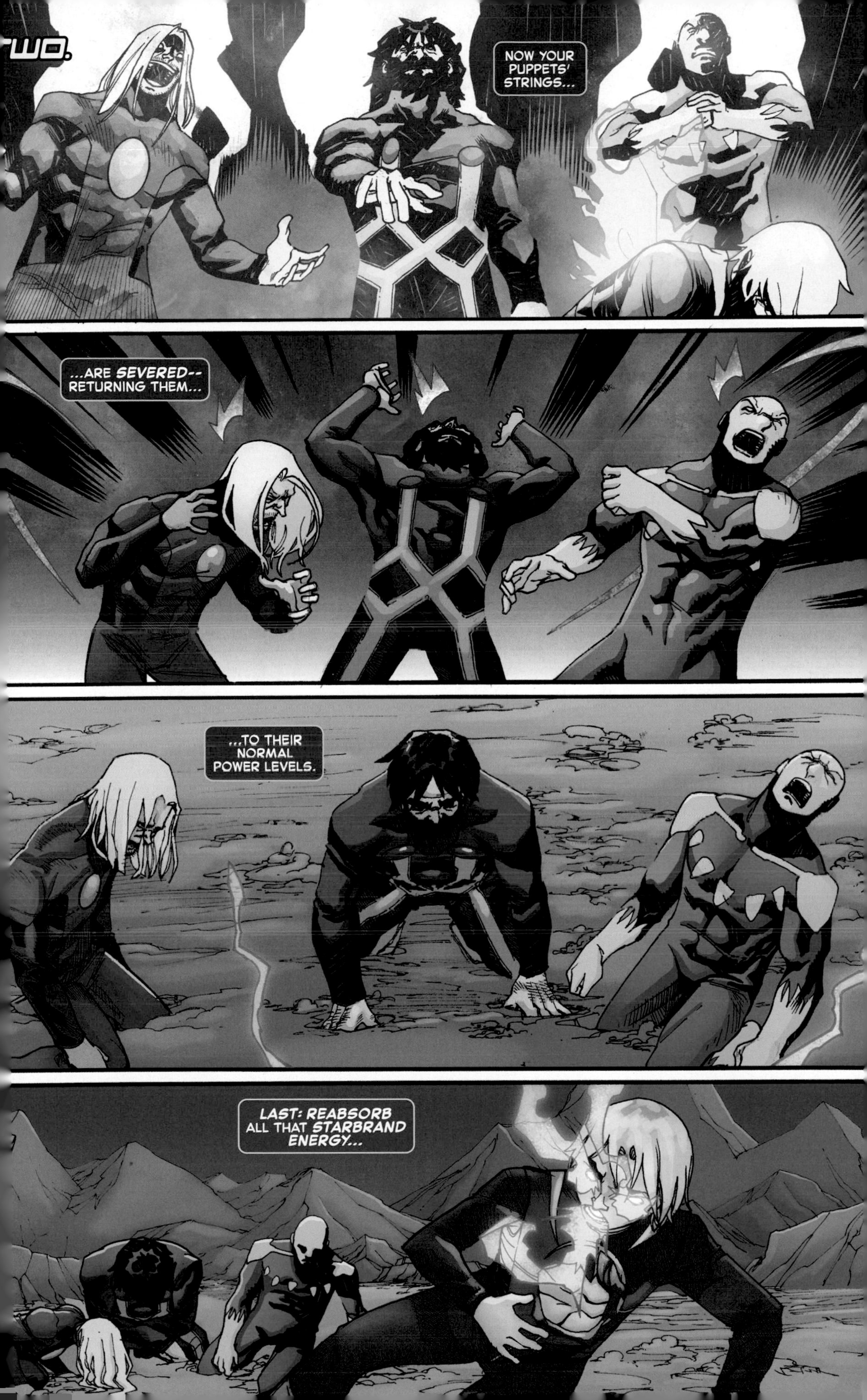
TWO.
NOW YOUR PUPPETS' STRINGS...
...ARE SEVERED-- RETURNING THEM...
...TO THEIR NORMAL POWER LEVELS.
LAST: REABSORB ALL THAT STARBRAND ENERGY...

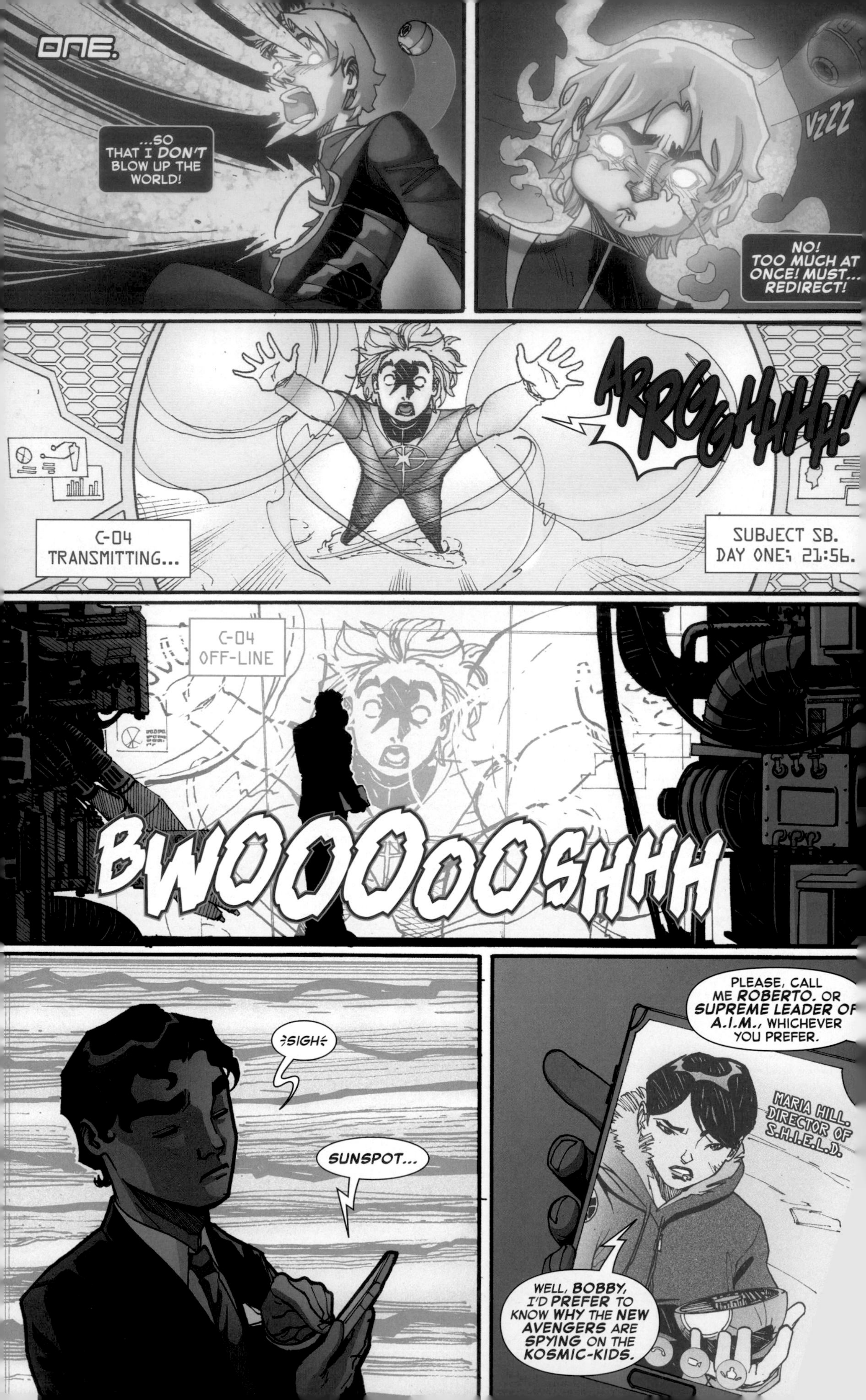
ONE.
...SO THAT I DON'T BLOW UP THE WORLD!
VZZZ
NO! TOO MUCH AT ONCE! MUST... REDIRECT!
ARRGGHHHH!
C-04 TRANSMITTING...
SUBJECT SB. DAY ONE; 21:56.
C-04 OFF-LINE
BWOOOOOOSHHH
SIGH
SUNSPOT...
PLEASE, CALL ME ROBERTO. OR SUPREME LEADER OF A.I.M., WHICHEVER YOU PREFER.
MARIA HILL. DIRECTOR OF S.H.I.E.L.D.
WELL, BOBBY, I'D PREFER TO KNOW WHY THE NEW AVENGERS ARE SPYING ON THE KOSMIC-KIDS.

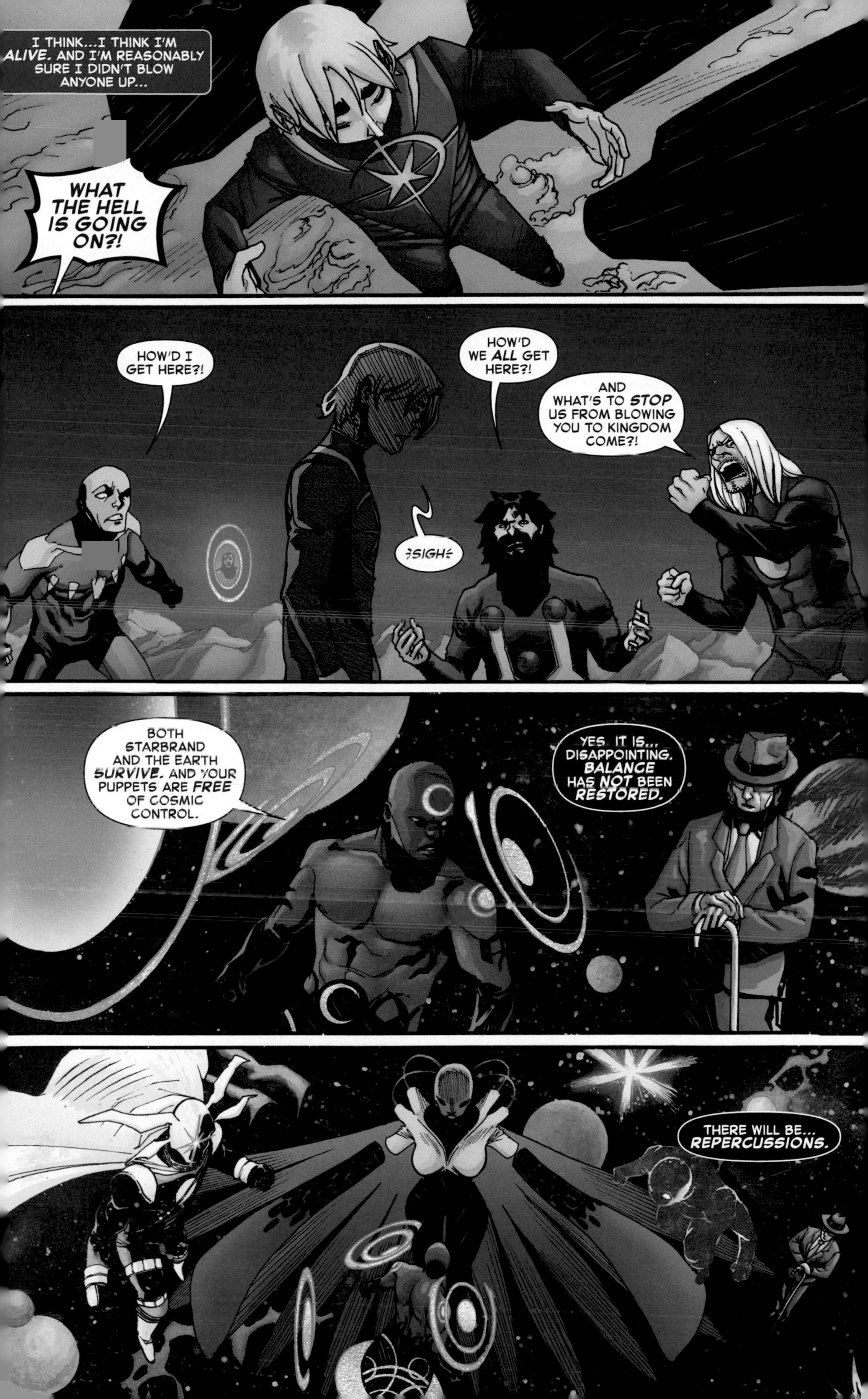
I THINK...I THINK I'M *ALIVE.* AND I'M REASONABLY SURE I DIDN'T BLOW ANYONE UP...
WHAT THE HELL IS GOING ON?!
HOW'D I GET HERE?!
HOW'D WE *ALL* GET HERE?!
AND WHAT'S TO *STOP* US FROM BLOWING YOU TO KINGDOM COME?!
SIGH
BOTH STARBRAND AND THE EARTH *SURVIVE.* AND YOUR PUPPETS ARE *FREE* OF COSMIC CONTROL.
YES. IT IS... DISAPPOINTING. *BALANCE* HAS *NOT* BEEN *RESTORED.*
THERE WILL BE... *REPERCUSSIONS.*

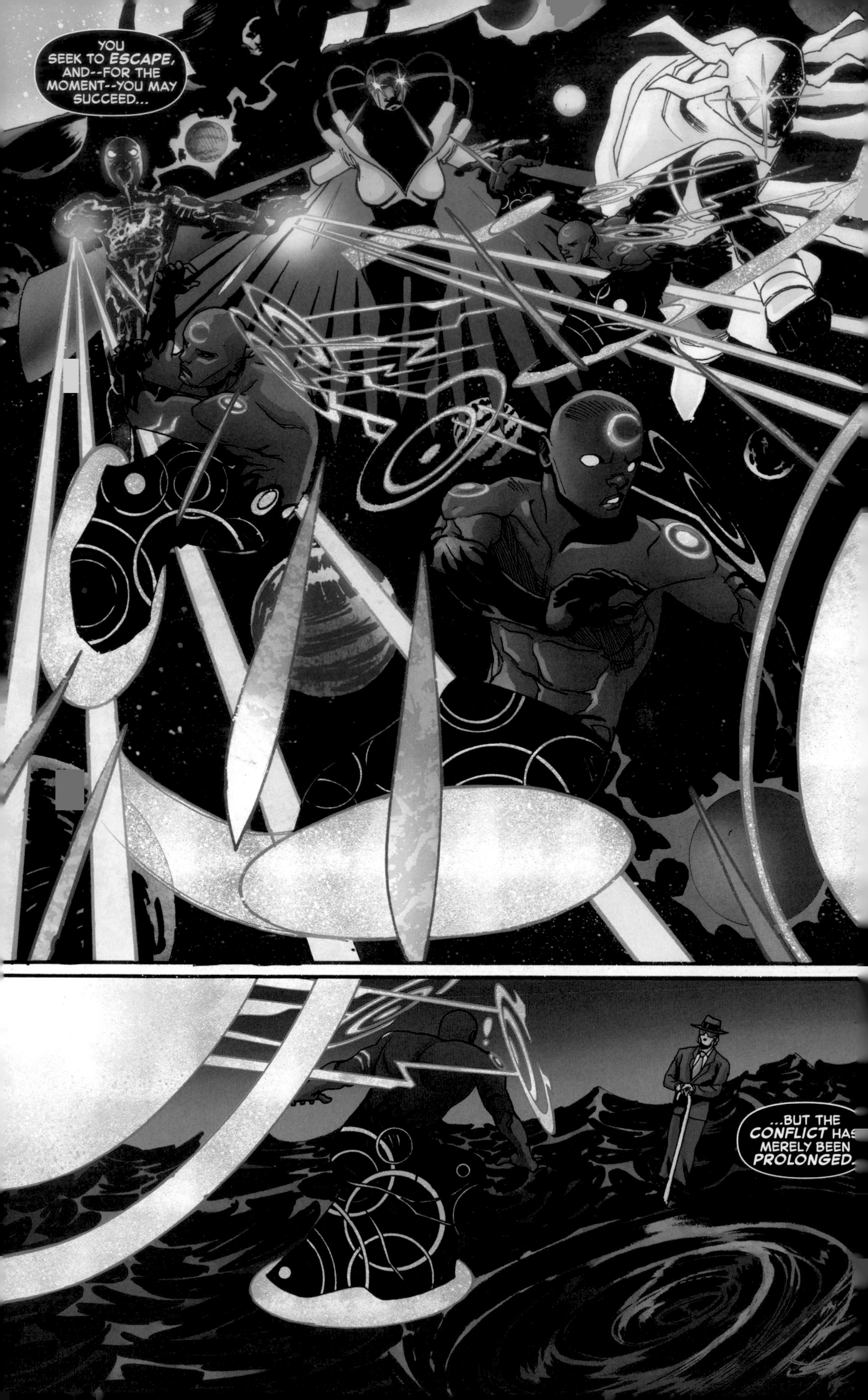
YOU SEEK TO ESCAPE, AND--FOR THE MOMENT--YOU MAY SUCCEED...
...BUT THE CONFLICT HAS MERELY BEEN PROLONGED.

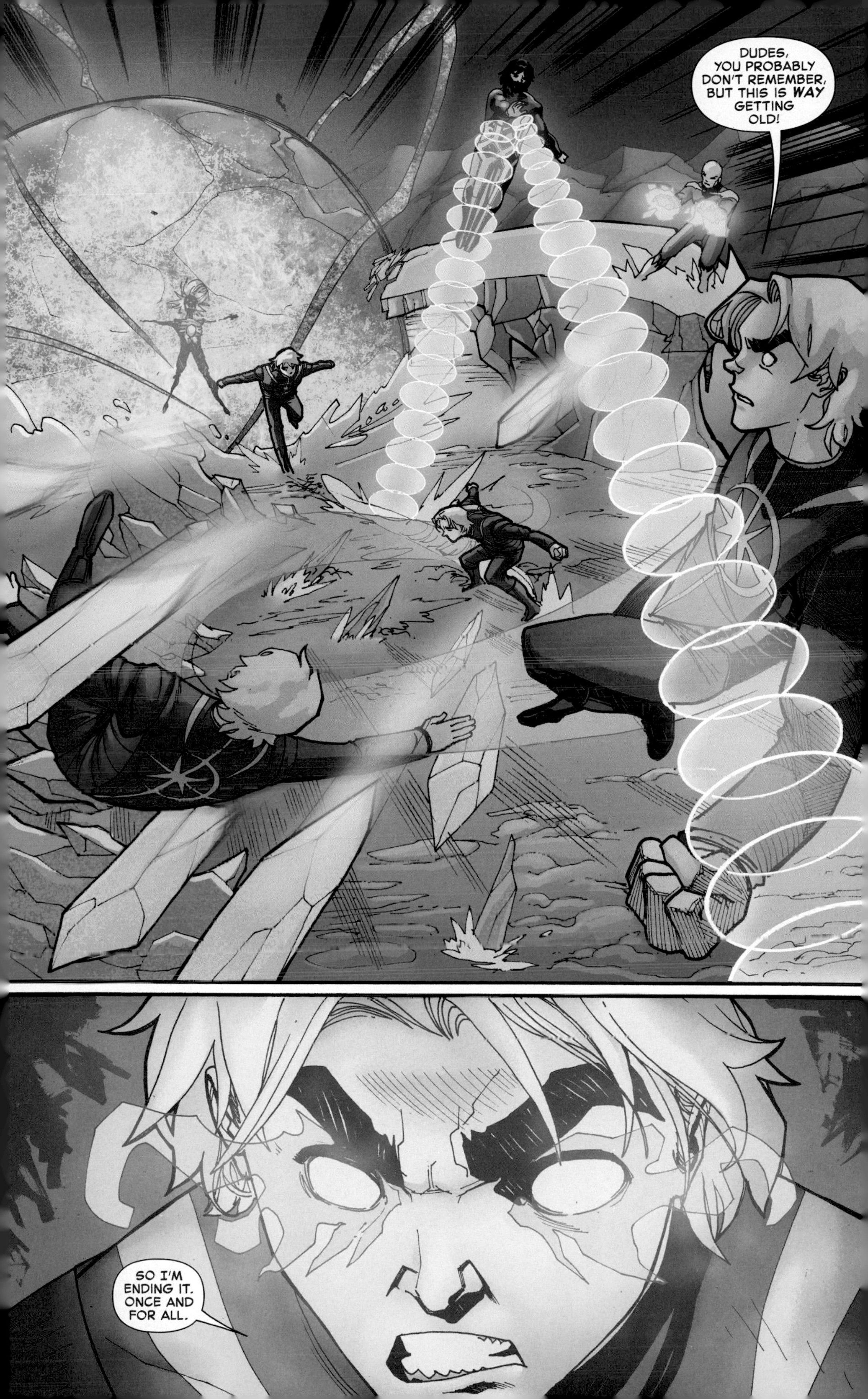
DUDES, YOU PROBABLY DON'T REMEMBER, BUT THIS IS WAY GETTING OLD!
SO I'M ENDING IT. ONCE AND FOR ALL.

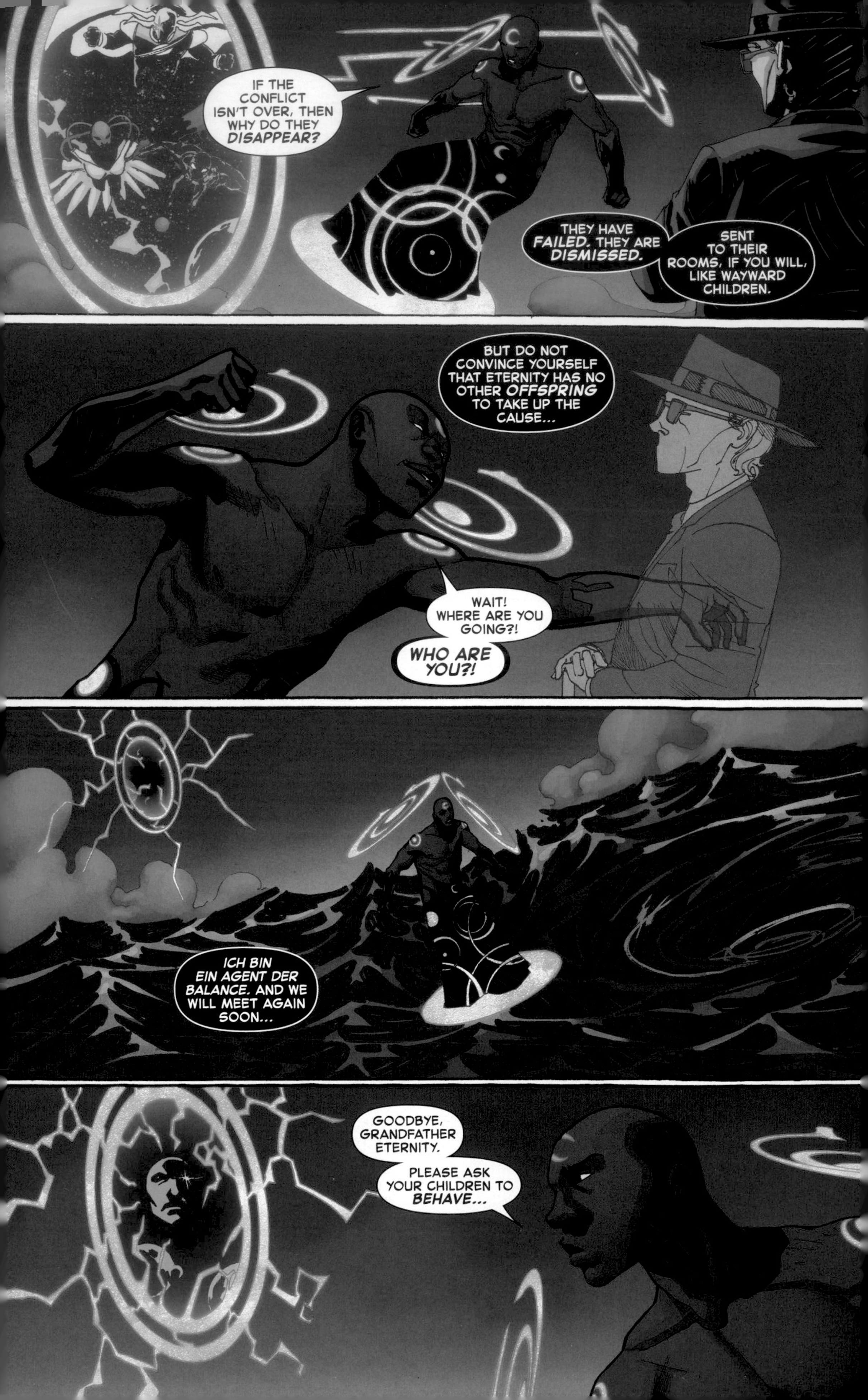
IF THE CONFLICT ISN'T OVER, THEN WHY DO THEY *DISAPPEAR?*
THEY HAVE *FAILED.* THEY ARE *DISMISSED.*
SENT TO THEIR ROOMS, IF YOU WILL, LIKE WAYWARD CHILDREN.
BUT DO NOT CONVINCE YOURSELF THAT ETERNITY HAS NO OTHER *OFFSPRING* TO TAKE UP THE CAUSE...
WAIT! WHERE ARE YOU GOING?!
WHO ARE YOU?!
ICH BIN EIN AGENT DER BALANCE. AND WE WILL MEET AGAIN SOON...
GOODBYE, GRANDFATHER ETERNITY.
PLEASE ASK YOUR CHILDREN TO *BEHAVE...*

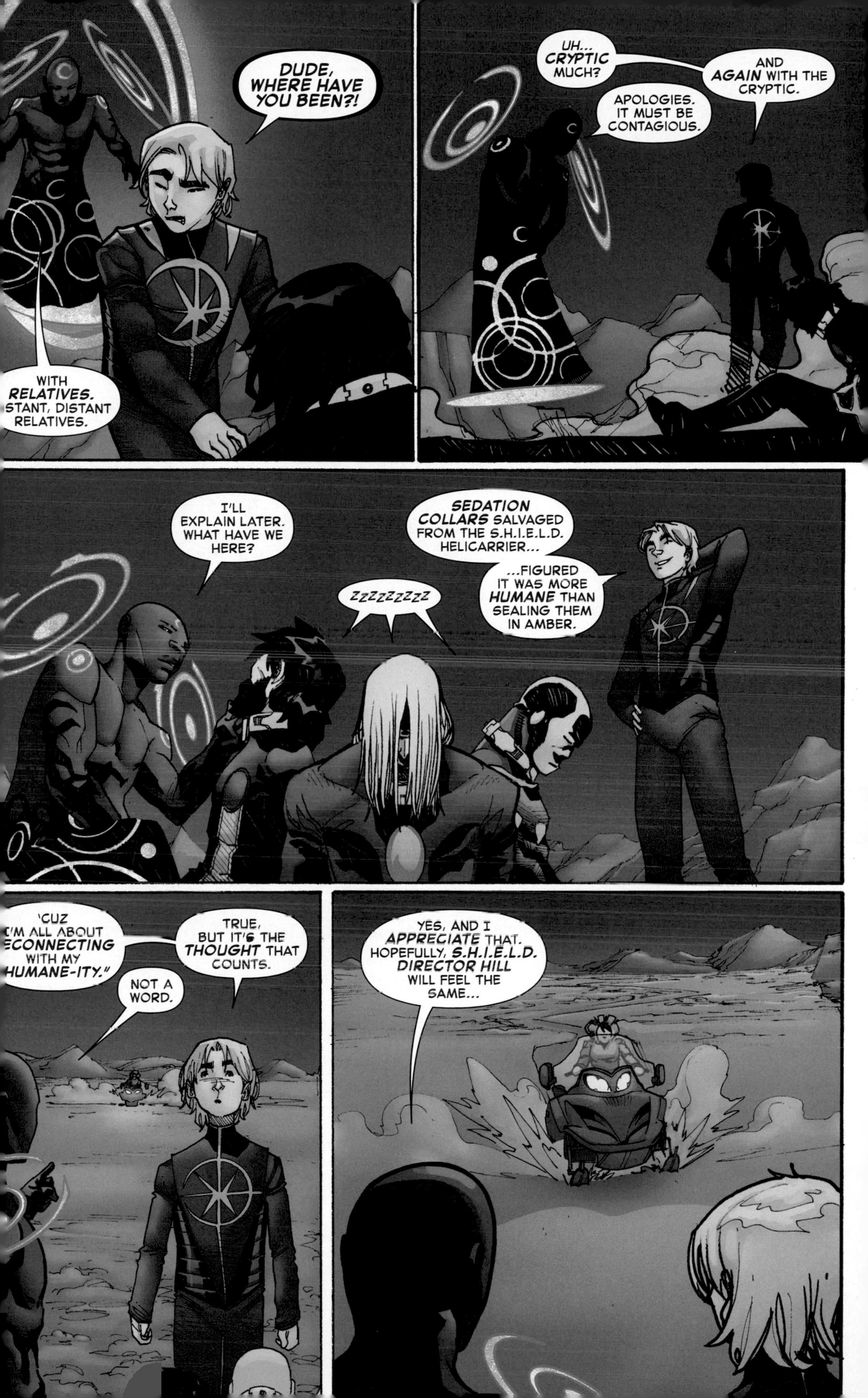
DUDE, WHERE HAVE YOU BEEN?!
WITH RELATIVES. STANT, DISTANT RELATIVES.
UH... CRYPTIC MUCH?
AND AGAIN WITH THE CRYPTIC.
APOLOGIES. IT MUST BE CONTAGIOUS.
I'LL EXPLAIN LATER. WHAT HAVE WE HERE?
SEDATION COLLARS SALVAGED FROM THE S.H.I.E.L.D. HELICARRIER...
...FIGURED IT WAS MORE HUMANE THAN SEALING THEM IN AMBER.
ZZZZZZZZZ
'CUZ I'M ALL ABOUT ECONNECTING WITH MY HUMANE-ITY."
TRUE, BUT IT'S THE THOUGHT THAT COUNTS.
NOT A WORD.
YES, AND I APPRECIATE THAT. HOPEFULLY, S.H.I.E.L.D. DIRECTOR HILL WILL FEEL THE SAME...

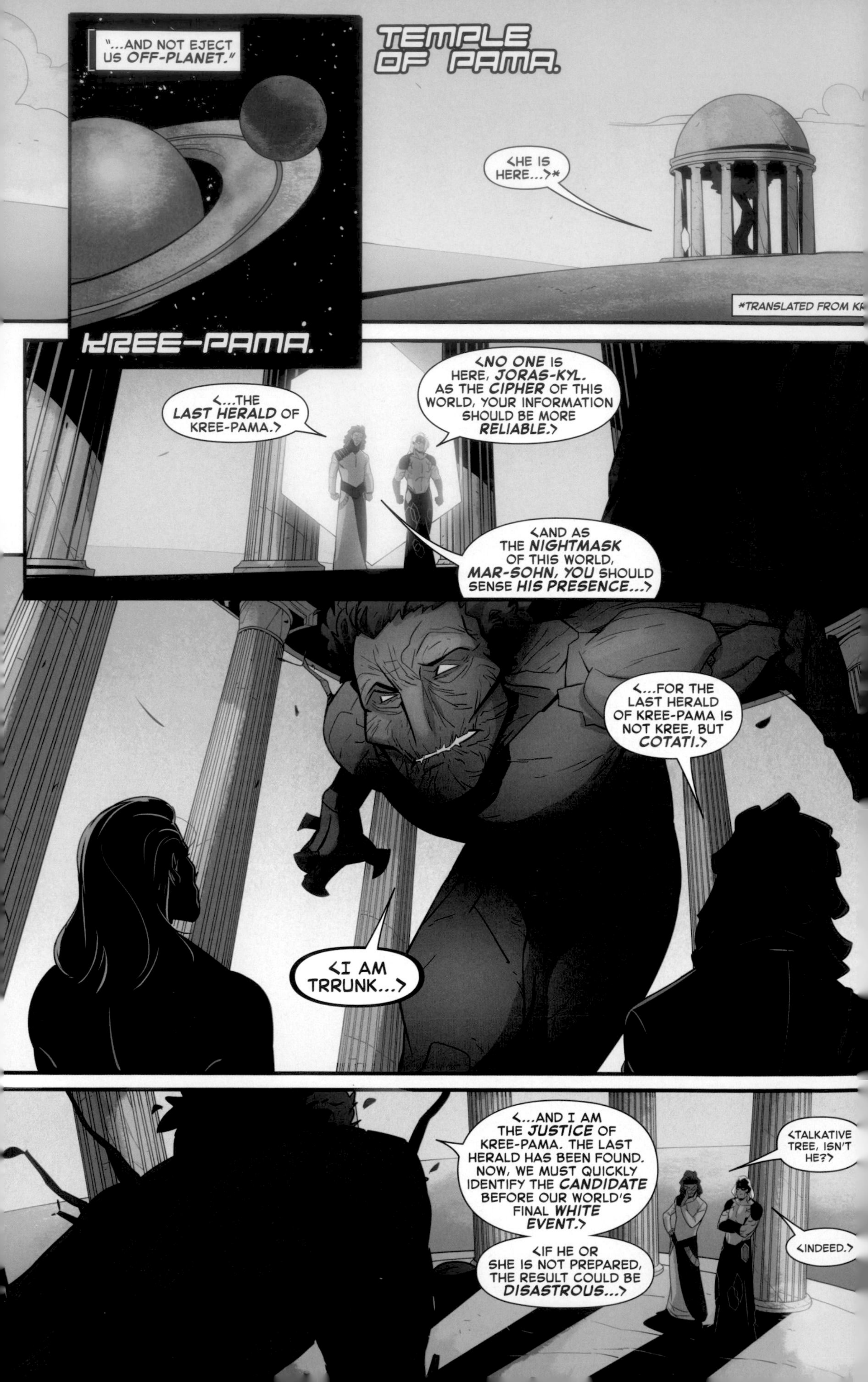
"...AND NOT EJECT US OFF-PLANET."
KREE-PAMA.
TEMPLE OF PAMA.
<HE IS HERE...>*
*TRANSLATED FROM KR
<...THE LAST HERALD OF KREE-PAMA.>
<NO ONE IS HERE, JORAS-KYL. AS THE CIPHER OF THIS WORLD, YOUR INFORMATION SHOULD BE MORE RELIABLE.>
<AND AS THE NIGHTMASK OF THIS WORLD, MAR-SOHN, YOU SHOULD SENSE HIS PRESENCE...>
<...FOR THE LAST HERALD OF KREE-PAMA IS NOT KREE, BUT COTATI.>
<I AM TRRUNK...>
<...AND I AM THE JUSTICE OF KREE-PAMA. THE LAST HERALD HAS BEEN FOUND. NOW, WE MUST QUICKLY IDENTIFY THE CANDIDATE BEFORE OUR WORLD'S FINAL WHITE EVENT.>
<IF HE OR SHE IS NOT PREPARED, THE RESULT COULD BE DISASTROUS...>
<TALKATIVE TREE, ISN'T HE?>
<INDEED.>

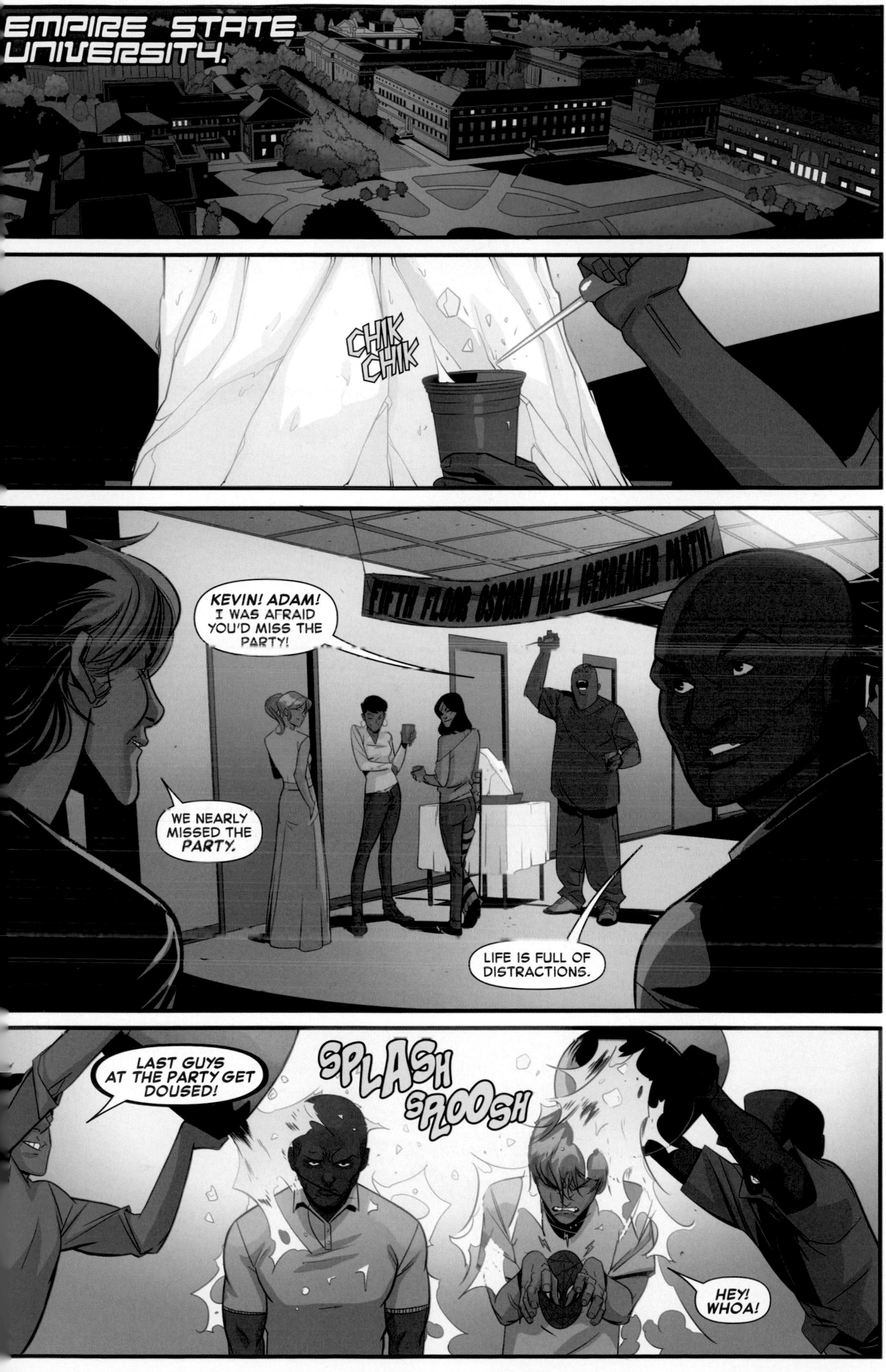
EMPIRE STATE UNIVERSITY.
CHIK CHIK
FIFTH FLOOR OSBORN HALL ICEBREAKER PARTY!
KEVIN! ADAM! I WAS AFRAID YOU'D MISS THE PARTY!
WE NEARLY MISSED THE PARTY.
LIFE IS FULL OF DISTRACTIONS.
LAST GUYS AT THE PARTY GET DOUSED!
SPLASH
SPLOOSH
HEY! WHOA!

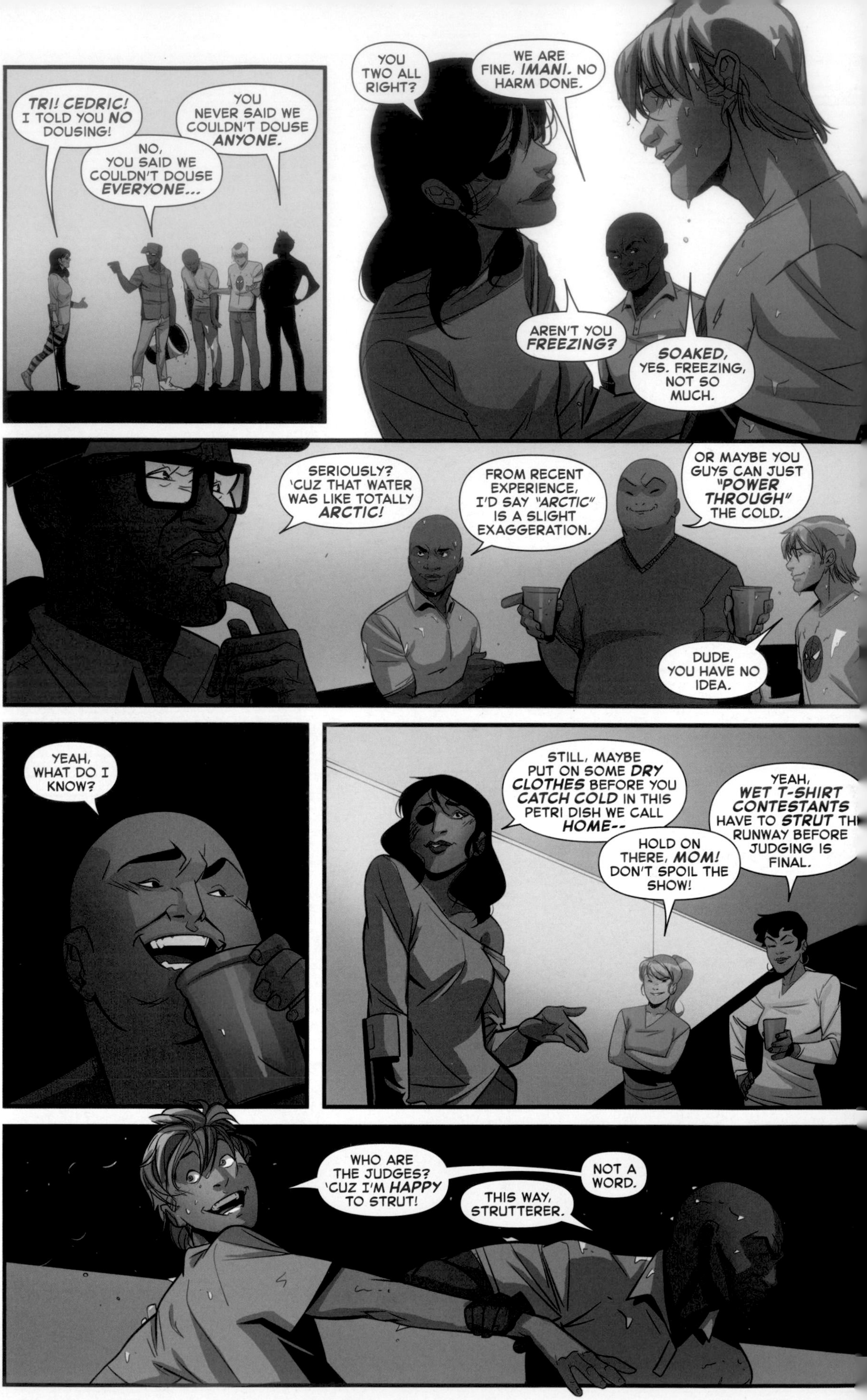
TRI! CEDRIC! I TOLD YOU NO DOUSING!
NO, YOU SAID WE COULDN'T DOUSE EVERYONE...
YOU NEVER SAID WE COULDN'T DOUSE ANYONE.
YOU TWO ALL RIGHT?
WE ARE FINE, IMANI. NO HARM DONE.
AREN'T YOU FREEZING?
SOAKED, YES. FREEZING, NOT SO MUCH.
SERIOUSLY? 'CUZ THAT WATER WAS LIKE TOTALLY ARCTIC!
FROM RECENT EXPERIENCE, I'D SAY "ARCTIC" IS A SLIGHT EXAGGERATION.
OR MAYBE YOU GUYS CAN JUST "POWER THROUGH" THE COLD.
DUDE, YOU HAVE NO IDEA.
YEAH, WHAT DO I KNOW?
STILL, MAYBE PUT ON SOME DRY CLOTHES BEFORE YOU CATCH COLD IN THIS PETRI DISH WE CALL HOME--
HOLD ON THERE, MOM! DON'T SPOIL THE SHOW!
YEAH, WET T-SHIRT CONTESTANTS HAVE TO STRUT THE RUNWAY BEFORE JUDGING IS FINAL.
WHO ARE THE JUDGES? 'CUZ I'M HAPPY TO STRUT!
NOT A WORD.
THIS WAY, STRUTTERER.

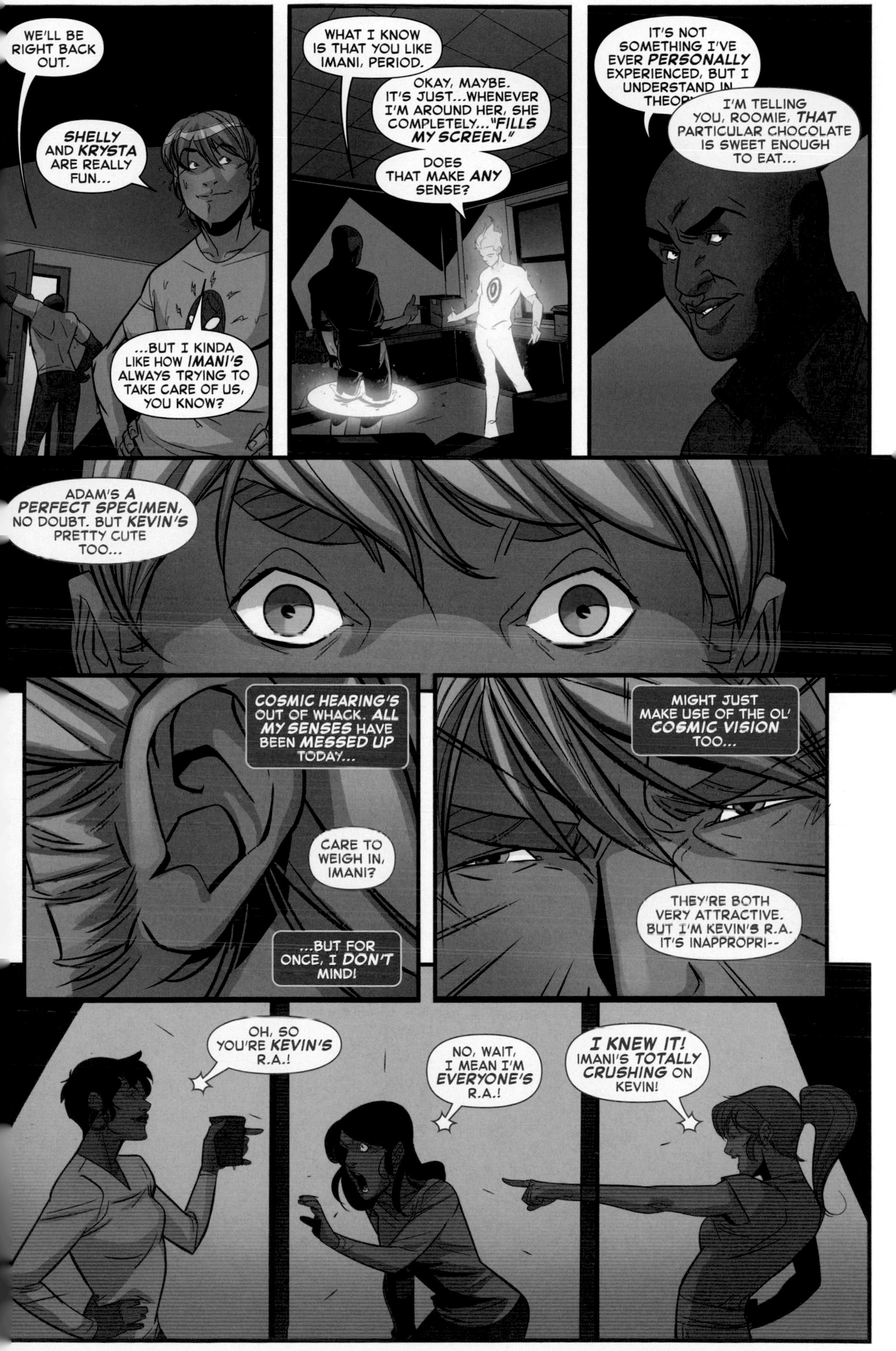
WE'LL BE RIGHT BACK OUT.
SHELLY AND KRYSTA ARE REALLY FUN...
...BUT I KINDA LIKE HOW IMANI'S ALWAYS TRYING TO TAKE CARE OF US, YOU KNOW?
WHAT I KNOW IS THAT YOU LIKE IMANI, PERIOD.
OKAY, MAYBE. IT'S JUST...WHENEVER I'M AROUND HER, SHE COMPLETELY..."FILLS MY SCREEN."
DOES THAT MAKE ANY SENSE?
IT'S NOT SOMETHING I'VE EVER PERSONALLY EXPERIENCED, BUT I UNDERSTAND IN
I'M TELLING YOU, ROOMIE, THAT PARTICULAR CHOCOLATE IS SWEET ENOUGH TO EAT...
ADAM'S A PERFECT SPECIMEN, NO DOUBT. BUT KEVIN'S PRETTY CUTE TOO...
COSMIC HEARING'S OUT OF WHACK. ALL MY SENSES HAVE BEEN MESSED UP TODAY...
CARE TO WEIGH IN, IMANI?
...BUT FOR ONCE, I DON'T MIND!
MIGHT JUST MAKE USE OF THE OL' COSMIC VISION TOO...
THEY'RE BOTH VERY ATTRACTIVE. BUT I'M KEVIN'S R.A. IT'S INAPPROPRI--
OH, SO YOU'RE KEVIN'S R.A.!
NO, WAIT, I MEAN I'M EVERYONE'S R.A.!
I KNEW IT! IMANI'S TOTALLY CRUSHING ON KEVIN!

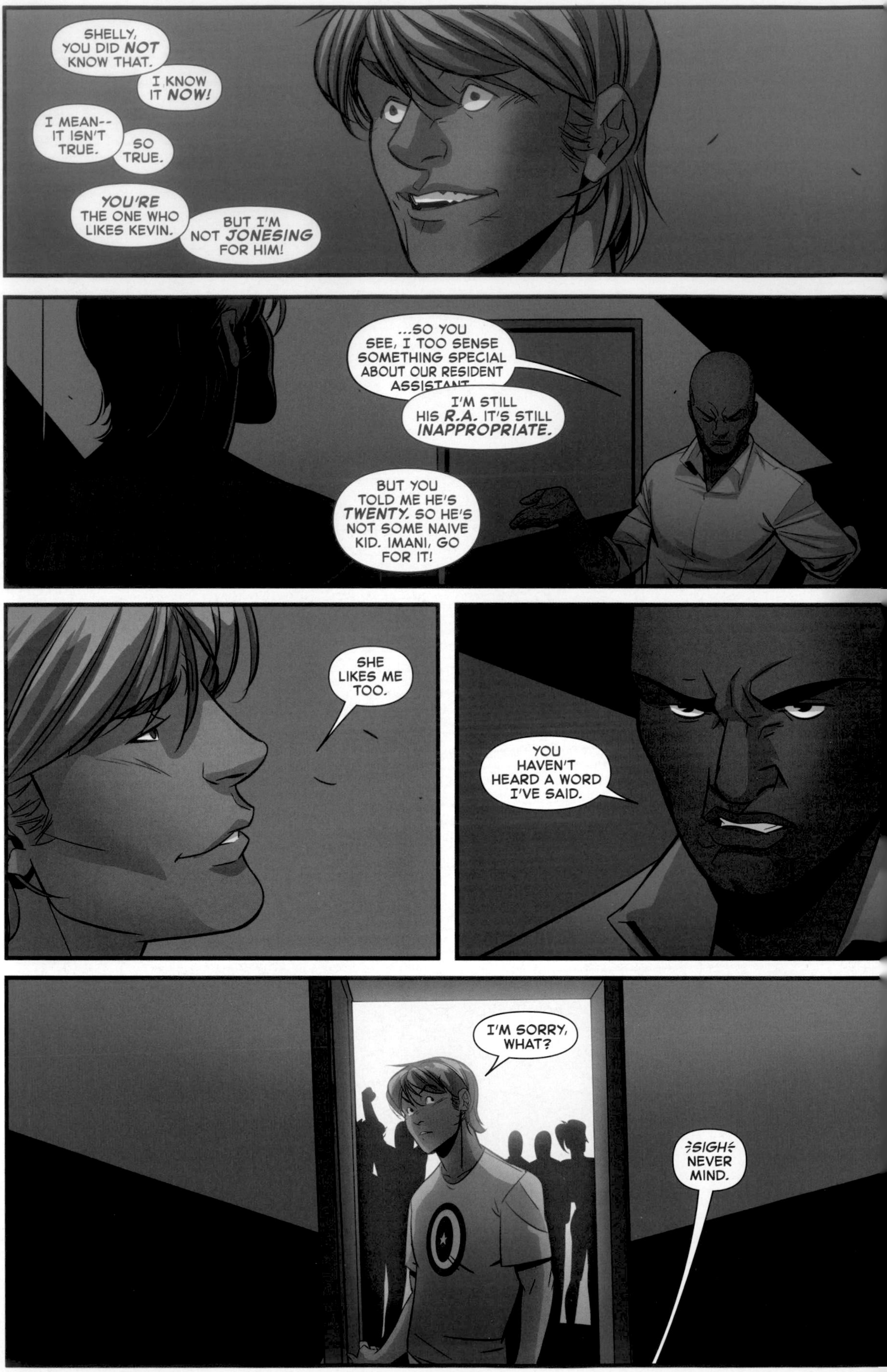
SHELLY, YOU DID NOT KNOW THAT.
I KNOW IT NOW!
I MEAN-- IT ISN'T TRUE.
SO TRUE.
YOU'RE THE ONE WHO LIKES KEVIN.
BUT I'M NOT JONESING FOR HIM!
...SO YOU SEE, I TOO SENSE SOMETHING SPECIAL ABOUT OUR RESIDENT ASSISTANT.
I'M STILL HIS R.A. IT'S STILL INAPPROPRIATE.
BUT YOU TOLD ME HE'S TWENTY. SO HE'S NOT SOME NAIVE KID. IMANI, GO FOR IT!
SHE LIKES ME TOO.
YOU HAVEN'T HEARD A WORD I'VE SAID.
I'M SORRY, WHAT?
SIGH NEVER MIND.

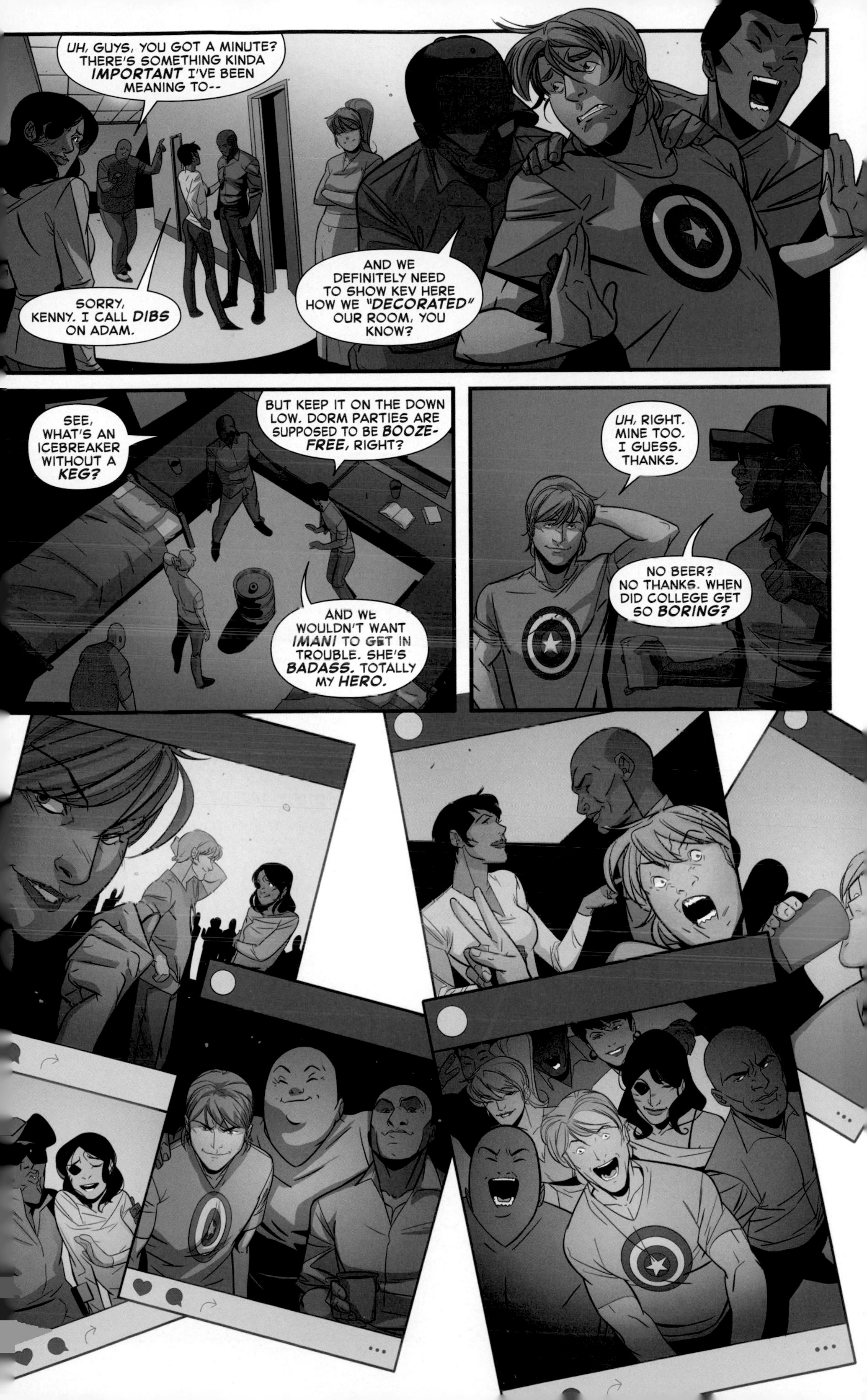
UH, GUYS, YOU GOT A MINUTE? THERE'S SOMETHING KINDA IMPORTANT I'VE BEEN MEANING TO--
SORRY, KENNY. I CALL DIBS ON ADAM.
AND WE DEFINITELY NEED TO SHOW KEV HERE HOW WE "DECORATED" OUR ROOM, YOU KNOW?
SEE, WHAT'S AN ICEBREAKER WITHOUT A KEG?
BUT KEEP IT ON THE DOWN LOW. DORM PARTIES ARE SUPPOSED TO BE BOOZE-FREE, RIGHT?
AND WE WOULDN'T WANT IMANI TO GET IN TROUBLE. SHE'S BADASS. TOTALLY MY HERO.
UH, RIGHT. MINE TOO. I GUESS. THANKS.
NO BEER? NO THANKS. WHEN DID COLLEGE GET SO BORING?

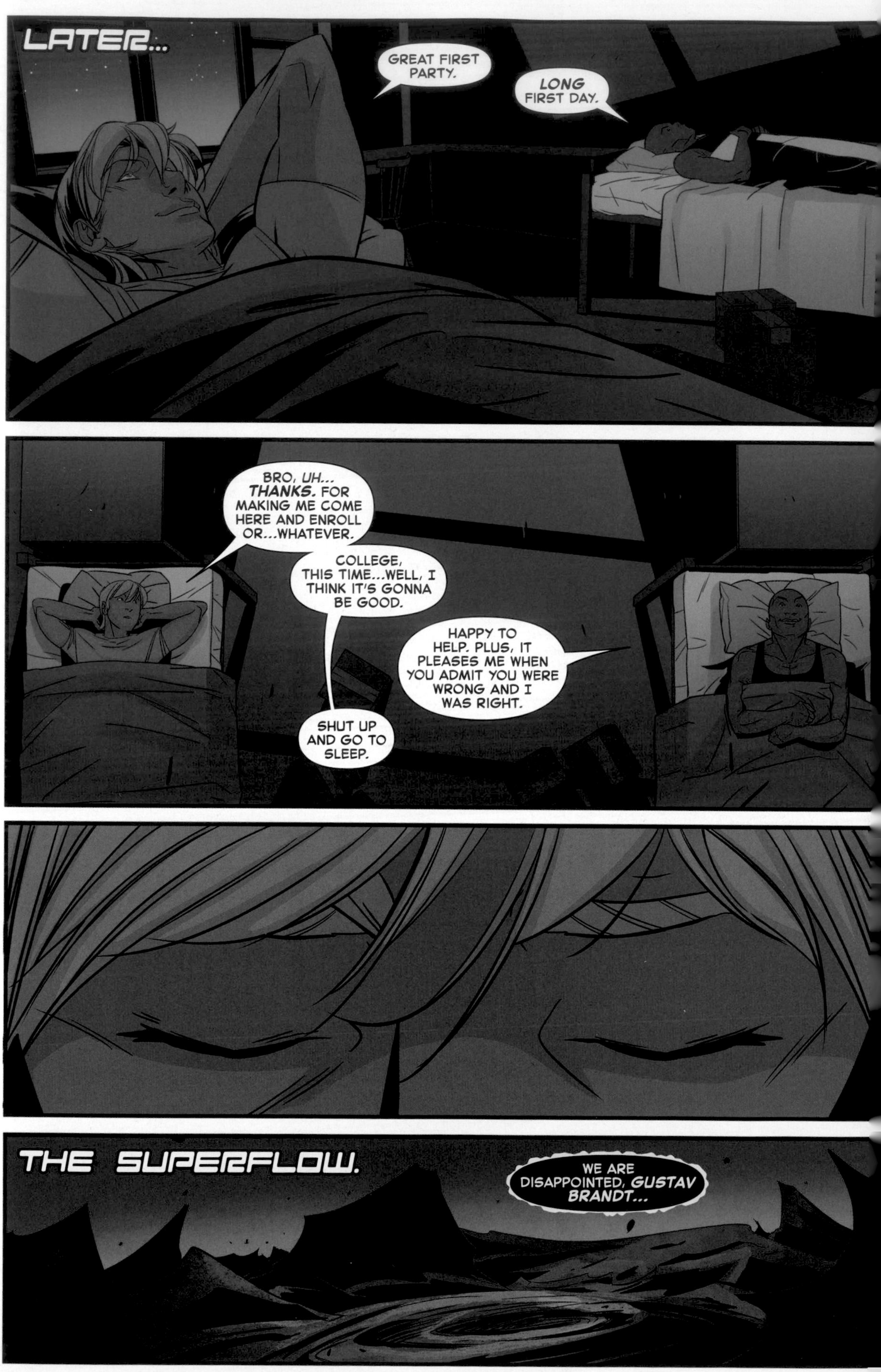
LATER...
GREAT FIRST PARTY.
LONG FIRST DAY.
BRO, UH... THANKS. FOR MAKING ME COME HERE AND ENROLL OR...WHATEVER.
COLLEGE, THIS TIME...WELL, I THINK IT'S GONNA BE GOOD.
HAPPY TO HELP. PLUS, IT PLEASES ME WHEN YOU ADMIT YOU WERE WRONG AND I WAS RIGHT.
SHUT UP AND GO TO SLEEP.
THE SUPERFLOW.
WE ARE DISAPPOINTED, GUSTAV BRANDT...

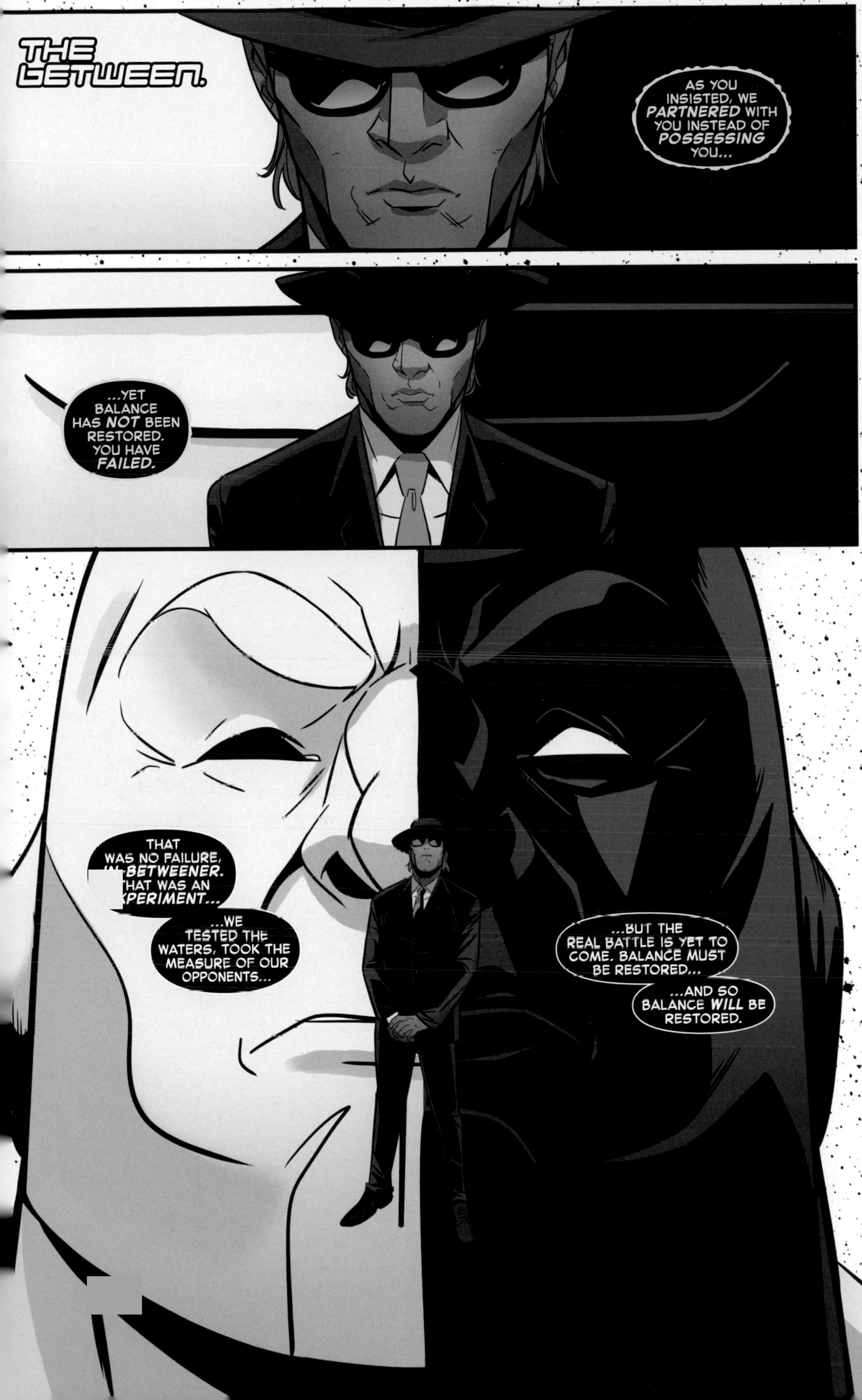
THE BETWEEN.
AS YOU INSISTED, WE PARTNERED WITH YOU INSTEAD OF POSSESSING YOU...
...YET BALANCE HAS NOT BEEN RESTORED. YOU HAVE FAILED.
THAT WAS NO FAILURE, IN-BETWEENER. THAT WAS AN EXPERIMENT...
...WE TESTED THE WATERS, TOOK THE MEASURE OF OUR OPPONENTS...
...BUT THE REAL BATTLE IS YET TO COME. BALANCE MUST BE RESTORED...
...AND SO BALANCE WILL BE RESTORED.

IT'S PROBABLY NOTHING

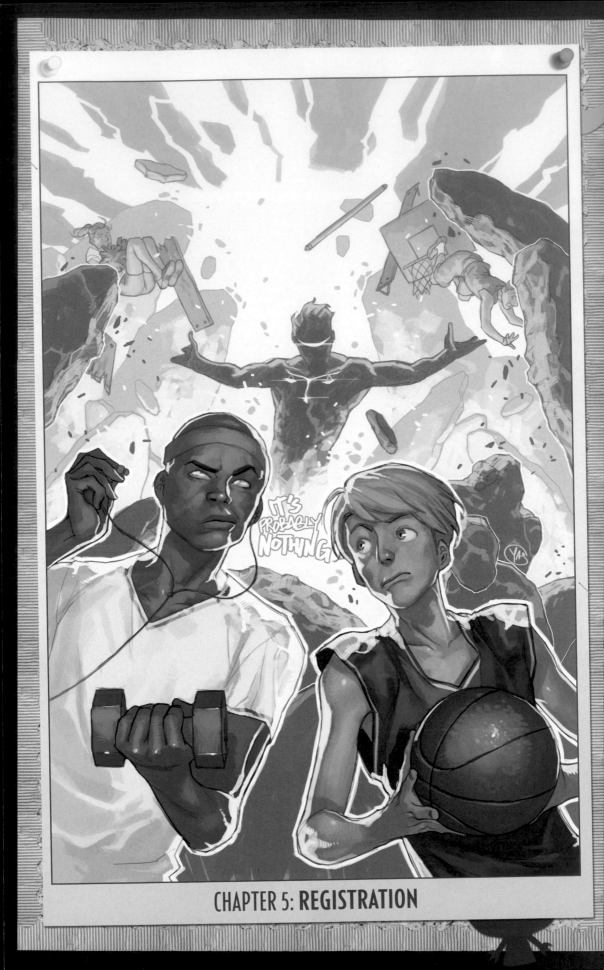

CHAPTER 5: REGISTRATION

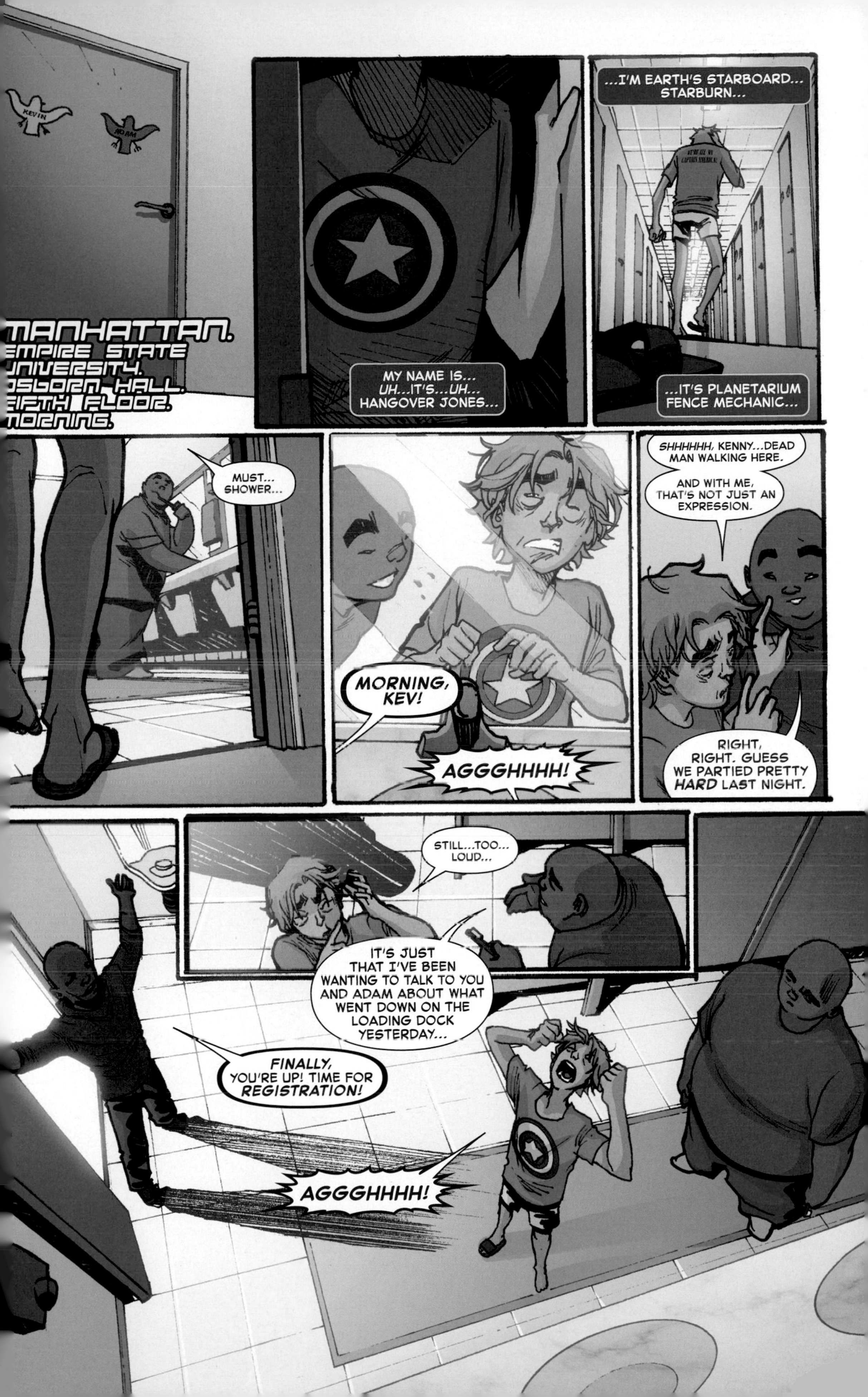
KEVIN
ADAM
MANHATTAN.
EMPIRE STATE
UNIVERSITY.
OSBORN HALL.
FIFTH FLOOR.
MORNING.
MY NAME IS... UH...IT'S...UH... HANGOVER JONES...
...I'M EARTH'S STARBOARD... STARBURN...
...IT'S PLANETARIUM FENCE MECHANIC...
MUST... SHOWER...
MORNING, KEV!
AGGGHHHH!
SHHHHHH, KENNY...DEAD MAN WALKING HERE.
AND WITH ME, THAT'S NOT JUST AN EXPRESSION.
RIGHT, RIGHT. GUESS WE PARTIED PRETTY HARD LAST NIGHT.
STILL...TOO... LOUD...
IT'S JUST THAT I'VE BEEN WANTING TO TALK TO YOU AND ADAM ABOUT WHAT WENT DOWN ON THE LOADING DOCK YESTERDAY...
FINALLY, YOU'RE UP! TIME FOR REGISTRATION!
AGGGHHHH!

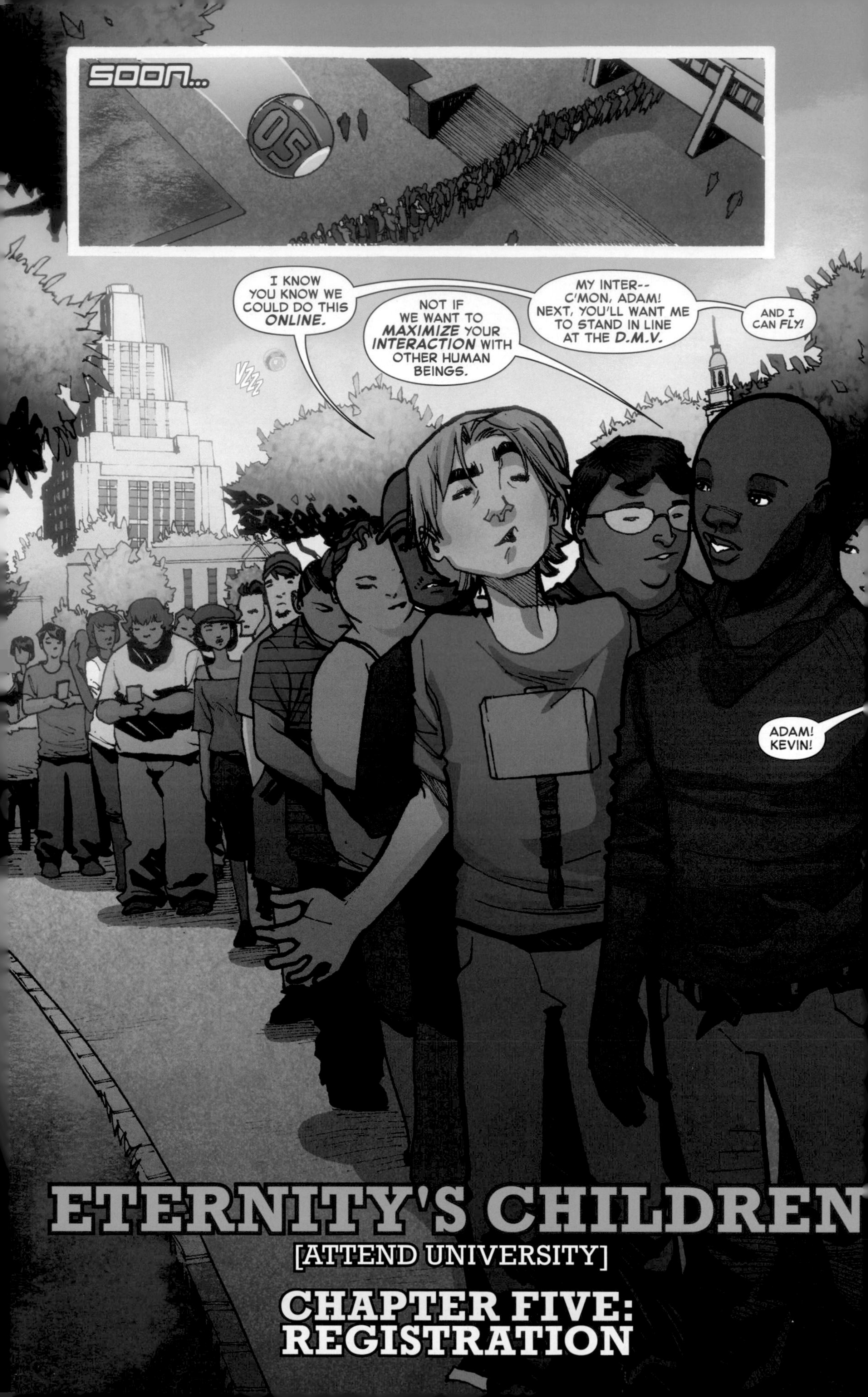
SOON...
I KNOW YOU KNOW WE COULD DO THIS ONLINE.
NOT IF WE WANT TO MAXIMIZE YOUR INTERACTION WITH OTHER HUMAN BEINGS.
MY INTER-- C'MON, ADAM! NEXT, YOU'LL WANT ME TO STAND IN LINE AT THE D.M.V.
AND I CAN FLY!
VZZZ
ADAM! KEVIN!
ETERNITY'S CHILDREN
[ATTEND UNIVERSITY]
CHAPTER FIVE: REGISTRATION

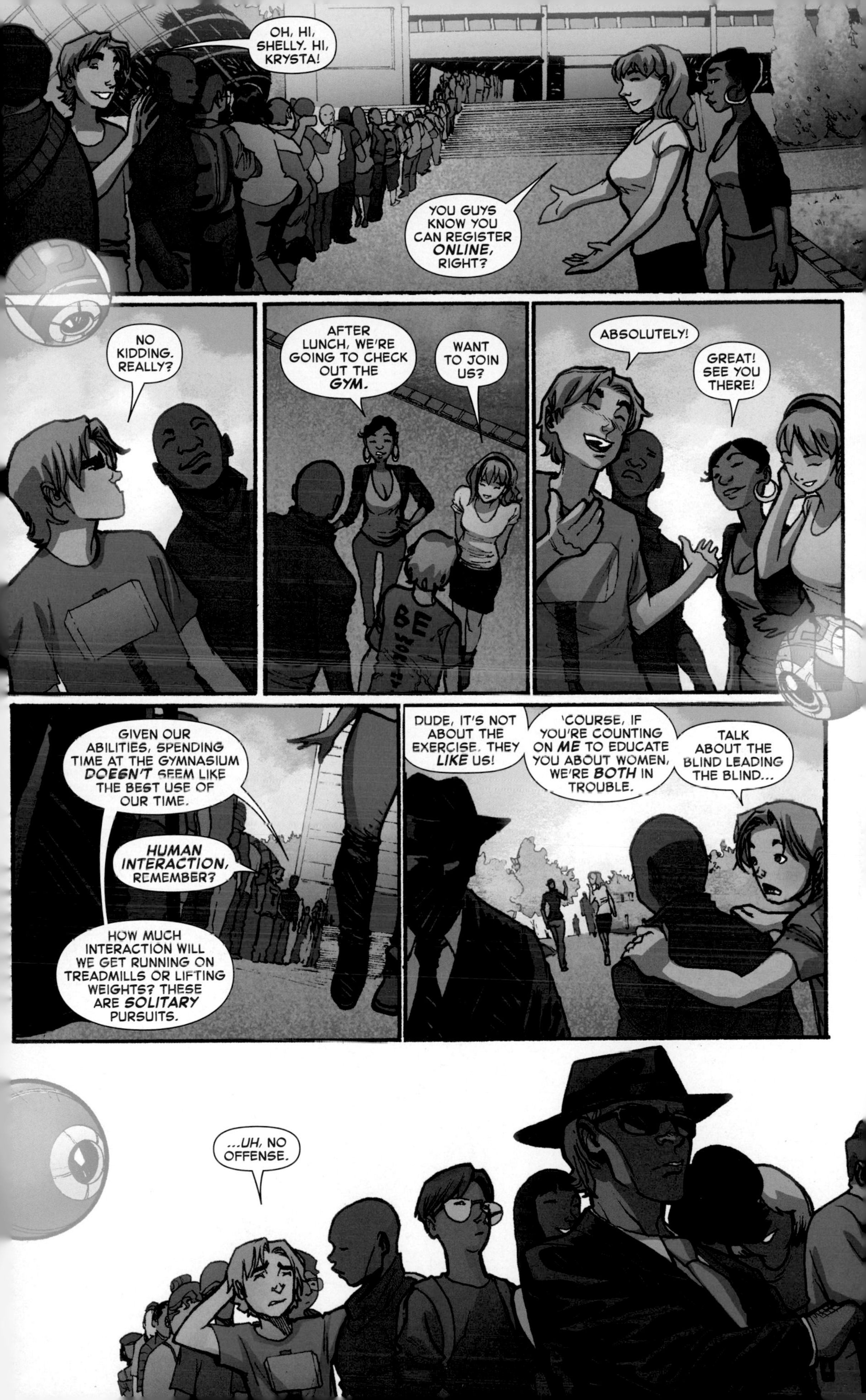
OH, HI, SHELLY. HI, KRYSTA!
YOU GUYS KNOW YOU CAN REGISTER ONLINE, RIGHT?
NO KIDDING. REALLY?
AFTER LUNCH, WE'RE GOING TO CHECK OUT THE GYM.
WANT TO JOIN US?
ABSOLUTELY!
GREAT! SEE YOU THERE!
GIVEN OUR ABILITIES, SPENDING TIME AT THE GYMNASIUM DOESN'T SEEM LIKE THE BEST USE OF OUR TIME.
HUMAN INTERACTION, REMEMBER?
HOW MUCH INTERACTION WILL WE GET RUNNING ON TREADMILLS OR LIFTING WEIGHTS? THESE ARE SOLITARY PURSUITS.
DUDE, IT'S NOT ABOUT THE EXERCISE. THEY LIKE US!
'COURSE, IF YOU'RE COUNTING ON ME TO EDUCATE YOU ABOUT WOMEN, WE'RE BOTH IN TROUBLE.
TALK ABOUT THE BLIND LEADING THE BLIND...
...UH, NO OFFENSE.

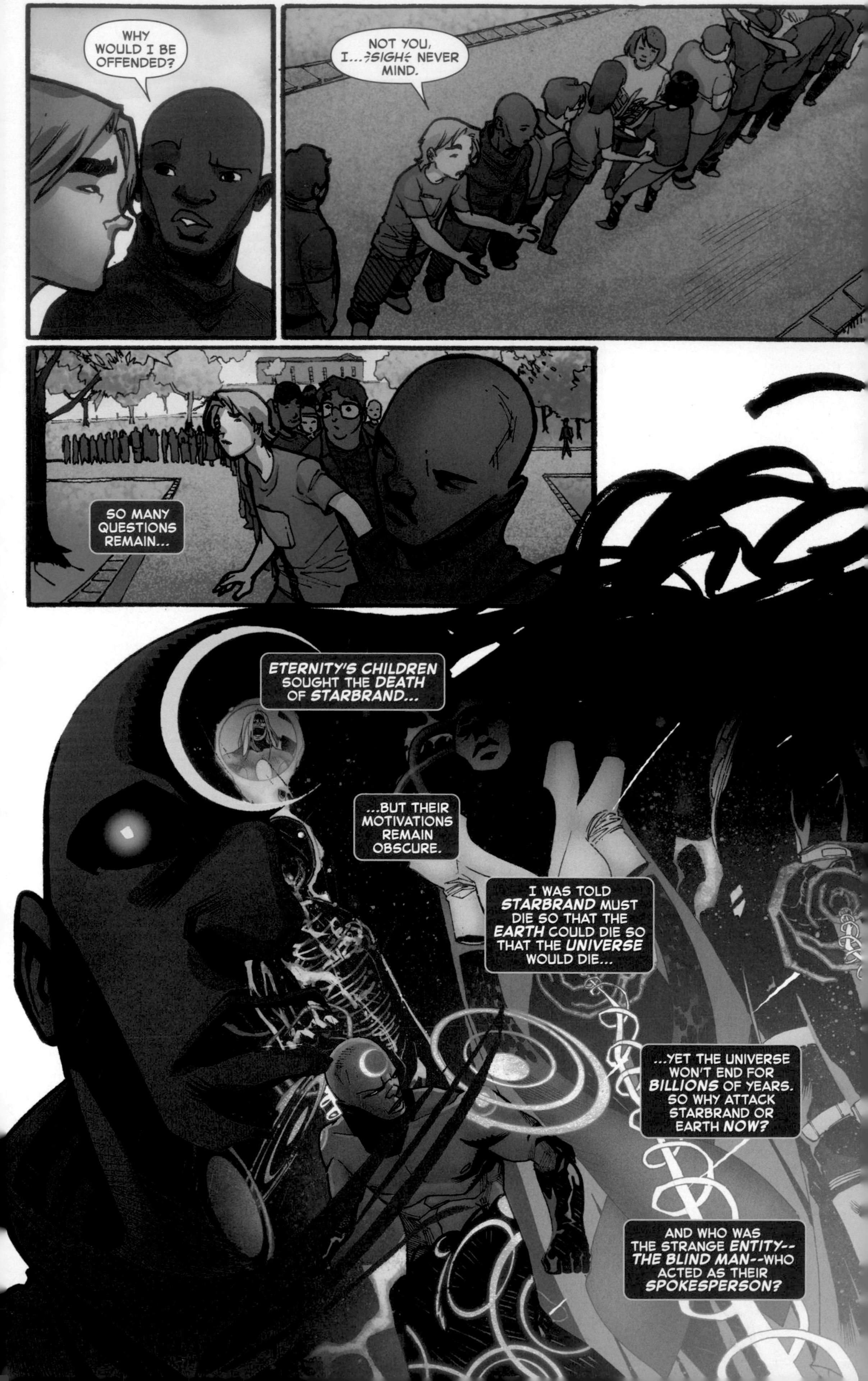
WHY WOULD I BE OFFENDED?
NOT YOU, I...⊰SIGH⊱ NEVER MIND.
SO MANY QUESTIONS REMAIN...
ETERNITY'S CHILDREN SOUGHT THE DEATH OF STARBRAND...
...BUT THEIR MOTIVATIONS REMAIN OBSCURE.
I WAS TOLD STARBRAND MUST DIE SO THAT THE EARTH COULD DIE SO THAT THE UNIVERSE WOULD DIE...
...YET THE UNIVERSE WON'T END FOR BILLIONS OF YEARS. SO WHY ATTACK STARBRAND OR EARTH NOW?
AND WHO WAS THE STRANGE ENTITY--THE BLIND MAN--WHO ACTED AS THEIR SPOKESPERSON?

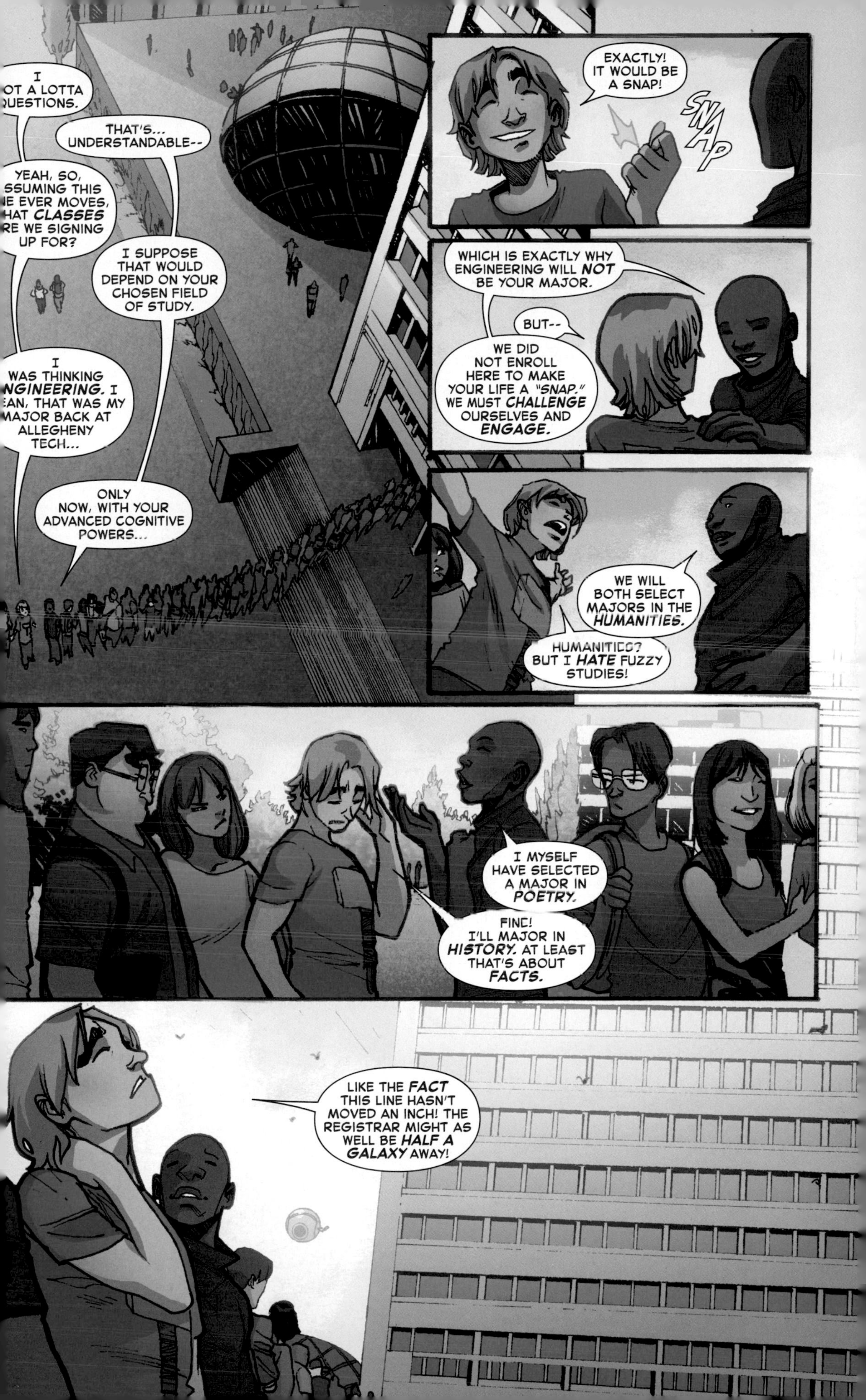

I OT A LOTTA QUESTIONS.
THAT'S... UNDERSTANDABLE--
YEAH, SO, SSUMING THIS E EVER MOVES, HAT CLASSES RE WE SIGNING UP FOR?
I SUPPOSE THAT WOULD DEPEND ON YOUR CHOSEN FIELD OF STUDY.
I WAS THINKING NGINEERING. I EAN, THAT WAS MY MAJOR BACK AT ALLEGHENY TECH...
ONLY NOW, WITH YOUR ADVANCED COGNITIVE POWERS...
EXACTLY! IT WOULD BE A SNAP!
SNAP
WHICH IS EXACTLY WHY ENGINEERING WILL NOT BE YOUR MAJOR.
BUT--
WE DID NOT ENROLL HERE TO MAKE YOUR LIFE A "SNAP." WE MUST CHALLENGE OURSELVES AND ENGAGE.
WE WILL BOTH SELECT MAJORS IN THE HUMANITIES.
HUMANITIES? BUT I HATE FUZZY STUDIES!
I MYSELF HAVE SELECTED A MAJOR IN POETRY.
FINE! I'LL MAJOR IN HISTORY. AT LEAST THAT'S ABOUT FACTS.
LIKE THE FACT THIS LINE HASN'T MOVED AN INCH! THE REGISTRAR MIGHT AS WELL BE HALF A GALAXY AWAY!

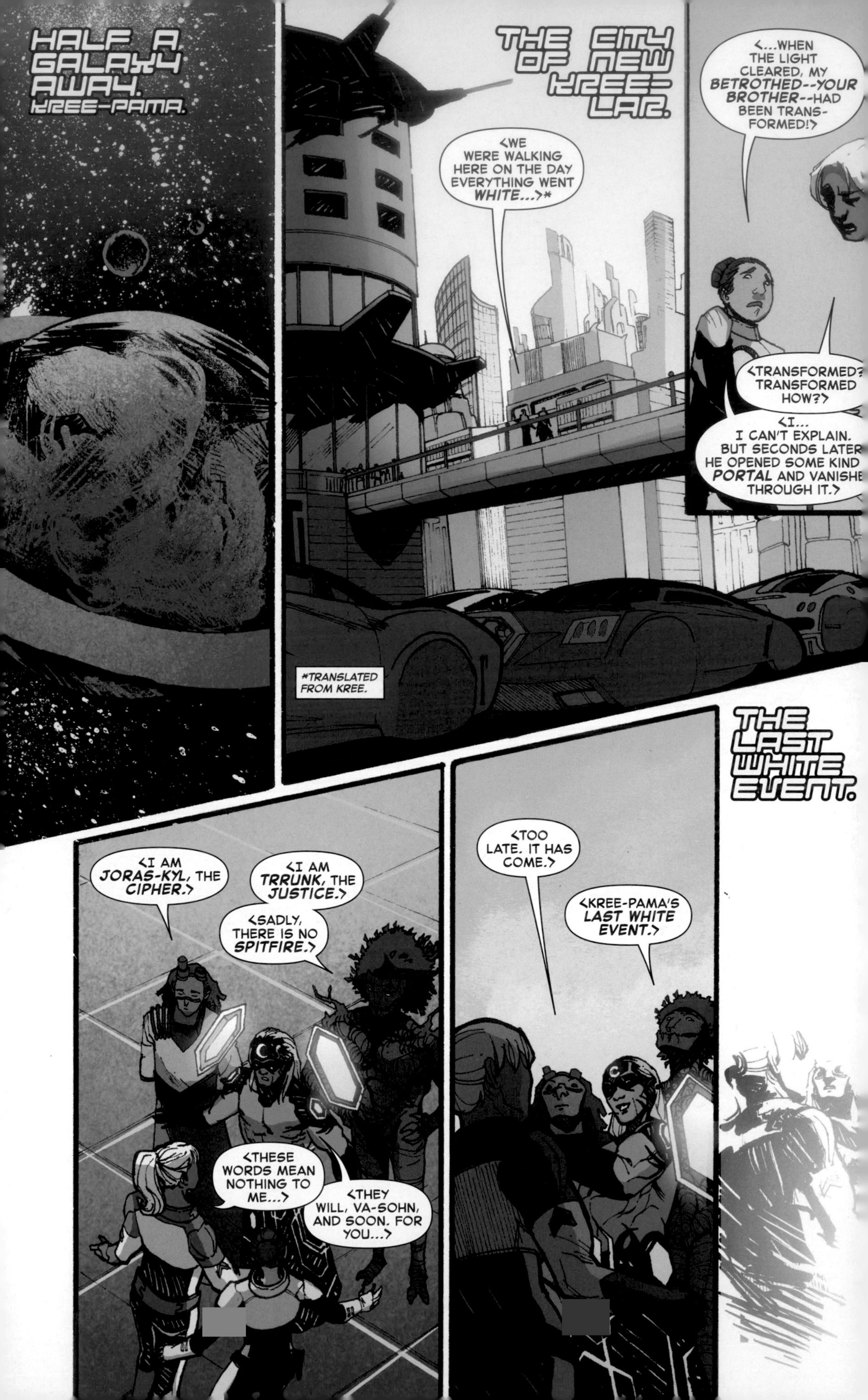
HALF A GALAXY AWAY. KREE-PAMA.
THE CITY OF NEW KREE-LAR.
<WE WERE WALKING HERE ON THE DAY EVERYTHING WENT WHITE...>*
*TRANSLATED FROM KREE.
<...WHEN THE LIGHT CLEARED, MY BETROTHED--YOUR BROTHER--HAD BEEN TRANSFORMED!>
<TRANSFORMED? TRANSFORMED HOW?>
<I... I CAN'T EXPLAIN. BUT SECONDS LATER HE OPENED SOME KIND PORTAL AND VANISHE THROUGH IT.>
THE LAST WHITE EVENT.
<I AM JORAS-KYL, THE CIPHER.>
<I AM TRRUNK, THE JUSTICE.>
<SADLY, THERE IS NO SPITFIRE.>
<THESE WORDS MEAN NOTHING TO ME...>
<THEY WILL, VA-SOHN, AND SOON. FOR YOU...>
<TOO LATE. IT HAS COME.>
<KREE-PAMA'S LAST WHITE EVENT.>

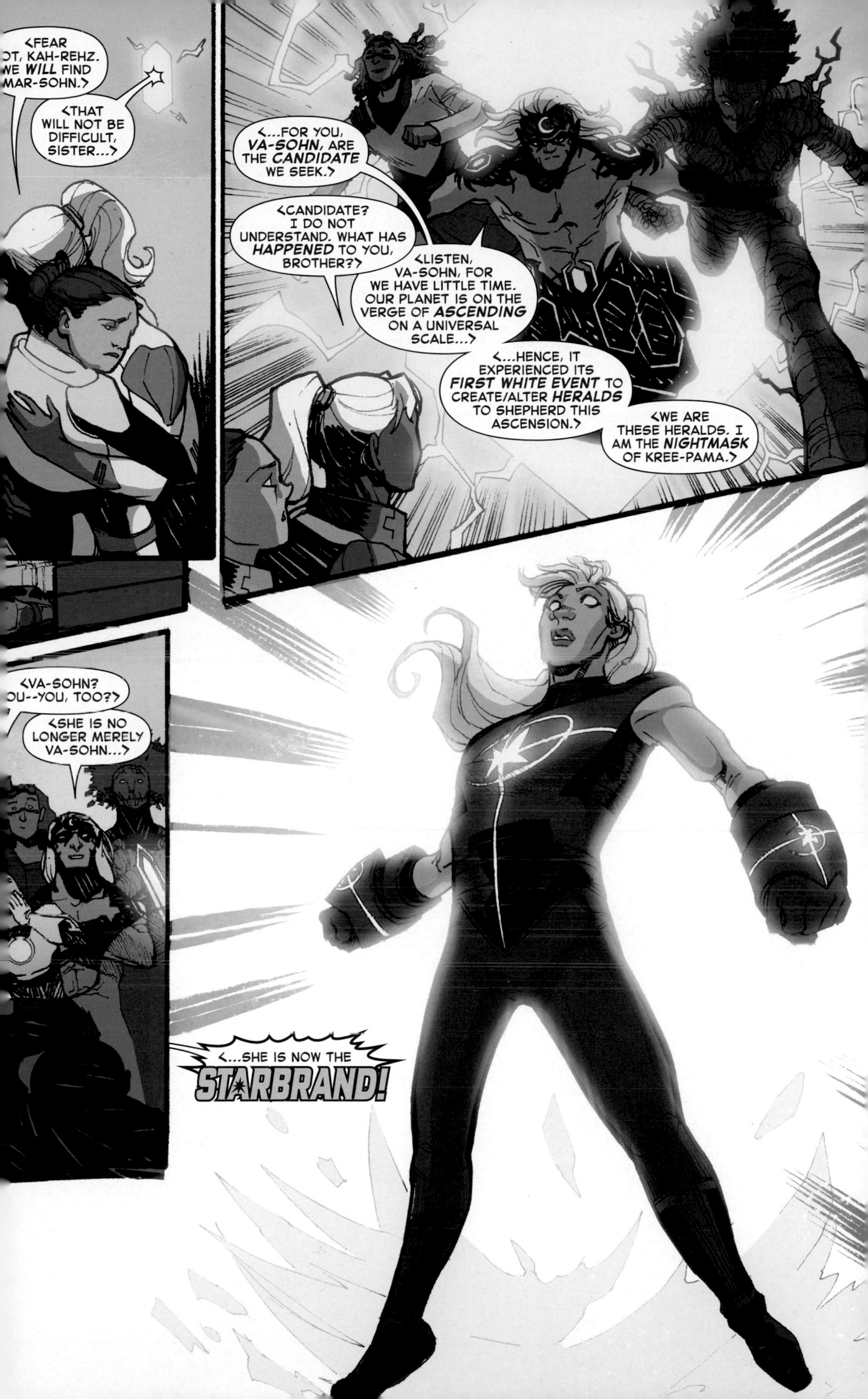

<FEAR NOT, KAH-REHZ. WE WILL FIND MAR-SOHN.>
<THAT WILL NOT BE DIFFICULT, SISTER...>
<...FOR YOU, VA-SOHN, ARE THE CANDIDATE WE SEEK.>
<CANDIDATE? I DO NOT UNDERSTAND. WHAT HAS HAPPENED TO YOU, BROTHER?>
<LISTEN, VA-SOHN, FOR WE HAVE LITTLE TIME. OUR PLANET IS ON THE VERGE OF ASCENDING ON A UNIVERSAL SCALE...>
<...HENCE, IT EXPERIENCED ITS FIRST WHITE EVENT TO CREATE/ALTER HERALDS TO SHEPHERD THIS ASCENSION.>
<WE ARE THESE HERALDS. I AM THE NIGHTMASK OF KREE-PAMA.>
<VA-SOHN? YOU--YOU, TOO?>
<SHE IS NO LONGER MERELY VA-SOHN...>
<...SHE IS NOW THE STARBRAND!

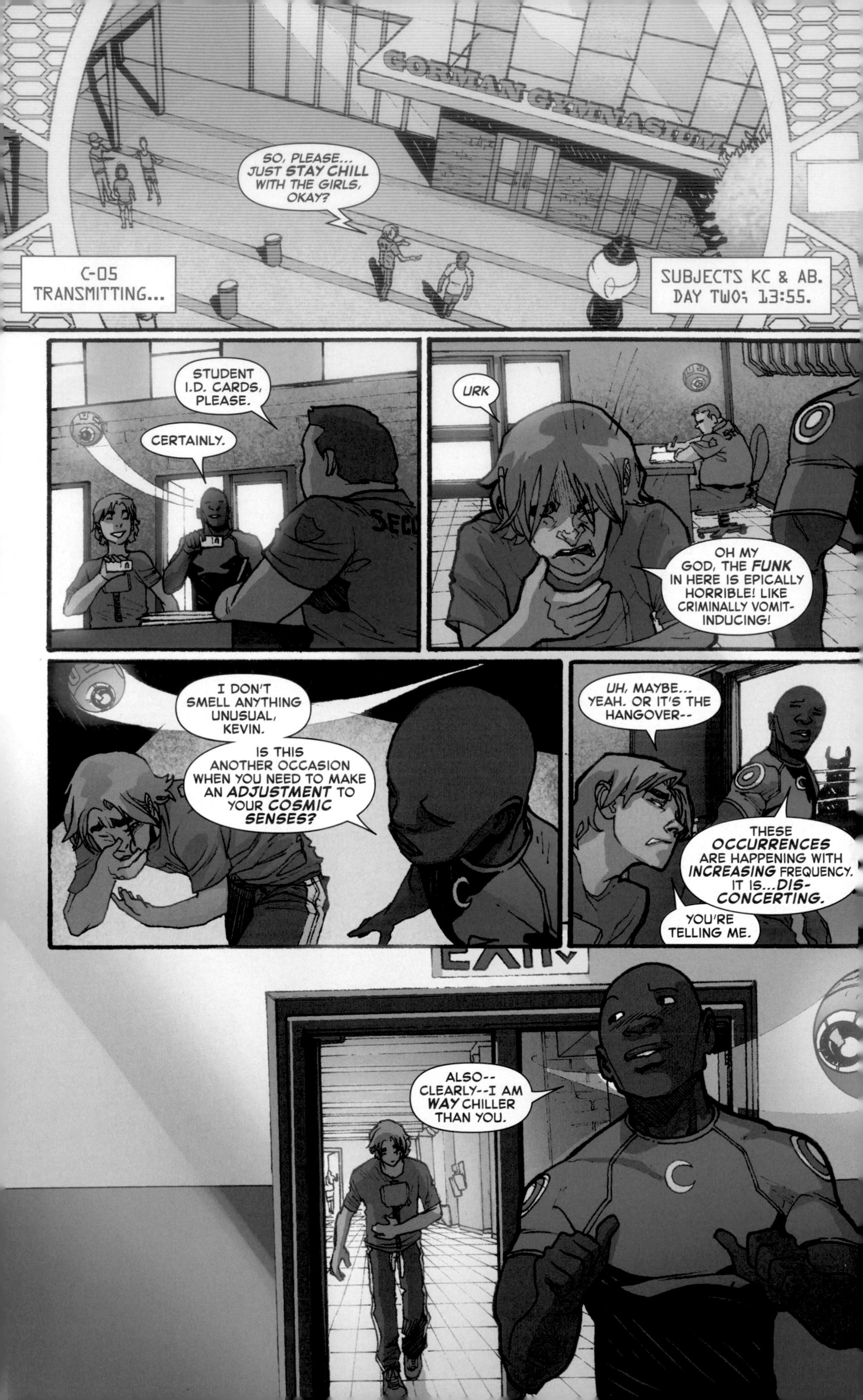
GORMAN GYMNASIUM
SO, PLEASE... JUST STAY CHILL WITH THE GIRLS, OKAY?
C-05 TRANSMITTING...
SUBJECTS KC & AB. DAY TWO: 13:55.
STUDENT I.D. CARDS, PLEASE.
CERTAINLY.
URK
OH MY GOD, THE FUNK IN HERE IS EPICALLY HORRIBLE! LIKE CRIMINALLY VOMIT-INDUCING!
I DON'T SMELL ANYTHING UNUSUAL, KEVIN.
IS THIS ANOTHER OCCASION WHEN YOU NEED TO MAKE AN ADJUSTMENT TO YOUR COSMIC SENSES?
UH, MAYBE... YEAH. OR IT'S THE HANGOVER--
THESE OCCURRENCES ARE HAPPENING WITH INCREASING FREQUENCY. IT IS...DIS-CONCERTING.
YOU'RE TELLING ME.
ALSO--CLEARLY--I AM WAY CHILLER THAN YOU.

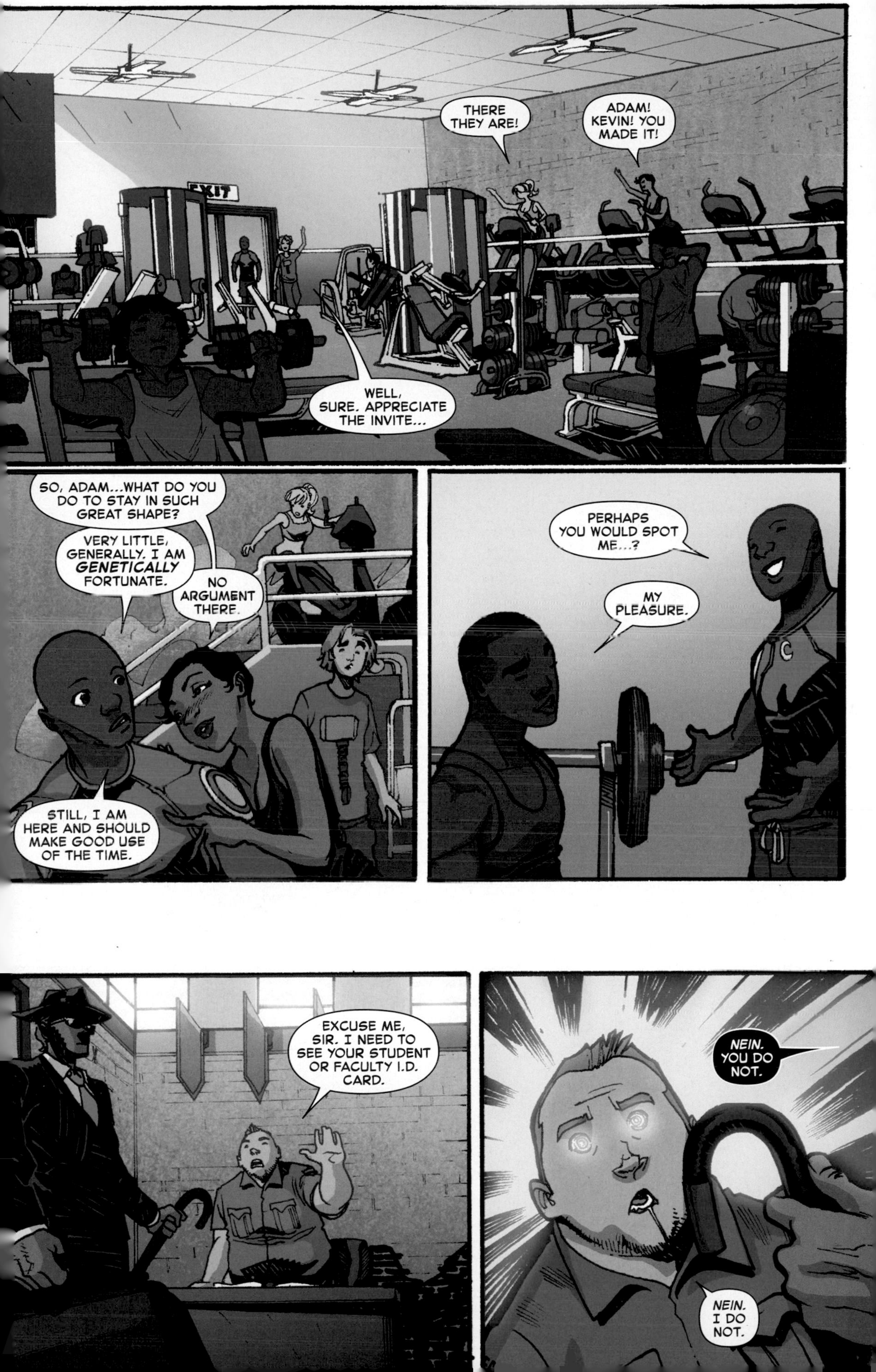
EXIT
THERE THEY ARE!
ADAM! KEVIN! YOU MADE IT!
WELL, SURE. APPRECIATE THE INVITE...
SO, ADAM...WHAT DO YOU DO TO STAY IN SUCH GREAT SHAPE?
VERY LITTLE, GENERALLY. I AM *GENETICALLY* FORTUNATE.
NO ARGUMENT THERE.
STILL, I AM HERE AND SHOULD MAKE GOOD USE OF THE TIME.
PERHAPS YOU WOULD SPOT ME...?
MY PLEASURE.
EXCUSE ME, SIR. I NEED TO SEE YOUR STUDENT OR FACULTY I.D. CARD.
NEIN. YOU DO NOT.
NEIN. I DO NOT.

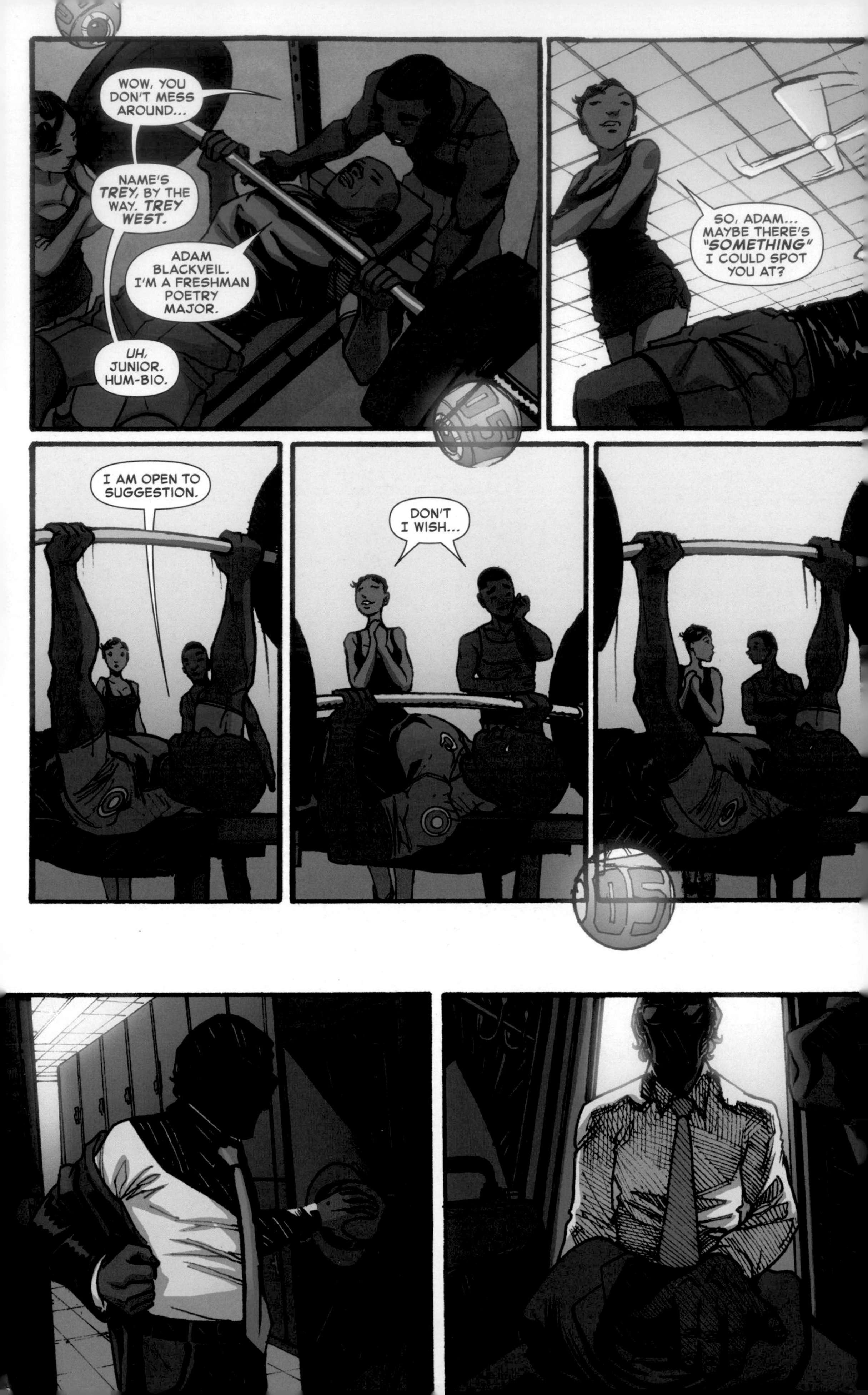
WOW, YOU DON'T MESS AROUND...
NAME'S TREY, BY THE WAY. TREY WEST.
ADAM BLACKVEIL. I'M A FRESHMAN POETRY MAJOR.
UH, JUNIOR. HUM-BIO.
SO, ADAM... MAYBE THERE'S "SOMETHING" I COULD SPOT YOU AT?
I AM OPEN TO SUGGESTION.
DON'T I WISH...

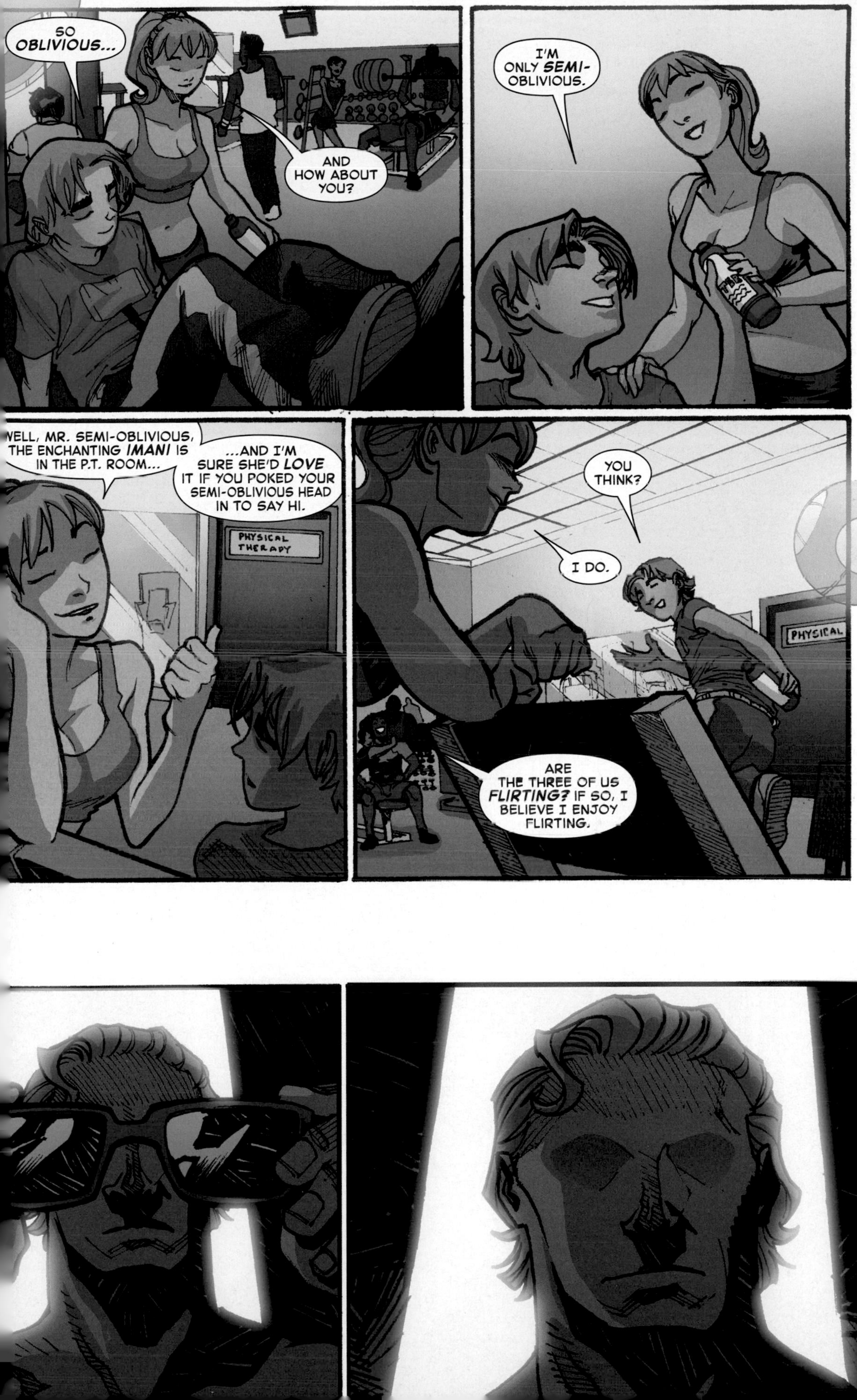
SO OBLIVIOUS...
AND HOW ABOUT YOU?
I'M ONLY SEMI-OBLIVIOUS.
WELL, MR. SEMI-OBLIVIOUS, THE ENCHANTING IMANI IS IN THE P.T. ROOM...
...AND I'M SURE SHE'D LOVE IT IF YOU POKED YOUR SEMI-OBLIVIOUS HEAD IN TO SAY HI.
PHYSICAL THERAPY
YOU THINK?
I DO.
PHYSICAL
ARE THE THREE OF US FLIRTING? IF SO, I BELIEVE I ENJOY FLIRTING.

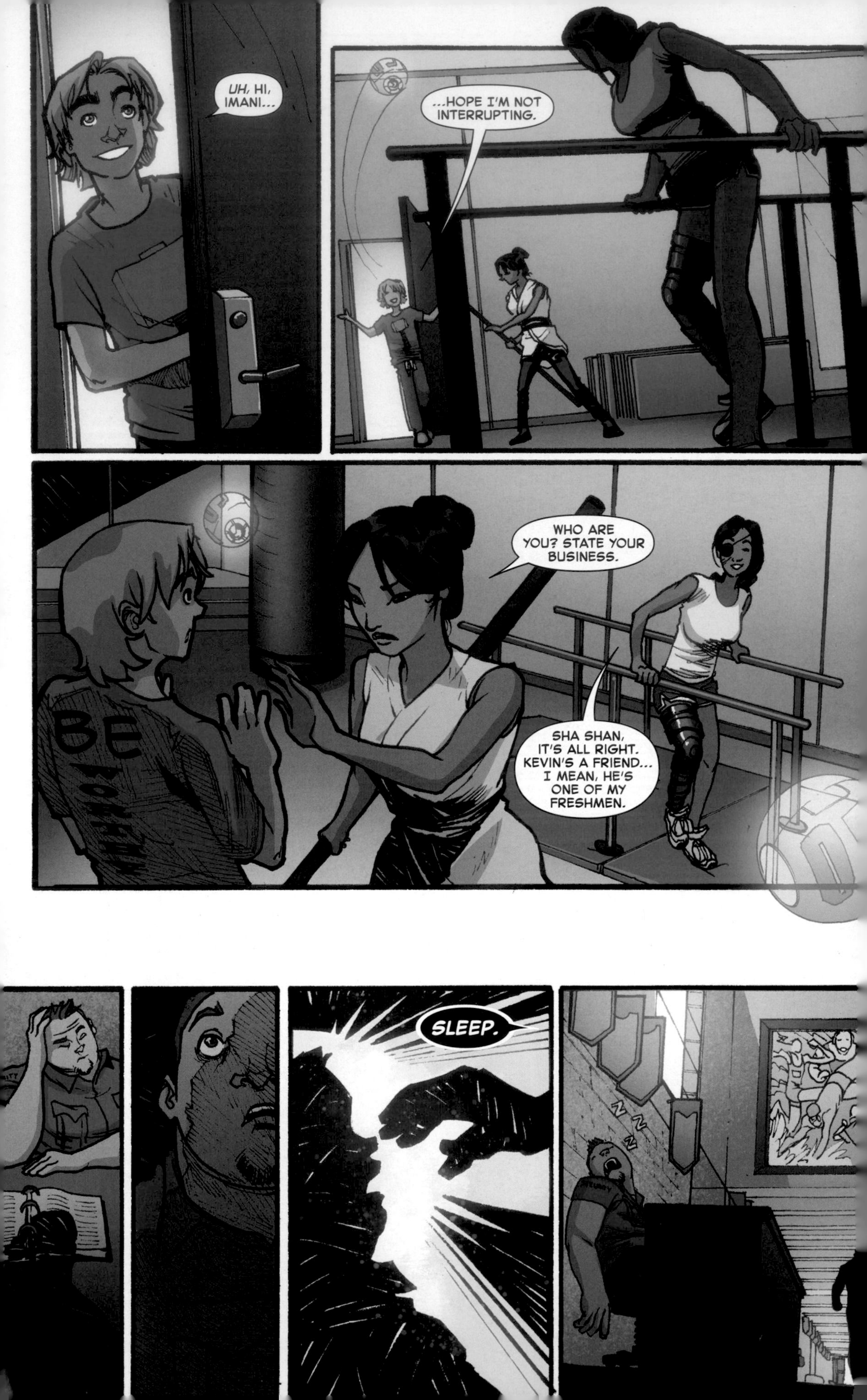
UH, HI, IMANI...
...HOPE I'M NOT INTERRUPTING.
WHO ARE YOU? STATE YOUR BUSINESS.
SHA SHAN, IT'S ALL RIGHT. KEVIN'S A FRIEND... I MEAN, HE'S ONE OF MY FRESHMEN.
SLEEP.

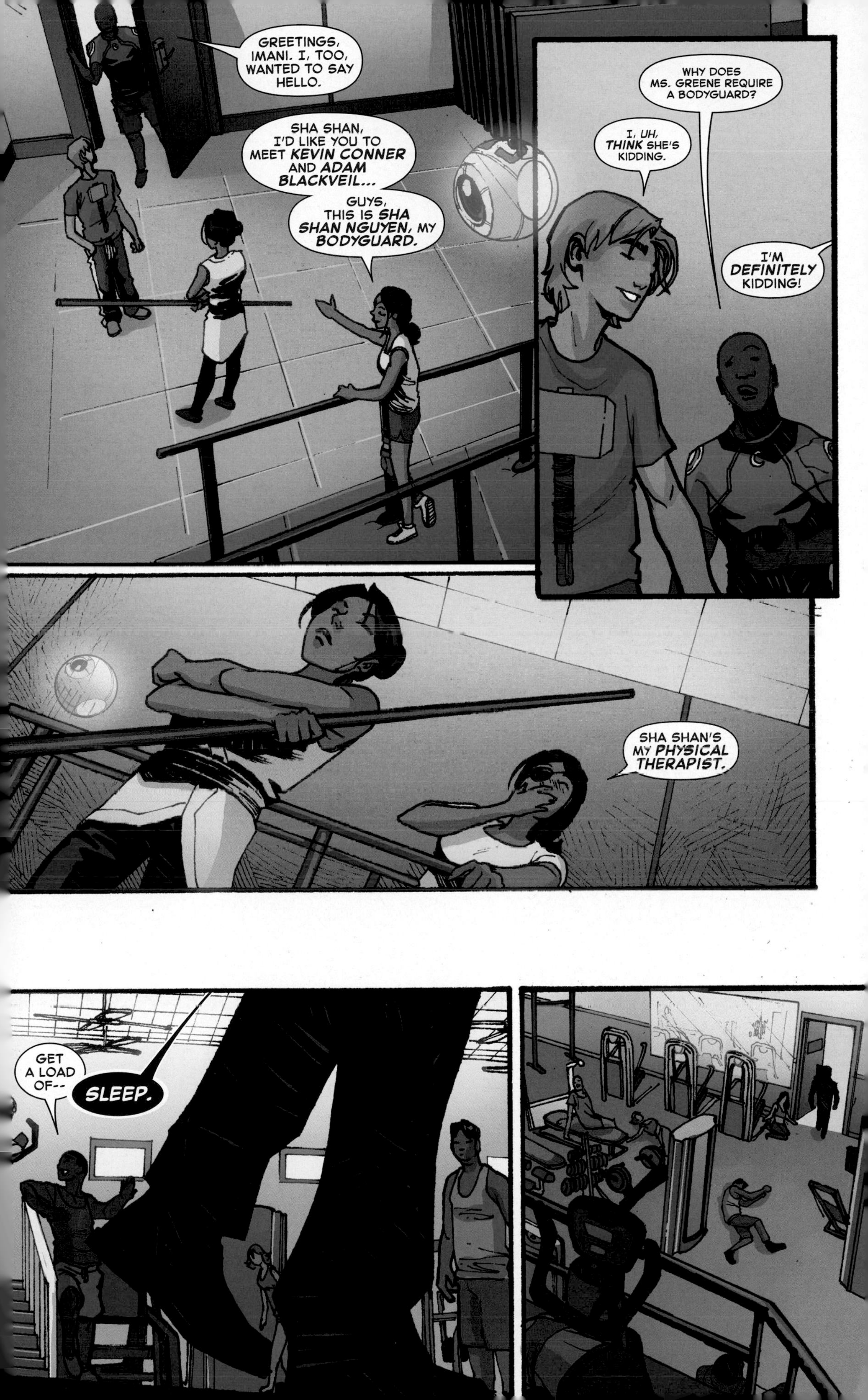
GREETINGS, IMANI. I, TOO, WANTED TO SAY HELLO.
SHA SHAN, I'D LIKE YOU TO MEET KEVIN CONNER AND ADAM BLACKVEIL...
GUYS, THIS IS SHA SHAN NGUYEN, MY BODYGUARD.
WHY DOES MS. GREENE REQUIRE A BODYGUARD?
I, UH, THINK SHE'S KIDDING.
I'M DEFINITELY KIDDING!
SHA SHAN'S MY PHYSICAL THERAPIST.
GET A LOAD OF--
SLEEP.

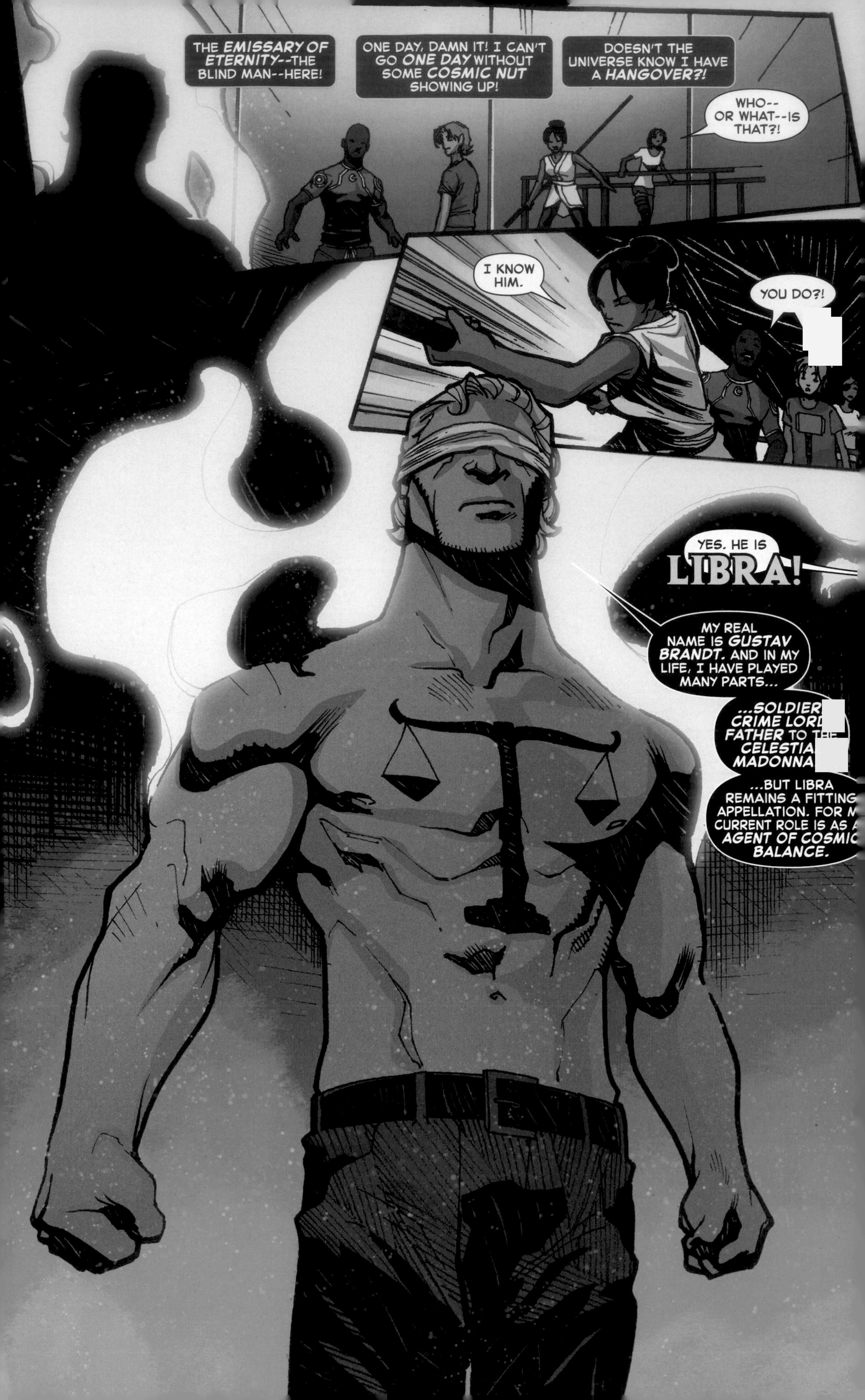
THE EMISSARY OF ETERNITY--THE BLIND MAN--HERE!
ONE DAY, DAMN IT! I CAN'T GO ONE DAY WITHOUT SOME COSMIC NUT SHOWING UP!
DOESN'T THE UNIVERSE KNOW I HAVE A HANGOVER?!
WHO-- OR WHAT--IS THAT?!
I KNOW HIM.
YOU DO?!
YES. HE IS LIBRA!
MY REAL NAME IS GUSTAV BRANDT. AND IN MY LIFE, I HAVE PLAYED MANY PARTS...
...SOLDIER CRIME LORD FATHER TO TH CELESTIA MADONNA
...BUT LIBRA REMAINS A FITTING APPELLATION. FOR M CURRENT ROLE IS AS A AGENT OF COSMIC BALANCE.

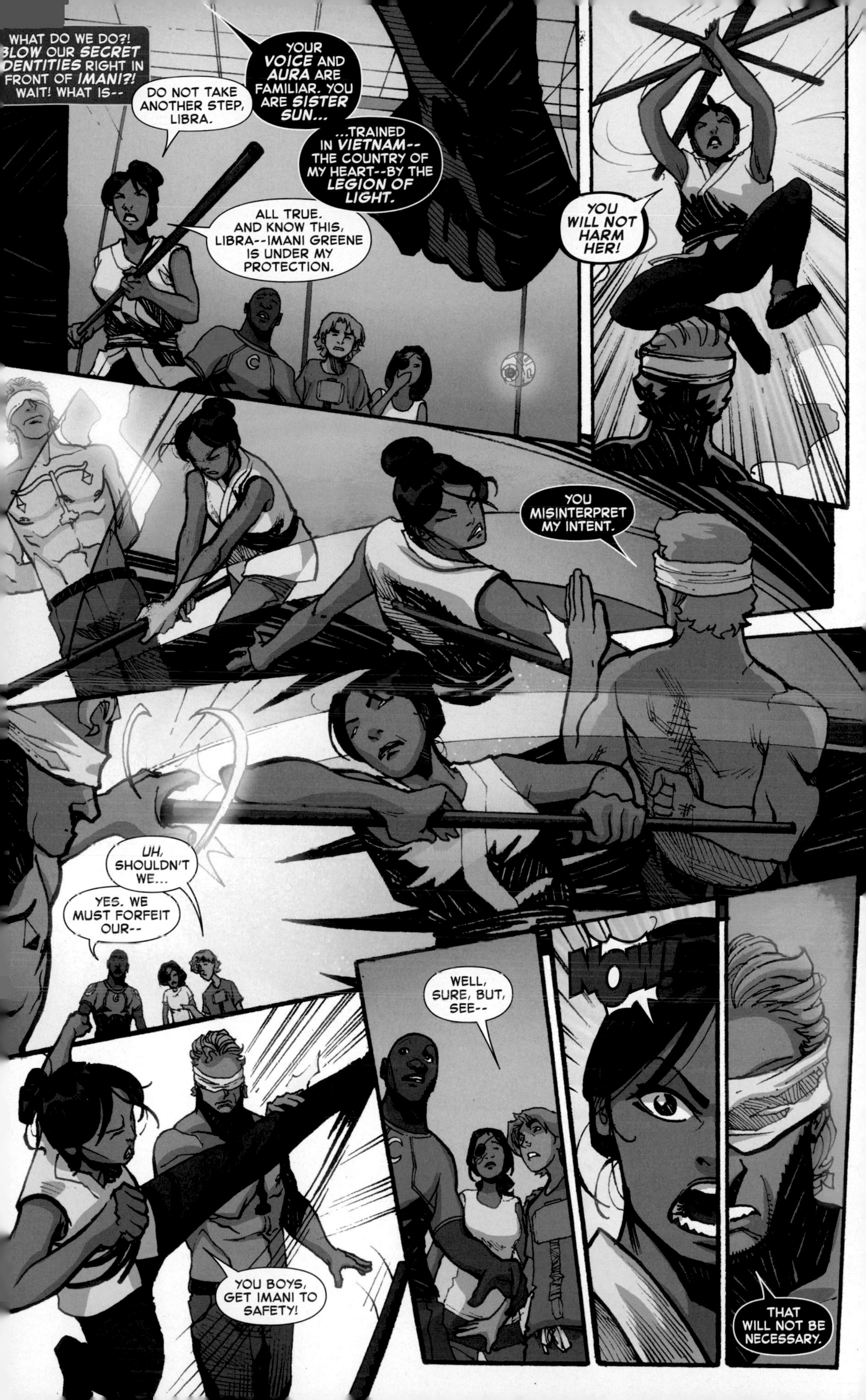
WHAT DO WE DO?! BLOW OUR SECRET IDENTITIES RIGHT IN FRONT OF IMANI?! WAIT! WHAT IS--
DO NOT TAKE ANOTHER STEP, LIBRA.
YOUR VOICE AND AURA ARE FAMILIAR. YOU ARE SISTER SUN...
...TRAINED IN VIETNAM-- THE COUNTRY OF MY HEART--BY THE LEGION OF LIGHT.
ALL TRUE. AND KNOW THIS, LIBRA--IMANI GREENE IS UNDER MY PROTECTION.
YOU WILL NOT HARM HER!
YOU MISINTERPRET MY INTENT.
UH, SHOULDN'T WE...
YES. WE MUST FORFEIT OUR--
YOU BOYS, GET IMANI TO SAFETY!
WELL, SURE, BUT, SEE--
NOW!
THAT WILL NOT BE NECESSARY.

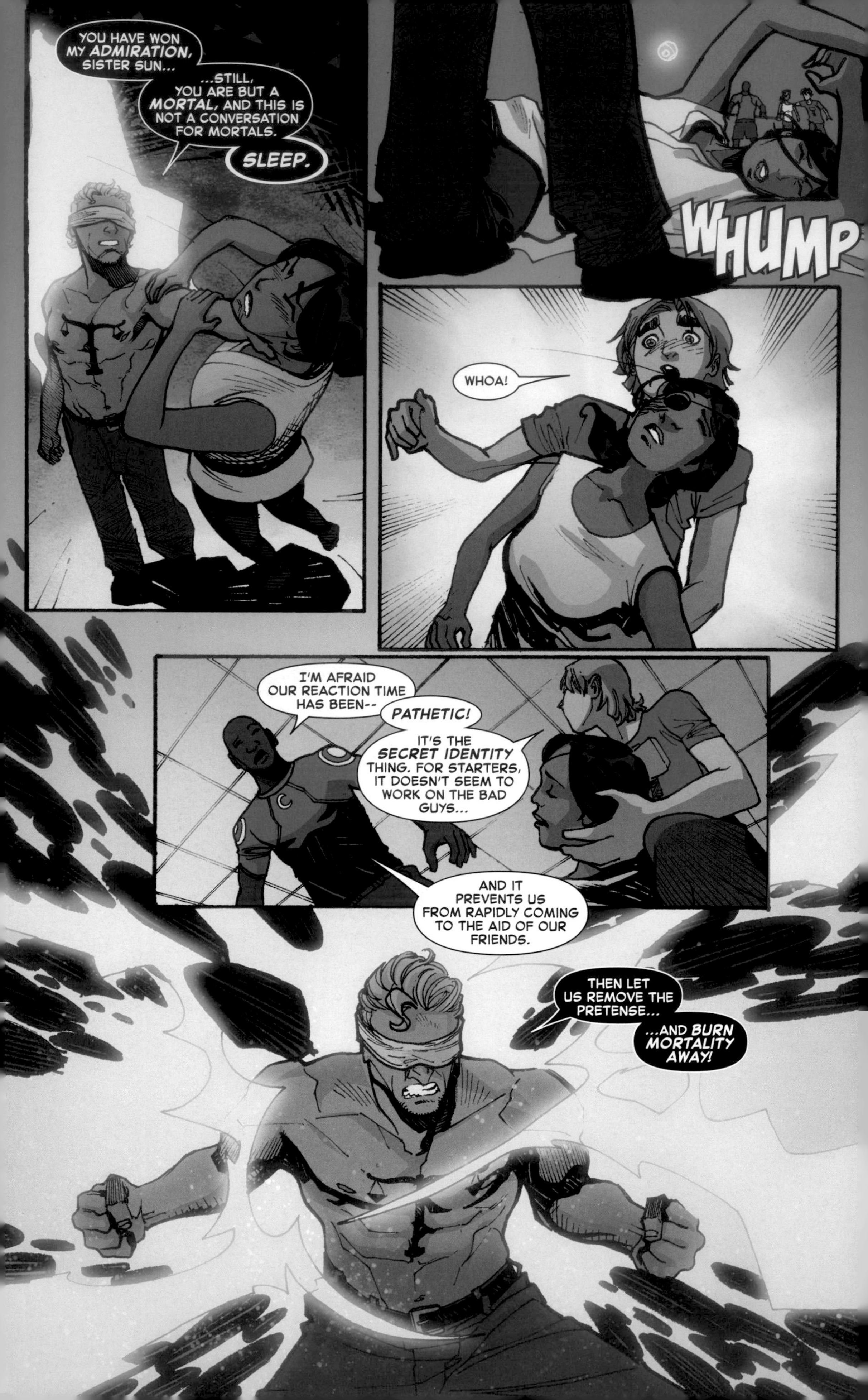
YOU HAVE WON MY ADMIRATION, SISTER SUN...
...STILL, YOU ARE BUT A MORTAL, AND THIS IS NOT A CONVERSATION FOR MORTALS.
SLEEP.
WHUMP
WHOA!
I'M AFRAID OUR REACTION TIME HAS BEEN--
PATHETIC!
IT'S THE SECRET IDENTITY THING. FOR STARTERS, IT DOESN'T SEEM TO WORK ON THE BAD GUYS...
AND IT PREVENTS US FROM RAPIDLY COMING TO THE AID OF OUR FRIENDS.
THEN LET US REMOVE THE PRETENSE...
...AND BURN MORTALITY AWAY!

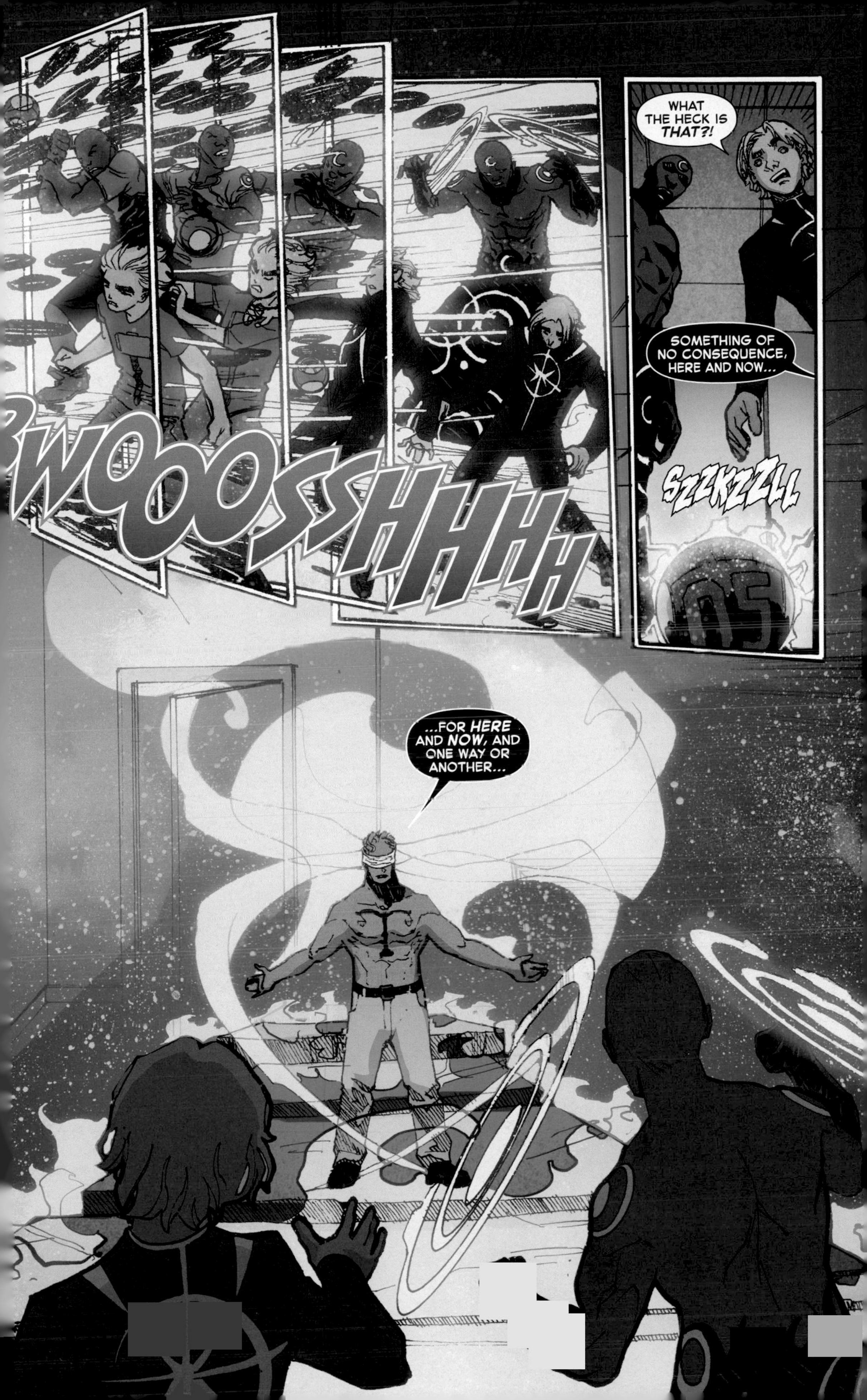
WOOOSSHHHHH
WHAT THE HECK IS THAT?!
SOMETHING OF NO CONSEQUENCE, HERE AND NOW...
SZZKZZLL
...FOR HERE AND NOW, AND ONE WAY OR ANOTHER...

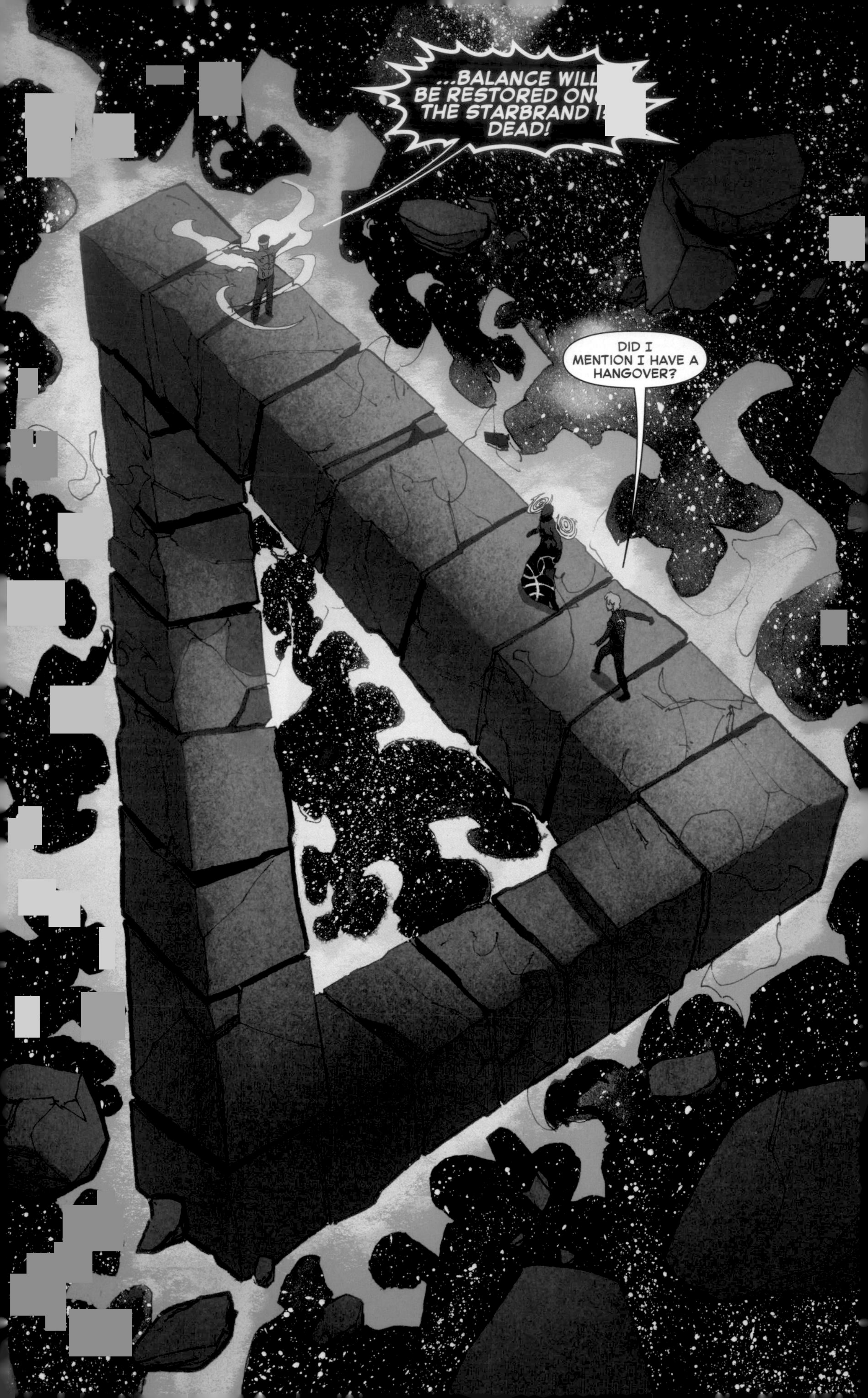
...BALANCE WILL BE RESTORED ONC THE STARBRAND I DEAD!
DID I MENTION I HAVE A HANGOVER?

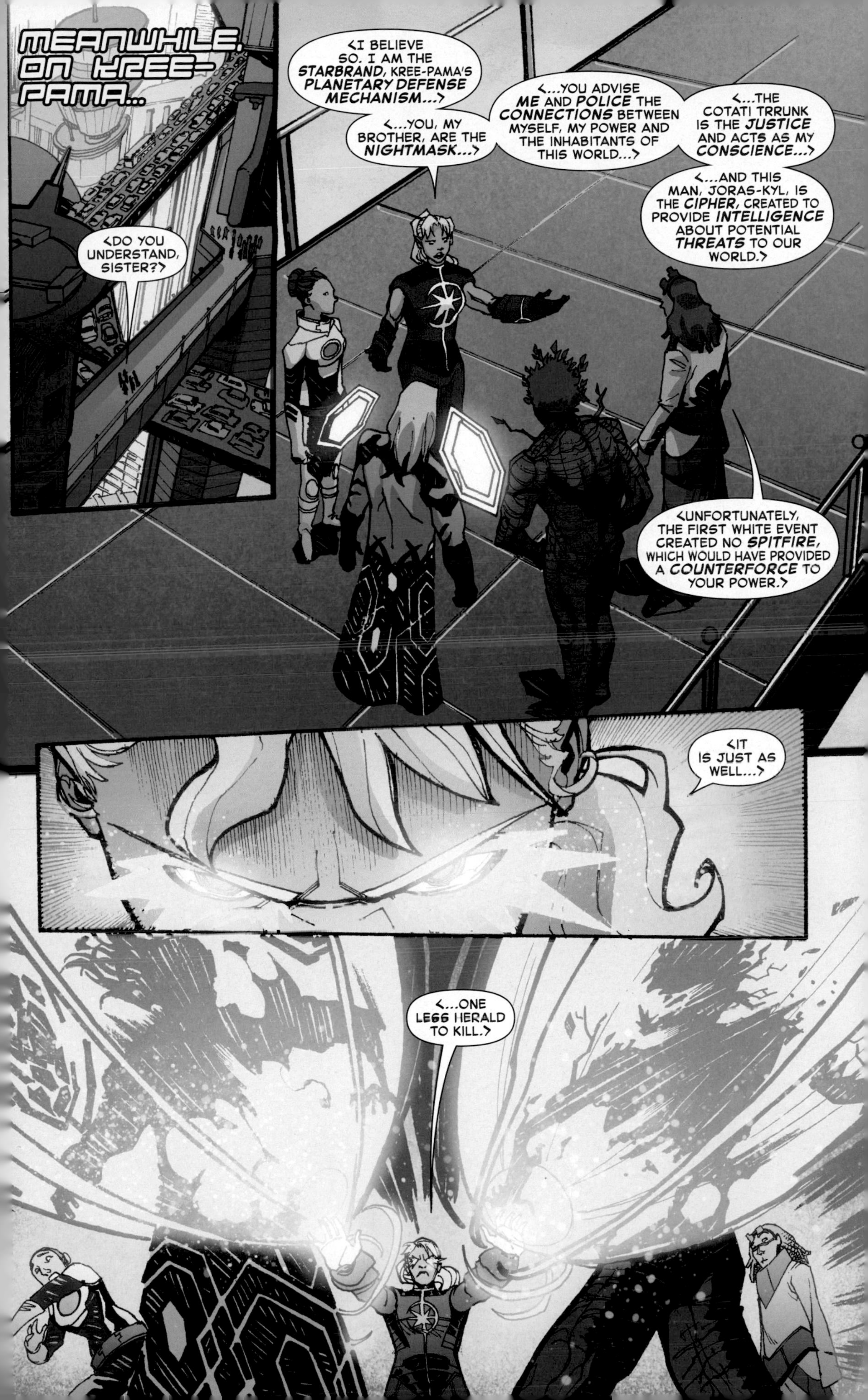
MEANWHILE, ON KREE-PAMA...
<DO YOU UNDERSTAND, SISTER?>
<I BELIEVE SO. I AM THE STARBRAND, KREE-PAMA'S PLANETARY DEFENSE MECHANISM...>
<...YOU, MY BROTHER, ARE THE NIGHTMASK...>
<...YOU ADVISE ME AND POLICE THE CONNECTIONS BETWEEN MYSELF, MY POWER AND THE INHABITANTS OF THIS WORLD...>
<...THE COTATI TRRUNK IS THE JUSTICE AND ACTS AS MY CONSCIENCE...>
<...AND THIS MAN, JORAS-KYL, IS THE CIPHER, CREATED TO PROVIDE INTELLIGENCE ABOUT POTENTIAL THREATS TO OUR WORLD.>
<UNFORTUNATELY, THE FIRST WHITE EVENT CREATED NO SPITFIRE, WHICH WOULD HAVE PROVIDED A COUNTERFORCE TO YOUR POWER.>
<IT IS JUST AS WELL...>
<...ONE LESS HERALD TO KILL.>

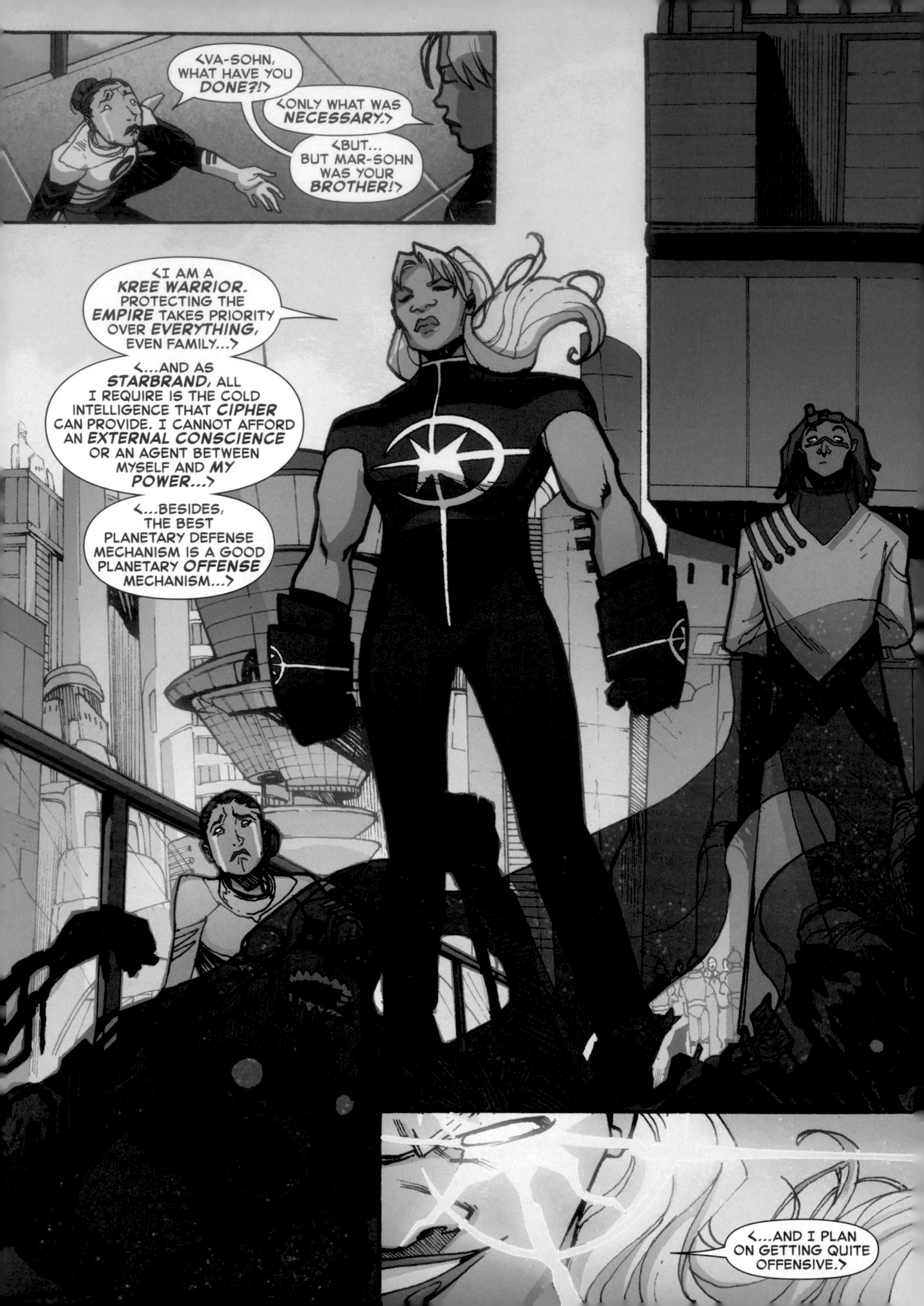

<VA-SOHN, WHAT HAVE YOU DONE?!>
<ONLY WHAT WAS NECESSARY.>
<BUT... BUT MAR-SOHN WAS YOUR BROTHER!>
<I AM A KREE WARRIOR. PROTECTING THE EMPIRE TAKES PRIORITY OVER EVERYTHING, EVEN FAMILY...>
<...AND AS STARBRAND, ALL I REQUIRE IS THE COLD INTELLIGENCE THAT CIPHER CAN PROVIDE. I CANNOT AFFORD AN EXTERNAL CONSCIENCE OR AN AGENT BETWEEN MYSELF AND MY POWER...>
<...BESIDES, THE BEST PLANETARY DEFENSE MECHANISM IS A GOOD PLANETARY OFFENSE MECHANISM...>
<...AND I PLAN ON GETTING QUITE OFFENSIVE.>

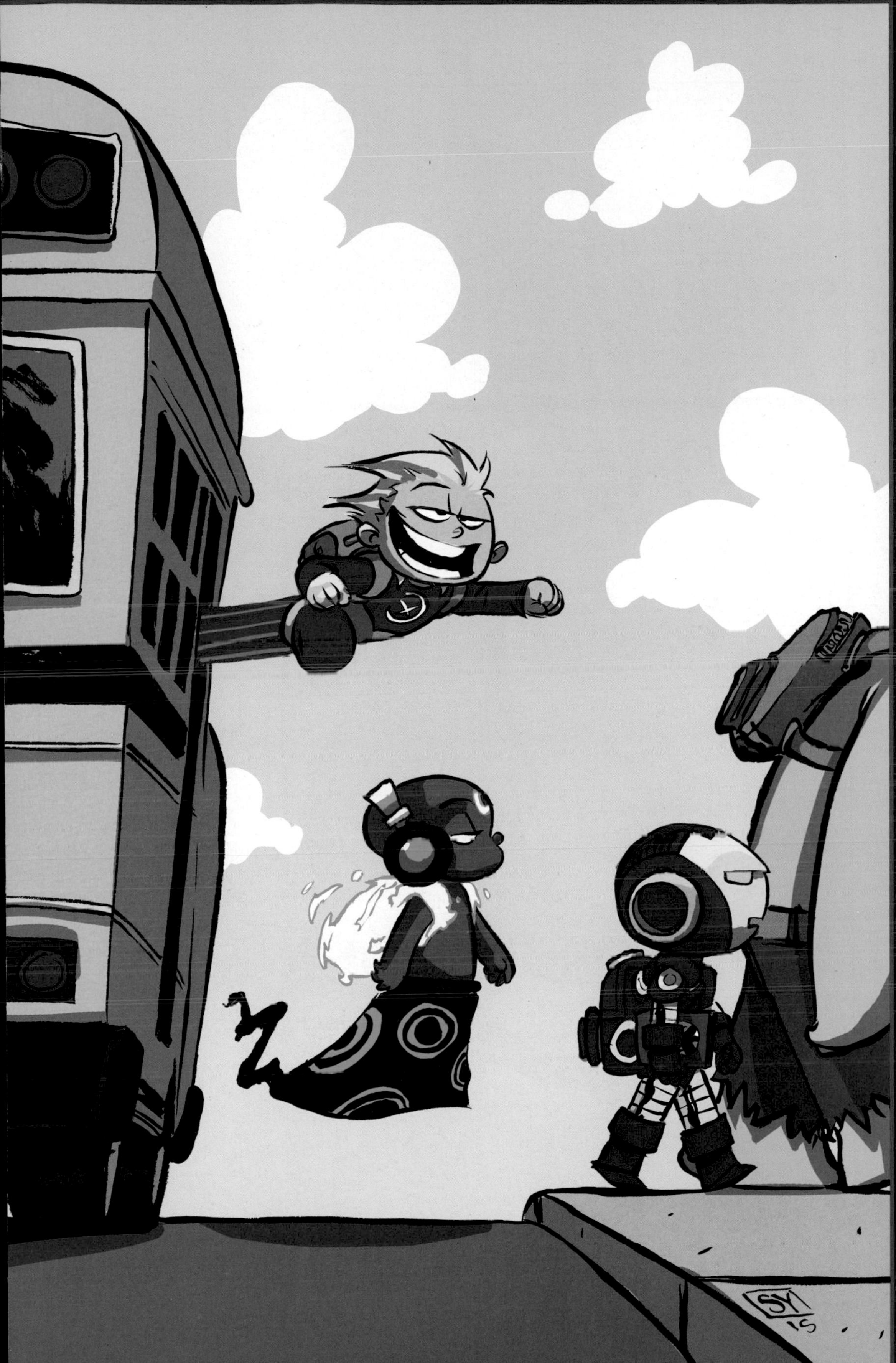
SY
'15

SKOTTIE YOUNG
1 VARIANT

CHAPTER 6: EVALUATION

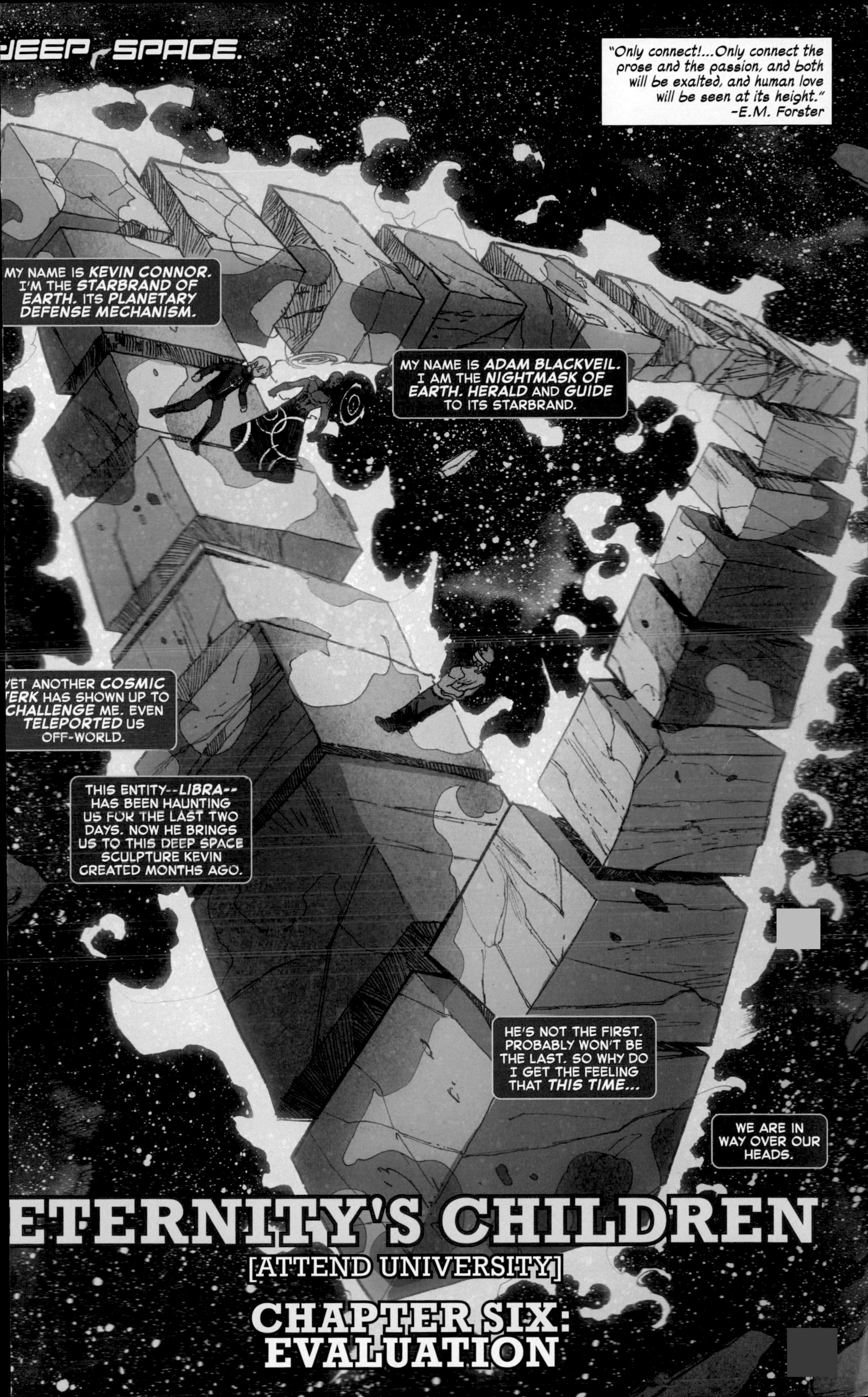
DEEP SPACE.
"Only connect!...Only connect the prose and the passion, and both will be exalted, and human love will be seen at its height." -E.M. Forster
MY NAME IS KEVIN CONNOR. I'M THE STARBRAND OF EARTH. ITS PLANETARY DEFENSE MECHANISM.
MY NAME IS ADAM BLACKVEIL. I AM THE NIGHTMASK OF EARTH. HERALD AND GUIDE TO ITS STARBRAND.
YET ANOTHER COSMIC JERK HAS SHOWN UP TO CHALLENGE ME. EVEN TELEPORTED US OFF-WORLD.
THIS ENTITY--LIBRA--HAS BEEN HAUNTING US FOR THE LAST TWO DAYS. NOW HE BRINGS US TO THIS DEEP SPACE SCULPTURE KEVIN CREATED MONTHS AGO.
HE'S NOT THE FIRST. PROBABLY WON'T BE THE LAST. SO WHY DO I GET THE FEELING THAT THIS TIME...
WE ARE IN WAY OVER OUR HEADS.
ETERNITY'S CHILDREN
[ATTEND UNIVERSITY]
CHAPTER SIX: EVALUATION

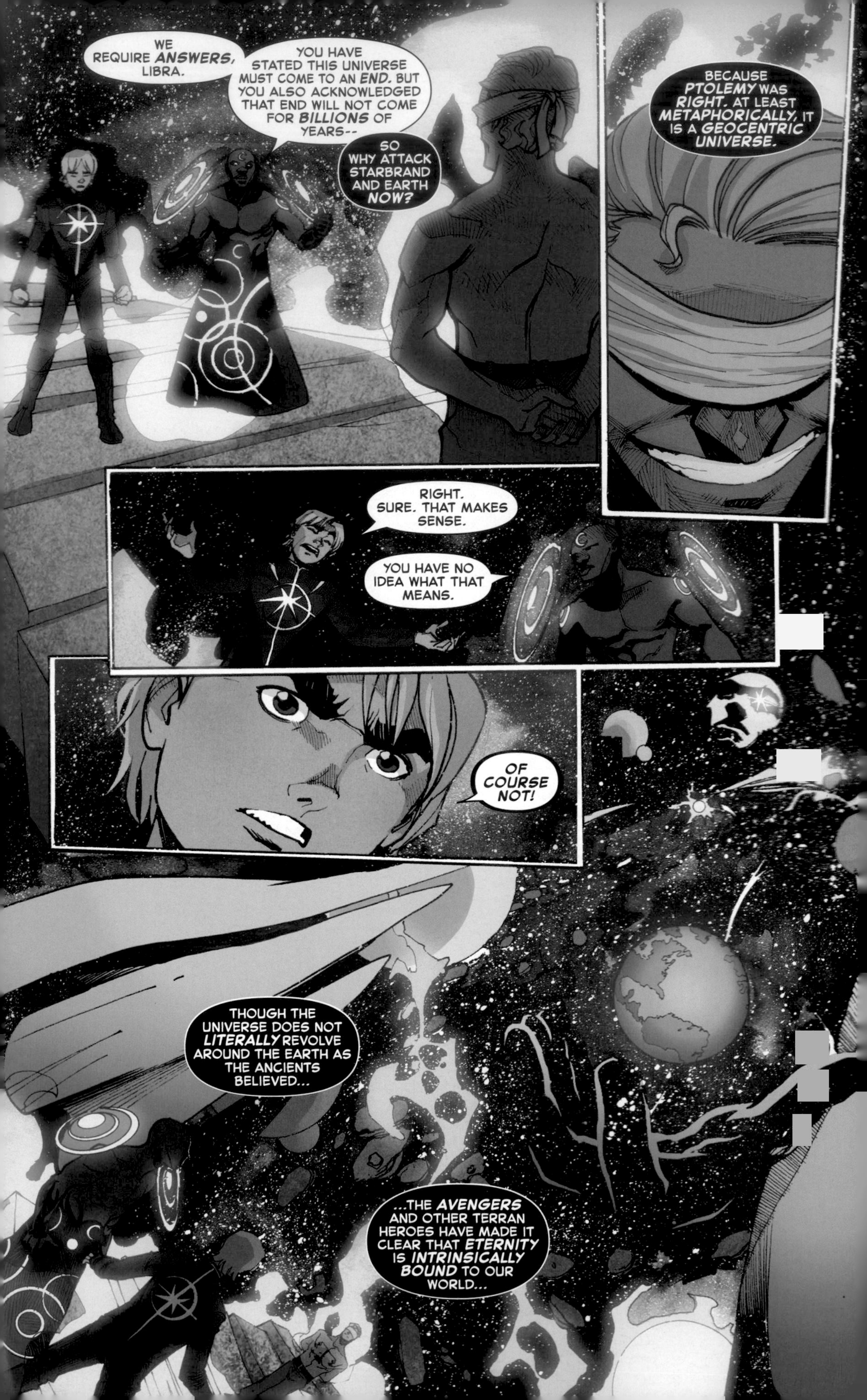
WE REQUIRE ANSWERS, LIBRA.
YOU HAVE STATED THIS UNIVERSE MUST COME TO AN END. BUT YOU ALSO ACKNOWLEDGED THAT END WILL NOT COME FOR BILLIONS OF YEARS--
SO WHY ATTACK STARBRAND AND EARTH NOW?
BECAUSE PTOLEMY WAS RIGHT. AT LEAST METAPHORICALLY, IT IS A GEOCENTRIC UNIVERSE.
RIGHT. SURE. THAT MAKES SENSE.
YOU HAVE NO IDEA WHAT THAT MEANS.
OF COURSE NOT!
THOUGH THE UNIVERSE DOES NOT LITERALLY REVOLVE AROUND THE EARTH AS THE ANCIENTS BELIEVED...
...THE AVENGERS AND OTHER TERRAN HEROES HAVE MADE IT CLEAR THAT ETERNITY IS INTRINSICALLY BOUND TO OUR WORLD...

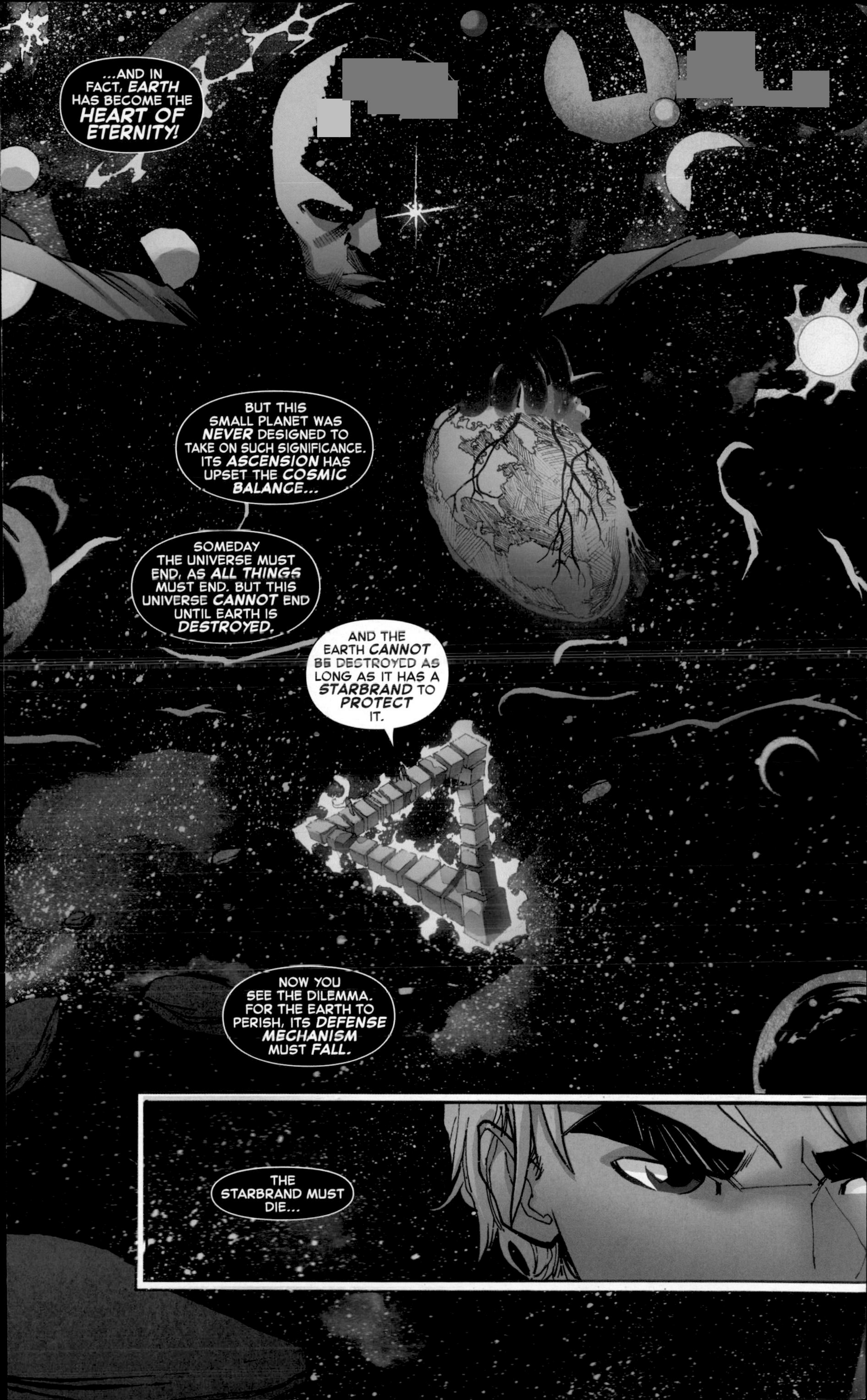
...AND IN FACT, EARTH HAS BECOME THE HEART OF ETERNITY!
BUT THIS SMALL PLANET WAS NEVER DESIGNED TO TAKE ON SUCH SIGNIFICANCE. ITS ASCENSION HAS UPSET THE COSMIC BALANCE...
SOMEDAY THE UNIVERSE MUST END, AS ALL THINGS MUST END. BUT THIS UNIVERSE CANNOT END UNTIL EARTH IS DESTROYED.
AND THE EARTH CANNOT BE DESTROYED AS LONG AS IT HAS A STARBRAND TO PROTECT IT.
NOW YOU SEE THE DILEMMA. FOR THE EARTH TO PERISH, ITS DEFENSE MECHANISM MUST FALL.
THE STARBRAND MUST DIE...

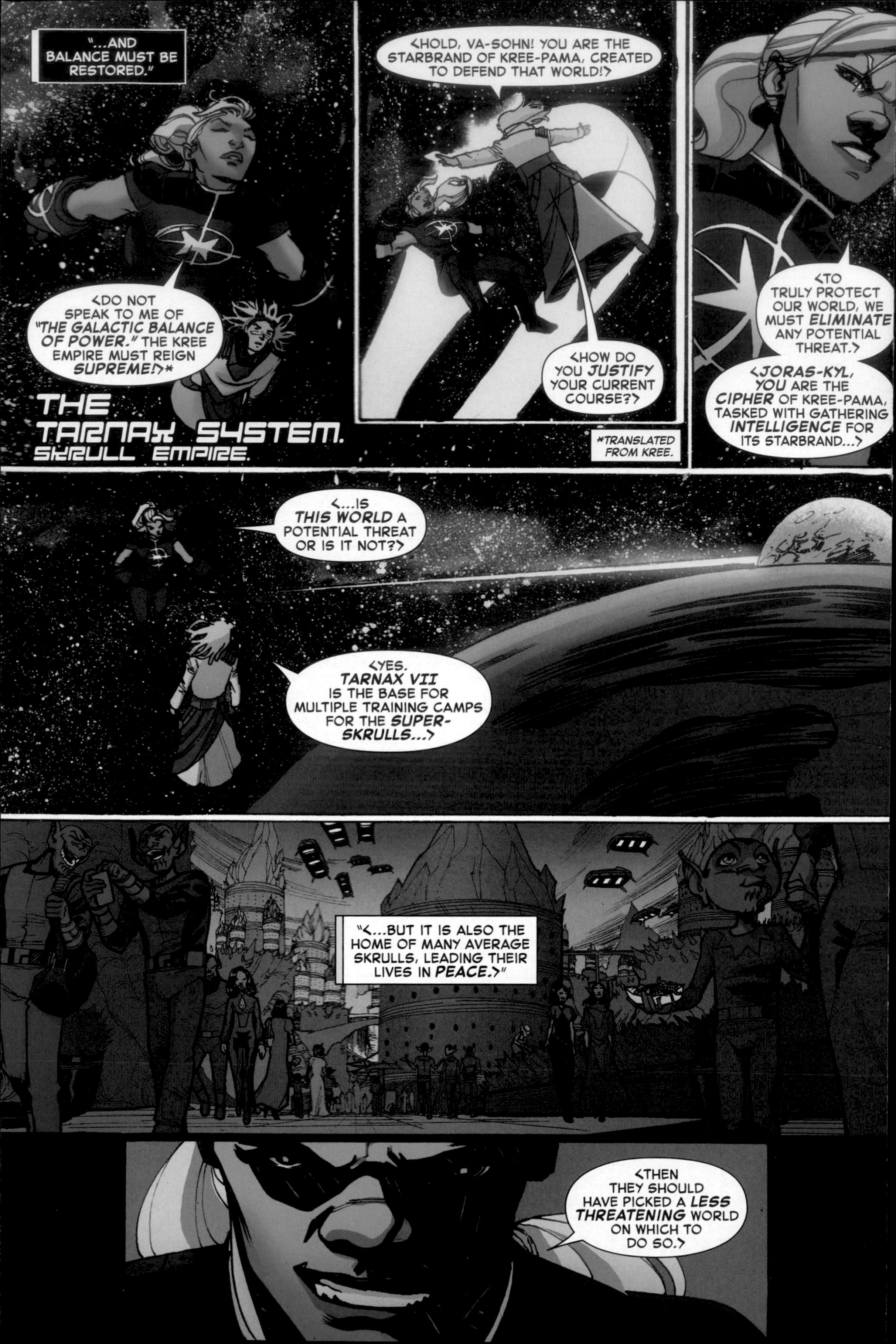
"...AND BALANCE MUST BE RESTORED."
<DO NOT SPEAK TO ME OF "THE GALACTIC BALANCE OF POWER." THE KREE EMPIRE MUST REIGN SUPREME!>*
THE TARNAX SYSTEM. SKRULL EMPIRE.
<HOLD, VA-SOHN! YOU ARE THE STARBRAND OF KREE-PAMA, CREATED TO DEFEND THAT WORLD!>
<HOW DO YOU JUSTIFY YOUR CURRENT COURSE?>
*TRANSLATED FROM KREE.
<TO TRULY PROTECT OUR WORLD, WE MUST ELIMINATE ANY POTENTIAL THREAT.>
<JORAS-KYL, YOU ARE THE CIPHER OF KREE-PAMA, TASKED WITH GATHERING INTELLIGENCE FOR ITS STARBRAND...>
<...IS THIS WORLD A POTENTIAL THREAT OR IS IT NOT?>
<YES. TARNAX VII IS THE BASE FOR MULTIPLE TRAINING CAMPS FOR THE SUPER-SKRULLS...>
"<...BUT IT IS ALSO THE HOME OF MANY AVERAGE SKRULLS, LEADING THEIR LIVES IN PEACE.>"
<THEN THEY SHOULD HAVE PICKED A LESS THREATENING WORLD ON WHICH TO DO SO.>

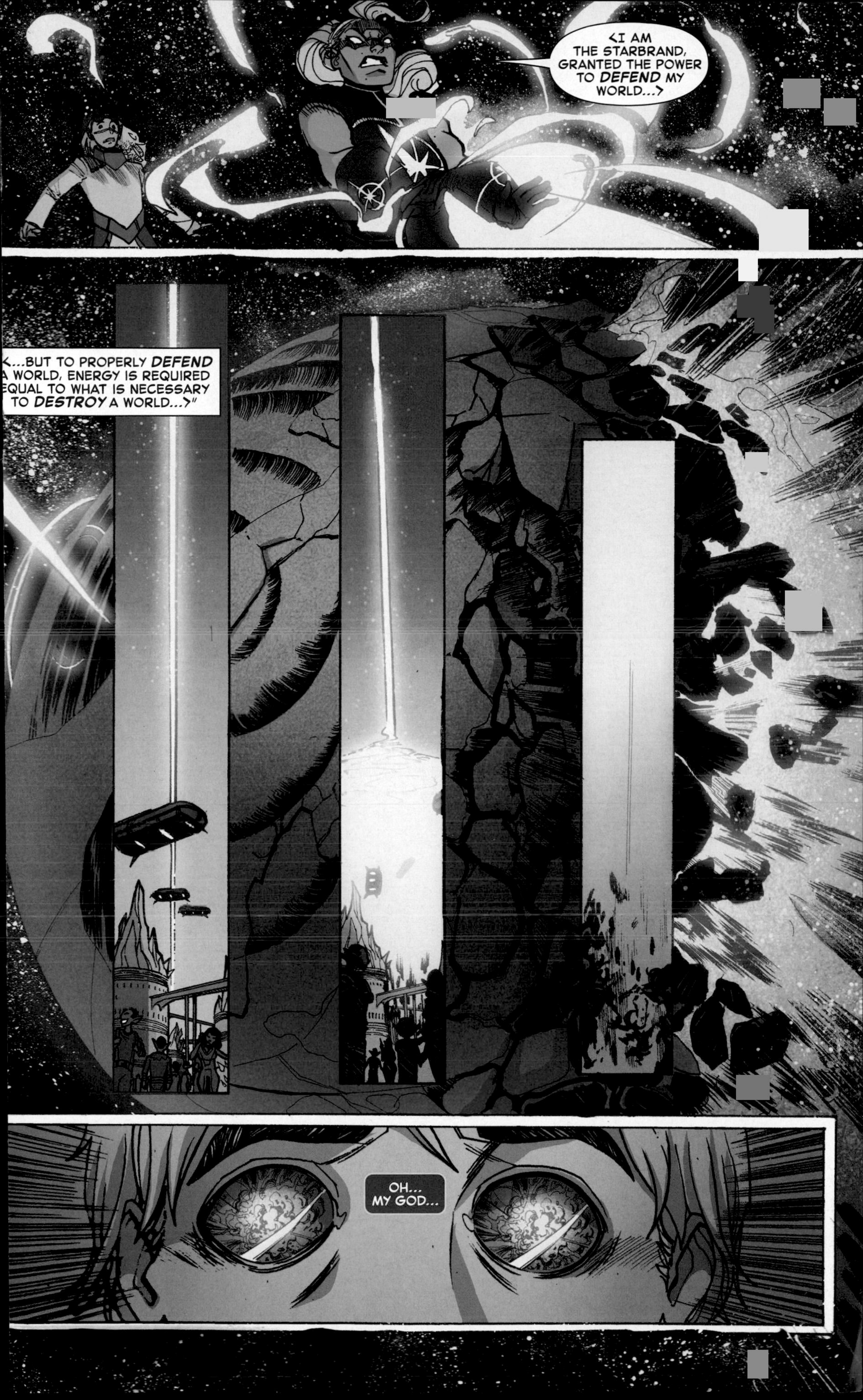
<I AM THE STARBRAND, GRANTED THE POWER TO DEFEND MY WORLD...>
<...BUT TO PROPERLY DEFEND A WORLD, ENERGY IS REQUIRED EQUAL TO WHAT IS NECESSARY TO DESTROY A WORLD...>"
OH... MY GOD...

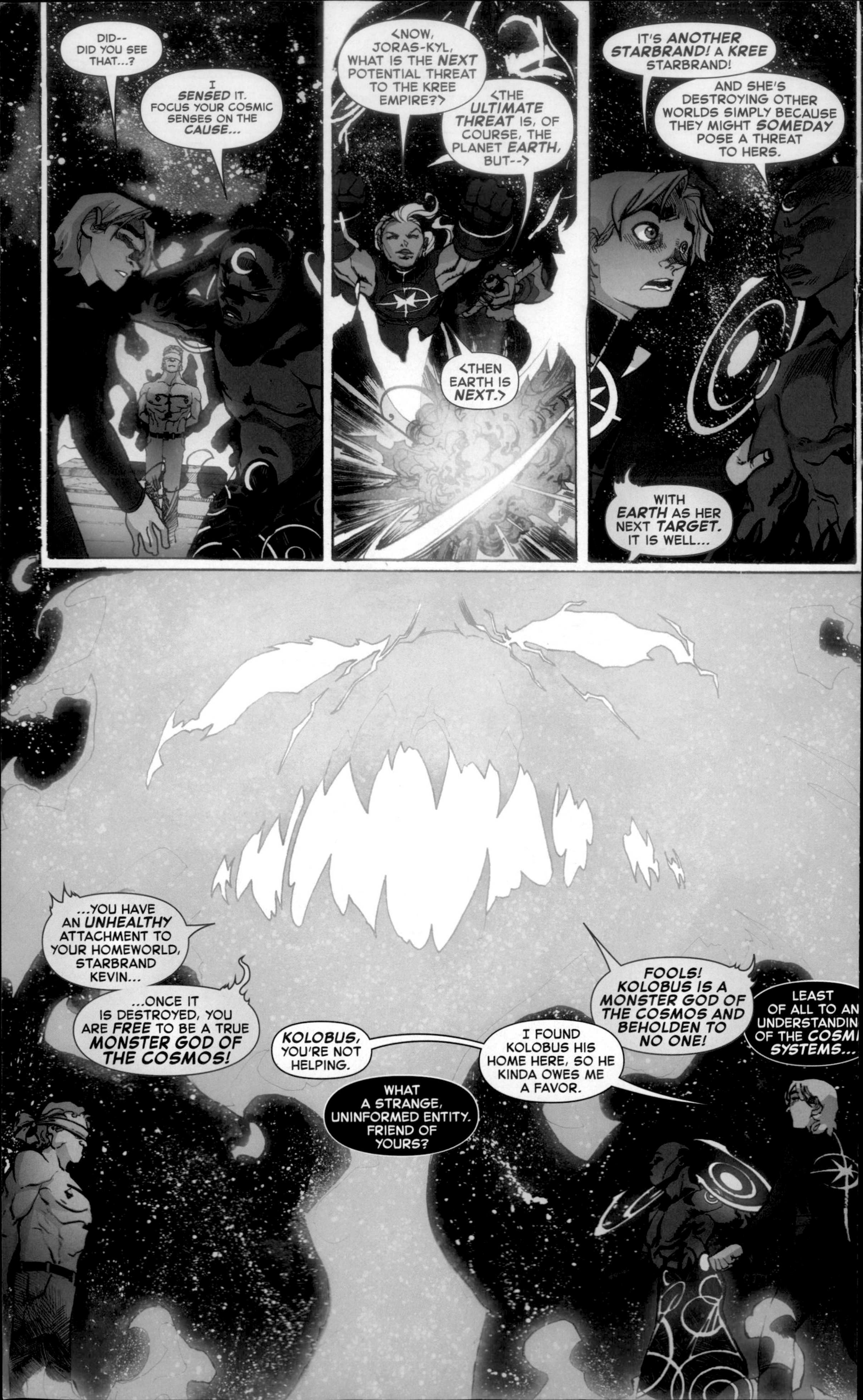
DID-- DID YOU SEE THAT...?
I SENSED IT. FOCUS YOUR COSMIC SENSES ON THE CAUSE...
<NOW, JORAS-KYL, WHAT IS THE NEXT POTENTIAL THREAT TO THE KREE EMPIRE?>
<THE ULTIMATE THREAT IS, OF COURSE, THE PLANET EARTH, BUT-->
<THEN EARTH IS NEXT.>
IT'S ANOTHER STARBRAND! A KREE STARBRAND!
AND SHE'S DESTROYING OTHER WORLDS SIMPLY BECAUSE THEY MIGHT SOMEDAY POSE A THREAT TO HERS.
WITH EARTH AS HER NEXT TARGET. IT IS WELL...
...YOU HAVE AN UNHEALTHY ATTACHMENT TO YOUR HOMEWORLD, STARBRAND KEVIN...
...ONCE IT IS DESTROYED, YOU ARE FREE TO BE A TRUE MONSTER GOD OF THE COSMOS!
KOLOBUS, YOU'RE NOT HELPING.
I FOUND KOLOBUS HIS HOME HERE, SO HE KINDA OWES ME A FAVOR.
FOOLS! KOLOBUS IS A MONSTER GOD OF THE COSMOS AND BEHOLDEN TO NO ONE!
LEAST OF ALL TO AN UNDERSTANDIN OF THE COSMI SYSTEMS...
WHAT A STRANGE, UNINFORMED ENTITY. FRIEND OF YOURS?

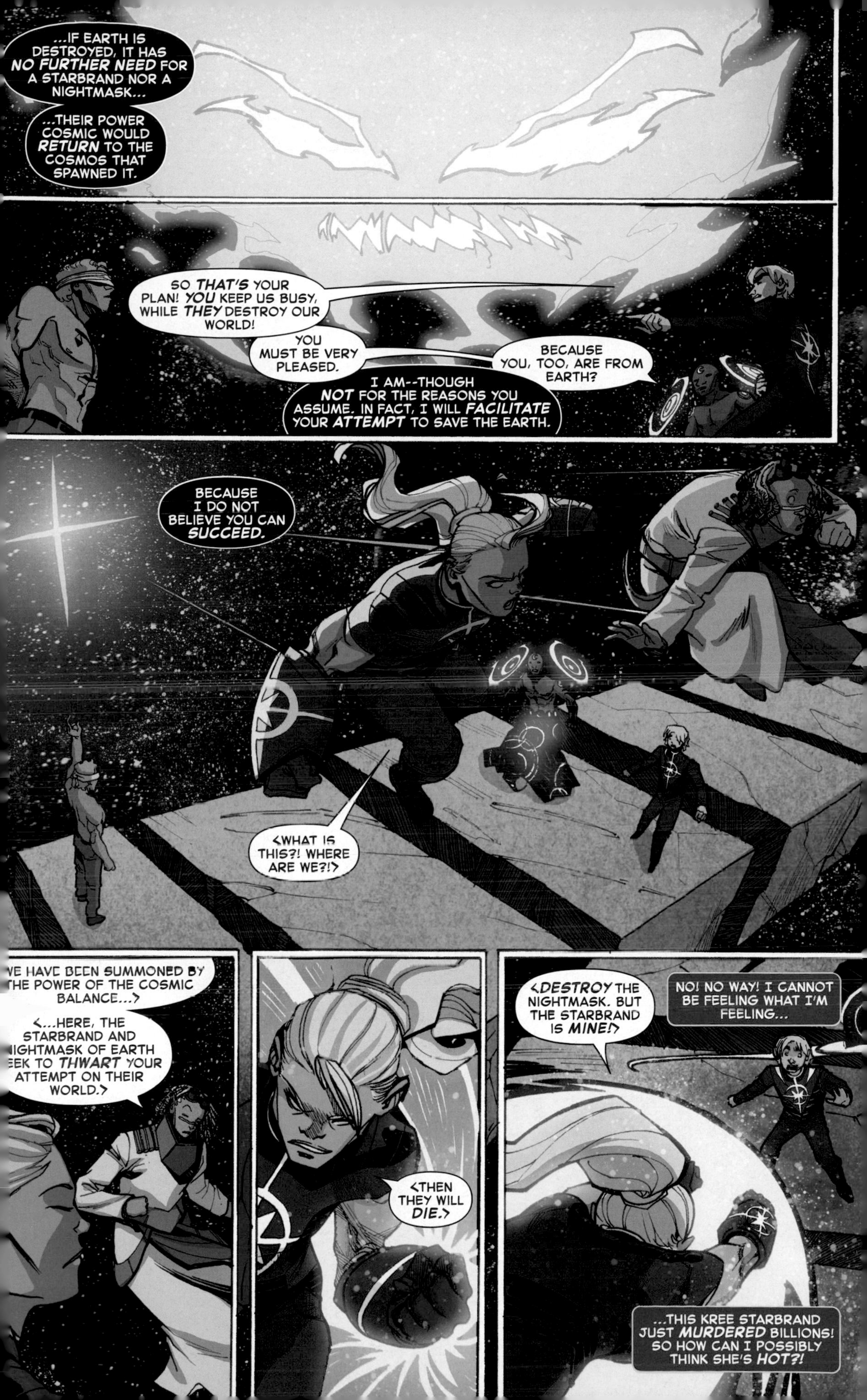
...IF EARTH IS DESTROYED, IT HAS NO FURTHER NEED FOR A STARBRAND NOR A NIGHTMASK...
...THEIR POWER COSMIC WOULD RETURN TO THE COSMOS THAT SPAWNED IT.
SO THAT'S YOUR PLAN! YOU KEEP US BUSY, WHILE THEY DESTROY OUR WORLD!
YOU MUST BE VERY PLEASED.
BECAUSE YOU, TOO, ARE FROM EARTH?
I AM--THOUGH NOT FOR THE REASONS YOU ASSUME. IN FACT, I WILL FACILITATE YOUR ATTEMPT TO SAVE THE EARTH.
BECAUSE I DO NOT BELIEVE YOU CAN SUCCEED.
<WHAT IS THIS?! WHERE ARE WE?!>
WE HAVE BEEN SUMMONED BY THE POWER OF THE COSMIC BALANCE...>
<...HERE, THE STARBRAND AND NIGHTMASK OF EARTH SEEK TO THWART YOUR ATTEMPT ON THEIR WORLD.>
<THEN THEY WILL DIE.>
<DESTROY THE NIGHTMASK. BUT THE STARBRAND IS MINE!>
NO! NO WAY! I CANNOT BE FEELING WHAT I'M FEELING...
...THIS KREE STARBRAND JUST MURDERED BILLIONS! SO HOW CAN I POSSIBLY THINK SHE'S HOT?!

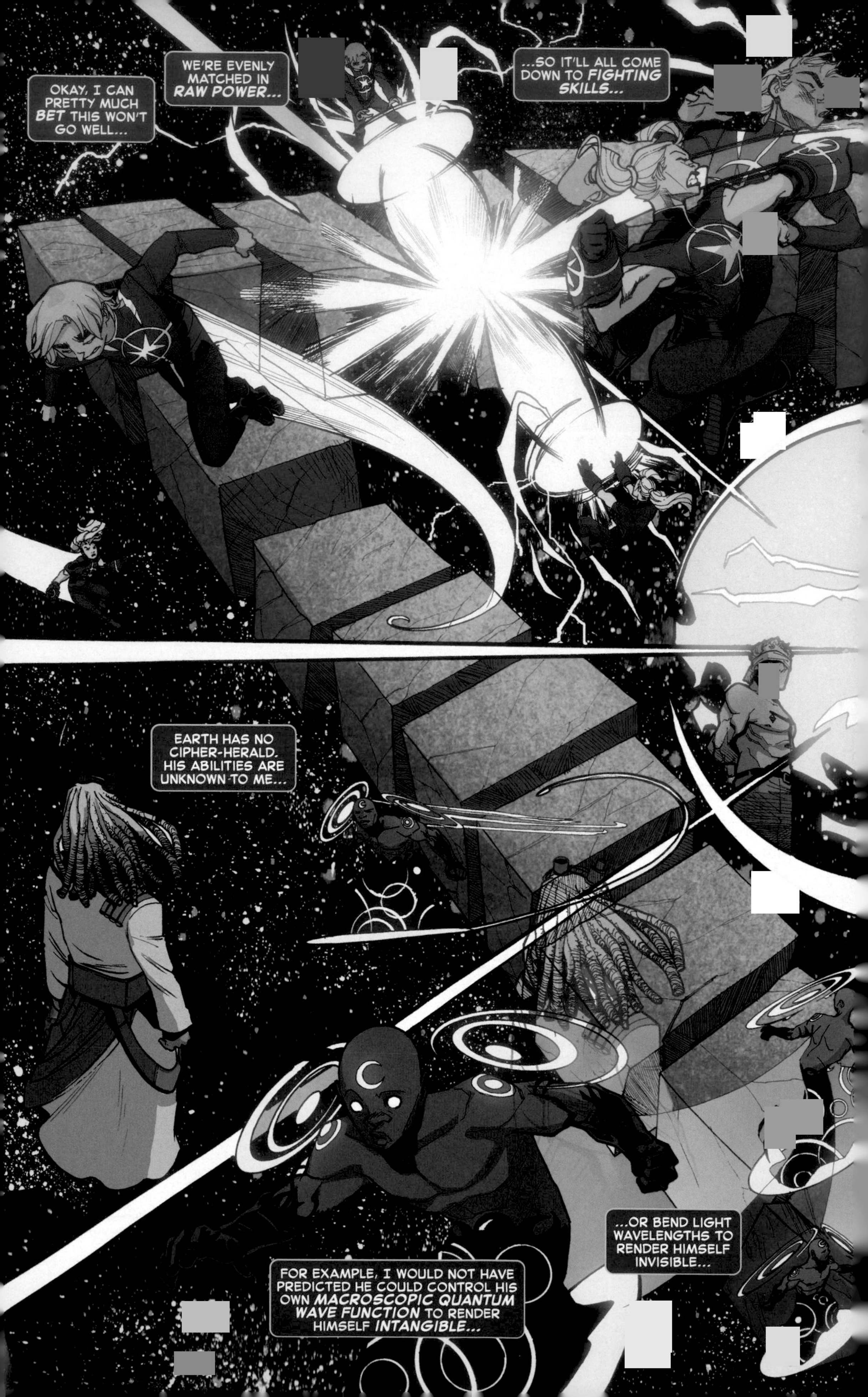
OKAY, I CAN PRETTY MUCH BET THIS WON'T GO WELL...
WE'RE EVENLY MATCHED IN RAW POWER...
...SO IT'LL ALL COME DOWN TO FIGHTING SKILLS...
EARTH HAS NO CIPHER-HERALD. HIS ABILITIES ARE UNKNOWN TO ME...
FOR EXAMPLE, I WOULD NOT HAVE PREDICTED HE COULD CONTROL HIS OWN MACROSCOPIC QUANTUM WAVE FUNCTION TO RENDER HIMSELF INTANGIBLE...
...OR BEND LIGHT WAVELENGTHS TO RENDER HIMSELF INVISIBLE...

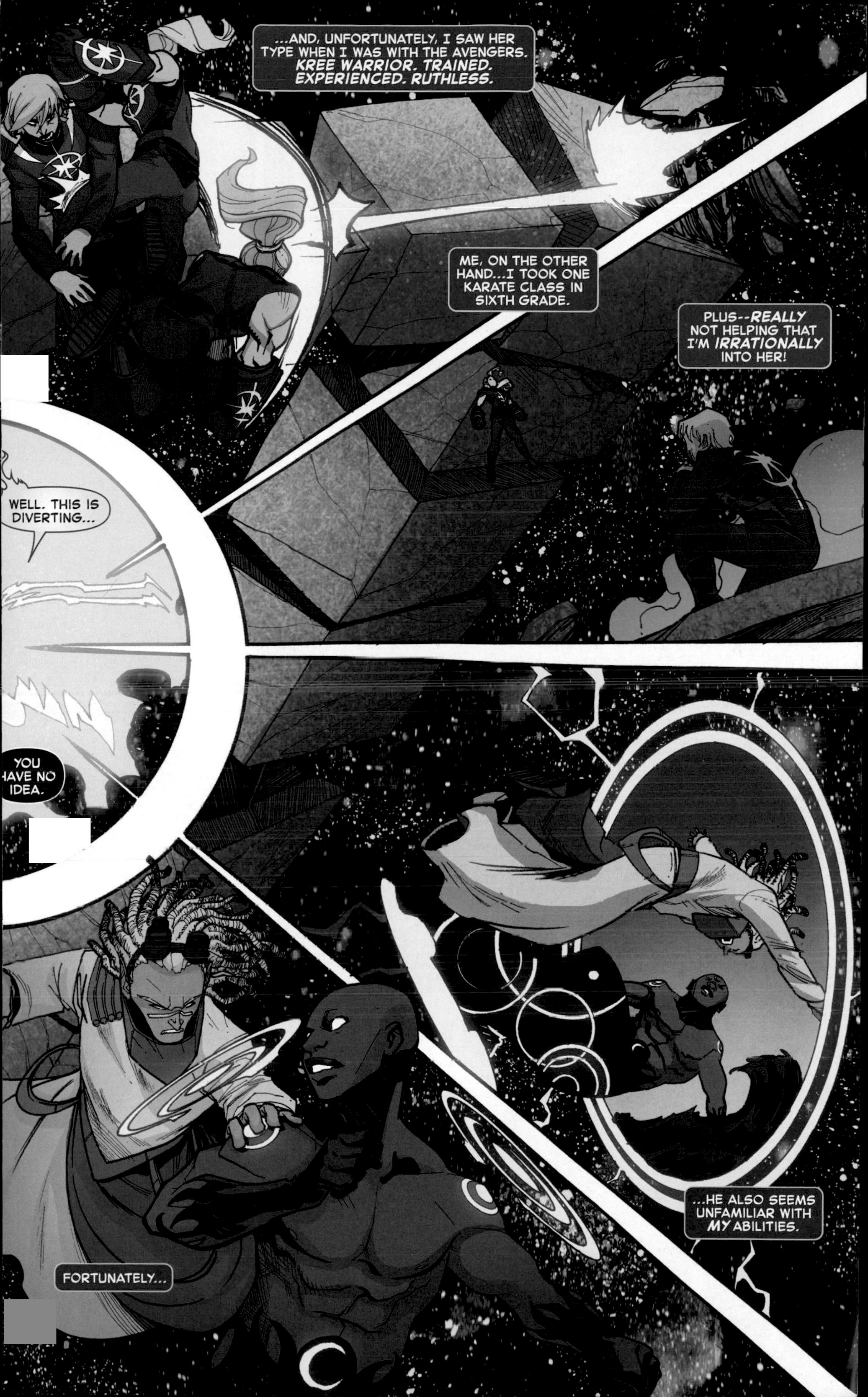
...AND, UNFORTUNATELY, I SAW HER TYPE WHEN I WAS WITH THE AVENGERS. KREE WARRIOR. TRAINED. EXPERIENCED. RUTHLESS.
ME, ON THE OTHER HAND...I TOOK ONE KARATE CLASS IN SIXTH GRADE.
PLUS--REALLY NOT HELPING THAT I'M IRRATIONALLY INTO HER!
WELL. THIS IS DIVERTING...
YOU HAVE NO IDEA.
FORTUNATELY...
...HE ALSO SEEMS UNFAMILIAR WITH MY ABILITIES.

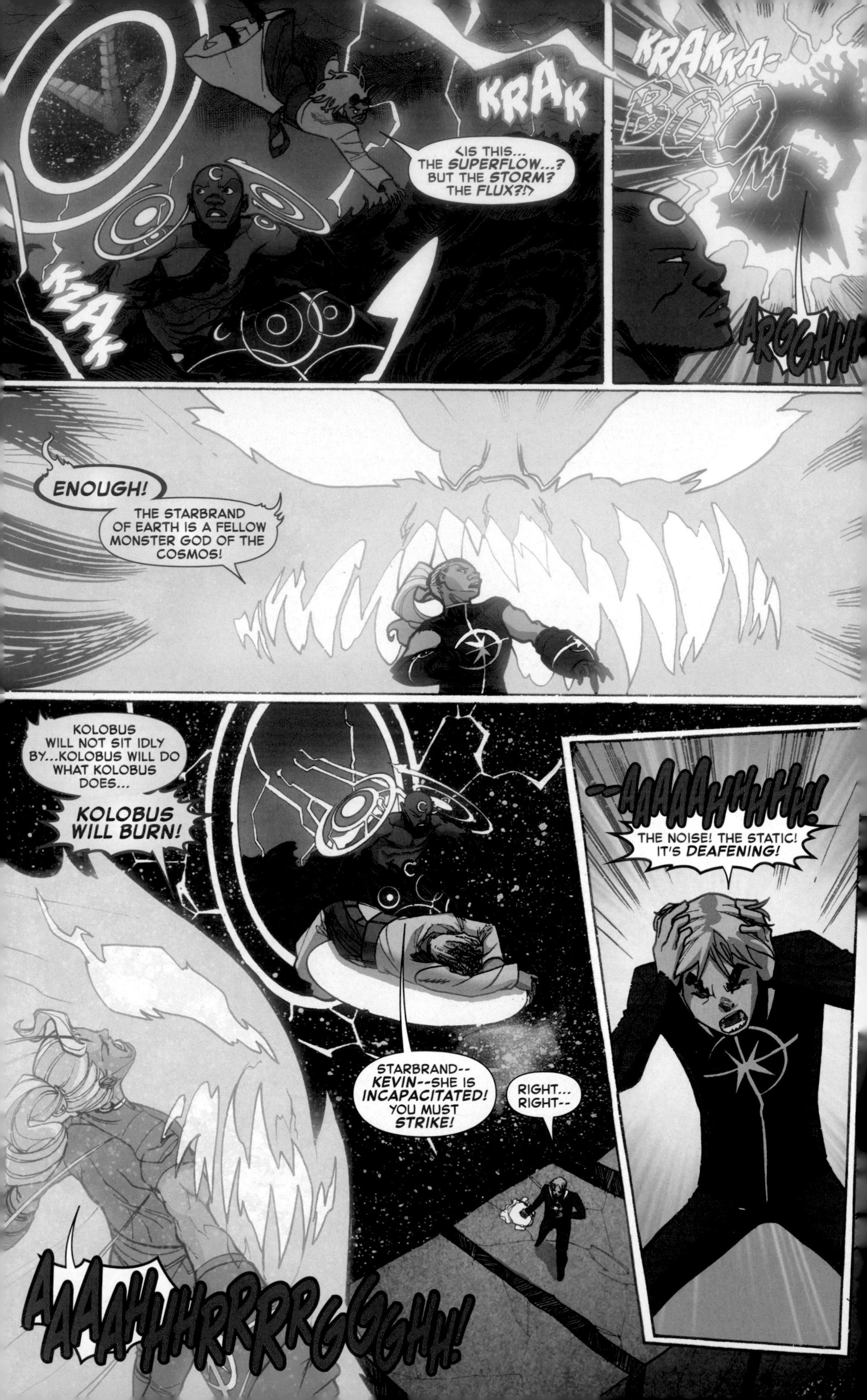
KRAK
<IS THIS... THE SUPERFLOW...? BUT THE STORM? THE FLUX?!>
KRAK
KRAKKA-BOOM
ARGGHHH
ENOUGH!
THE STARBRAND OF EARTH IS A FELLOW MONSTER GOD OF THE COSMOS!
KOLOBUS WILL NOT SIT IDLY BY...KOLOBUS WILL DO WHAT KOLOBUS DOES...
KOLOBUS WILL BURN!
--AAAAAHHHHH!
THE NOISE! THE STATIC! IT'S DEAFENING!
STARBRAND--KEVIN--SHE IS INCAPACITATED! YOU MUST STRIKE!
RIGHT... RIGHT--
AAAAHHHRRRRGGGHH!

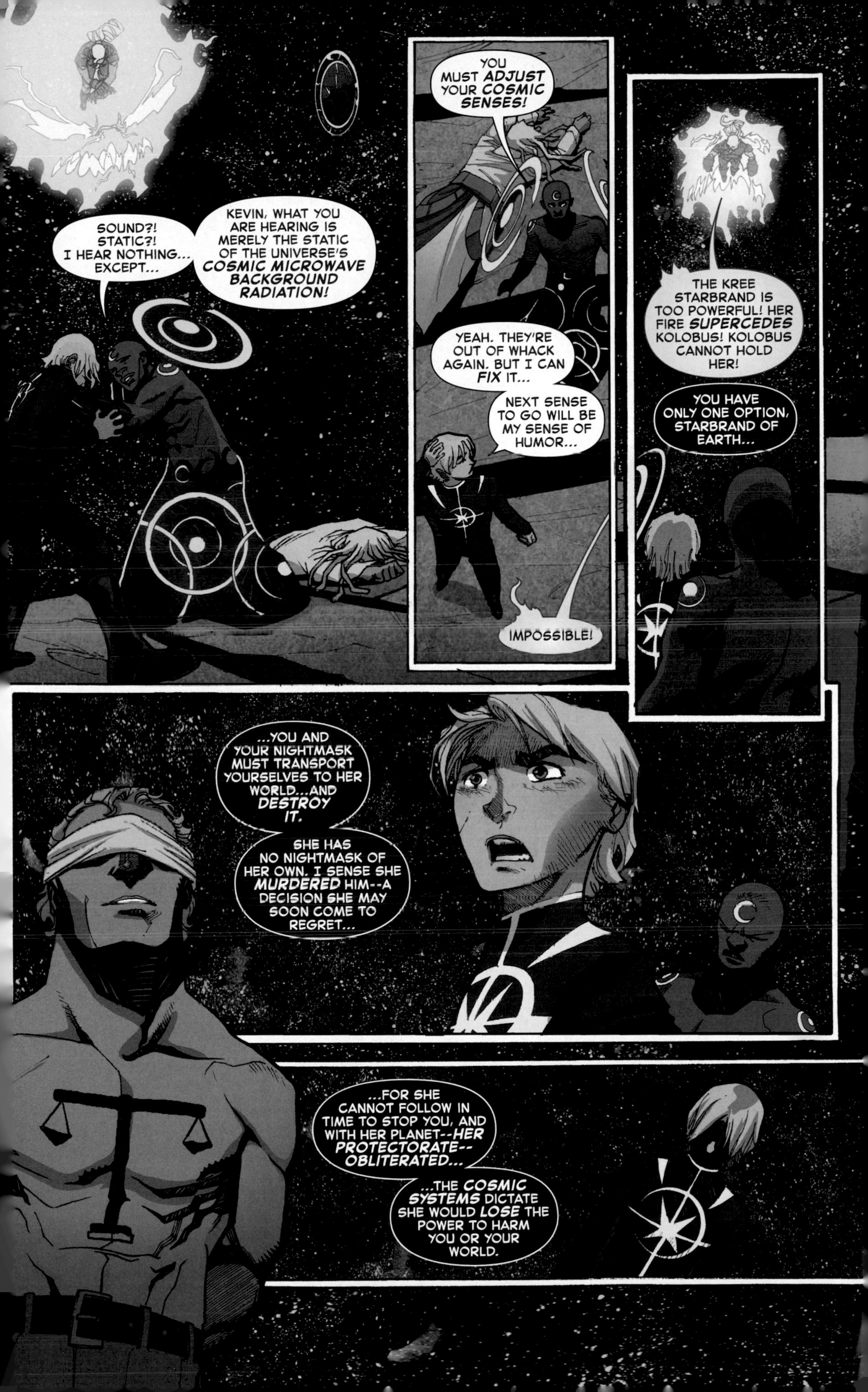
SOUND?! STATIC?! I HEAR NOTHING... EXCEPT...
KEVIN, WHAT YOU ARE HEARING IS MERELY THE STATIC OF THE UNIVERSE'S COSMIC MICROWAVE BACKGROUND RADIATION!
YOU MUST ADJUST YOUR COSMIC SENSES!
YEAH. THEY'RE OUT OF WHACK AGAIN. BUT I CAN FIX IT...
NEXT SENSE TO GO WILL BE MY SENSE OF HUMOR...
IMPOSSIBLE!
THE KREE STARBRAND IS TOO POWERFUL! HER FIRE SUPERCEDES KOLOBUS! KOLOBUS CANNOT HOLD HER!
YOU HAVE ONLY ONE OPTION, STARBRAND OF EARTH...
...YOU AND YOUR NIGHTMASK MUST TRANSPORT YOURSELVES TO HER WORLD...AND DESTROY IT.
SHE HAS NO NIGHTMASK OF HER OWN. I SENSE SHE MURDERED HIM--A DECISION SHE MAY SOON COME TO REGRET...
...FOR SHE CANNOT FOLLOW IN TIME TO STOP YOU, AND WITH HER PLANET--HER PROTECTORATE--OBLITERATED...
...THE COSMIC SYSTEMS DICTATE SHE WOULD LOSE THE POWER TO HARM YOU OR YOUR WORLD.

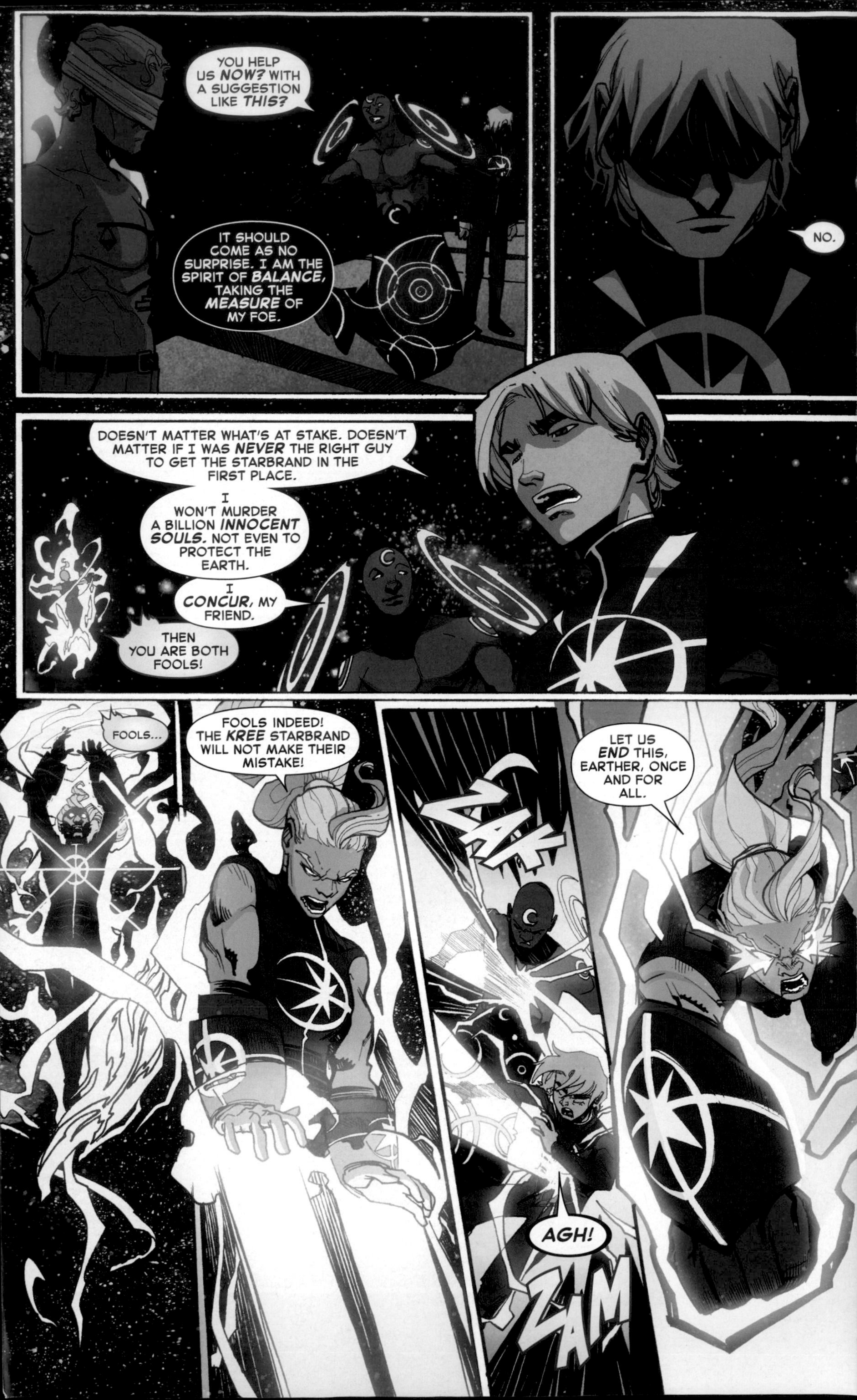

YOU HELP US NOW? WITH A SUGGESTION LIKE THIS?
IT SHOULD COME AS NO SURPRISE. I AM THE SPIRIT OF BALANCE, TAKING THE MEASURE OF MY FOE.
NO.
DOESN'T MATTER WHAT'S AT STAKE. DOESN'T MATTER IF I WAS NEVER THE RIGHT GUY TO GET THE STARBRAND IN THE FIRST PLACE.
I WON'T MURDER A BILLION INNOCENT SOULS. NOT EVEN TO PROTECT THE EARTH.
I CONCUR, MY FRIEND.
THEN YOU ARE BOTH FOOLS!
FOOLS...
FOOLS INDEED! THE KREE STARBRAND WILL NOT MAKE THEIR MISTAKE!
ZAK
LET US END THIS, EARTHER, ONCE AND FOR ALL.
AGH!
ZAM

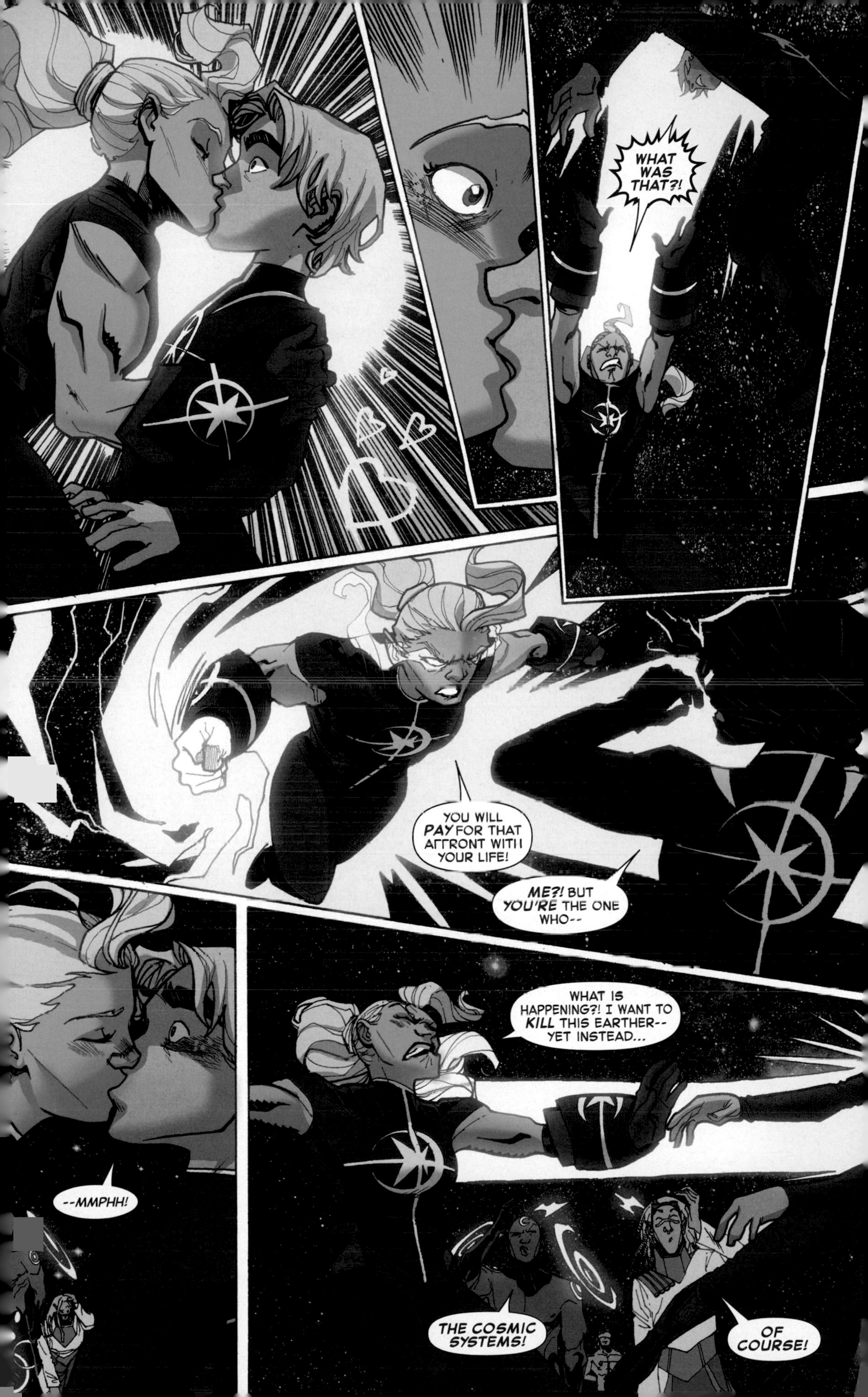
WHAT WAS THAT?!
YOU WILL PAY FOR THAT AFFRONT WITH YOUR LIFE!
ME?! BUT YOU'RE THE ONE WHO--
--MMPHH!
WHAT IS HAPPENING?! I WANT TO KILL THIS EARTHER-- YET INSTEAD...
THE COSMIC SYSTEMS!
OF COURSE!

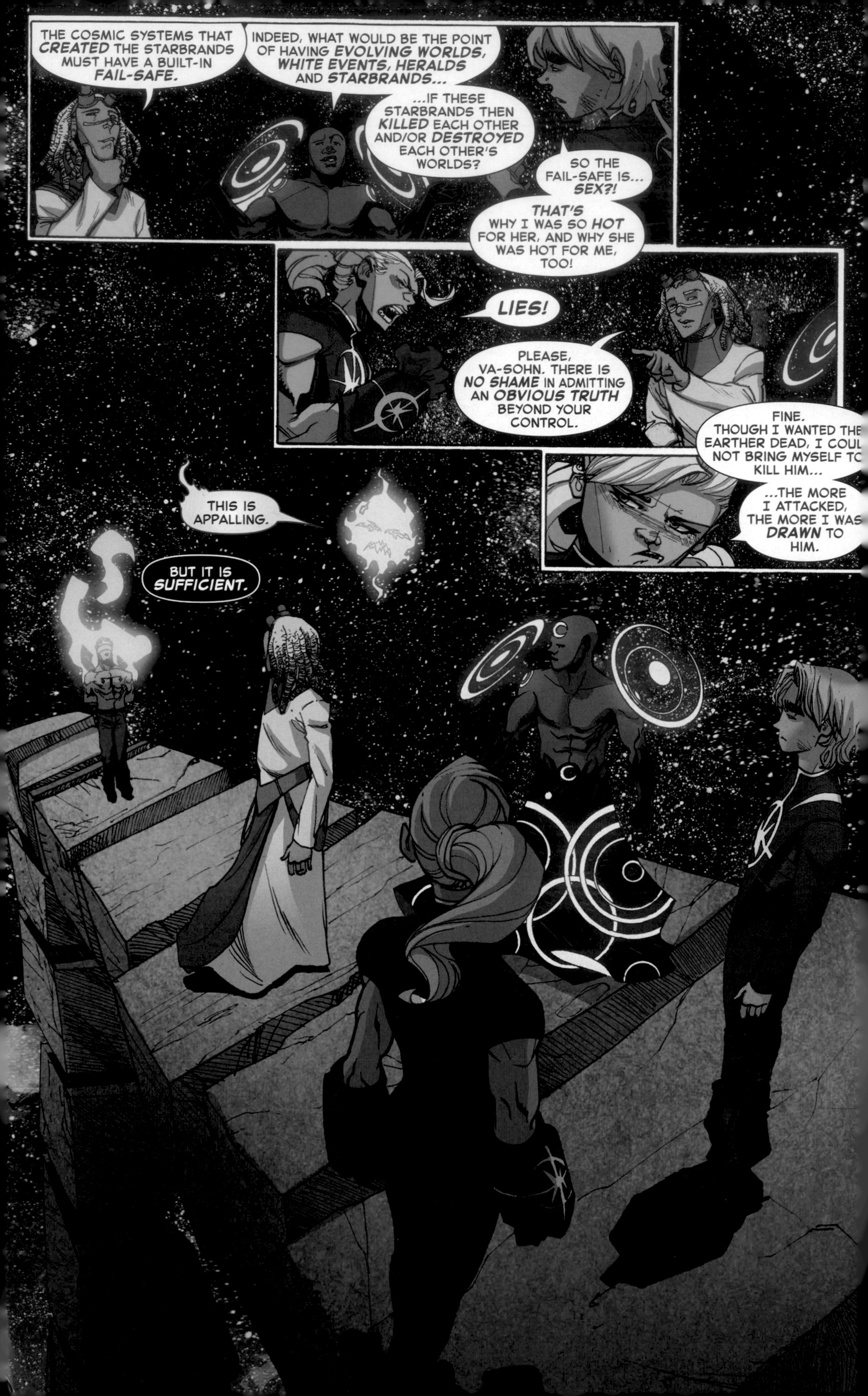
THE COSMIC SYSTEMS THAT CREATED THE STARBRANDS MUST HAVE A BUILT-IN FAIL-SAFE.
INDEED, WHAT WOULD BE THE POINT OF HAVING EVOLVING WORLDS, WHITE EVENTS, HERALDS AND STARBRANDS...
...IF THESE STARBRANDS THEN KILLED EACH OTHER AND/OR DESTROYED EACH OTHER'S WORLDS?
SO THE FAIL-SAFE IS... SEX?!
THAT'S WHY I WAS SO HOT FOR HER, AND WHY SHE WAS HOT FOR ME, TOO!
LIES!
PLEASE, VA-SOHN. THERE IS NO SHAME IN ADMITTING AN OBVIOUS TRUTH BEYOND YOUR CONTROL.
FINE. THOUGH I WANTED THE EARTHER DEAD, I COUL NOT BRING MYSELF TO KILL HIM...
...THE MORE I ATTACKED, THE MORE I WAS DRAWN TO HIM.
THIS IS APPALLING.
BUT IT IS SUFFICIENT.

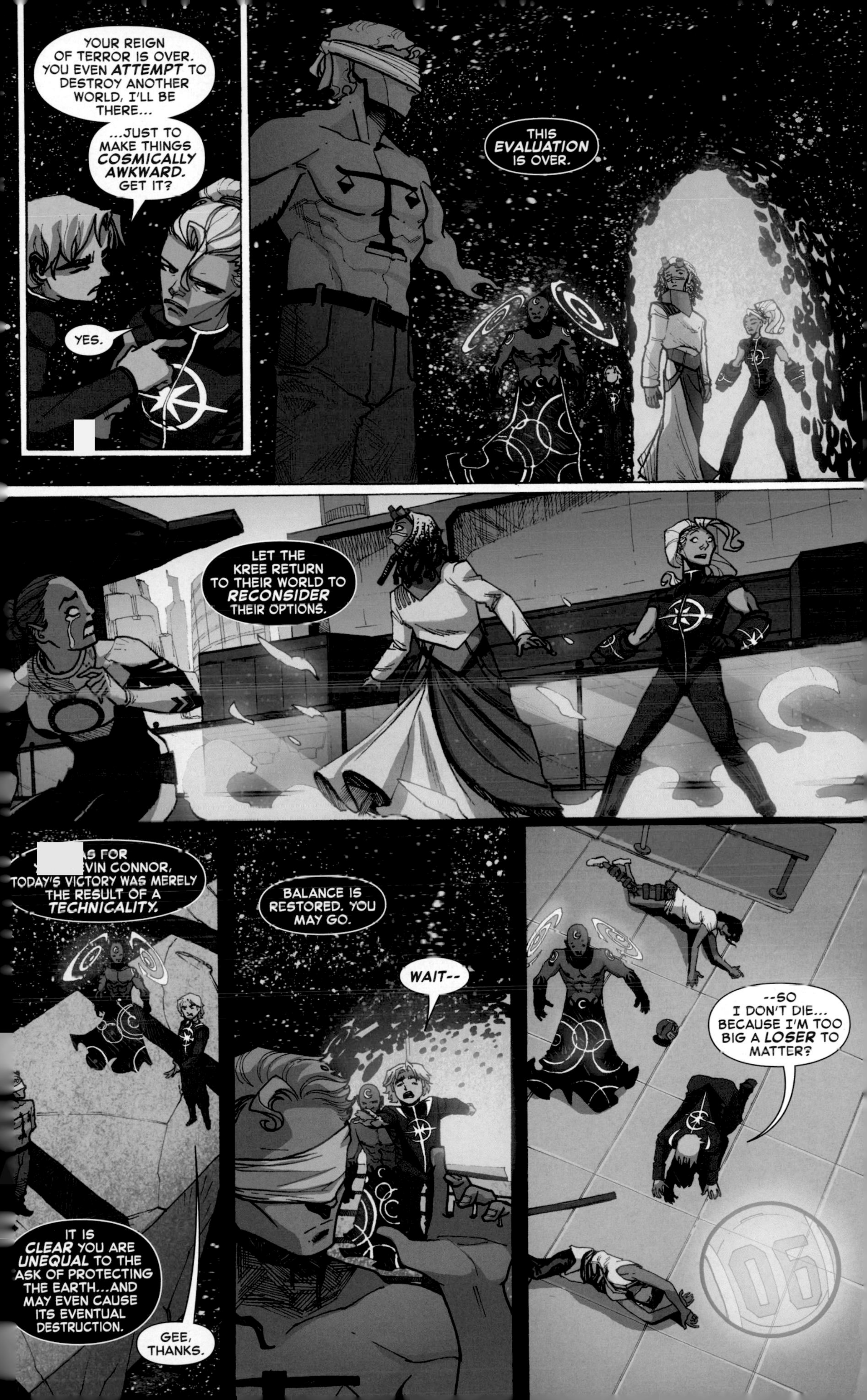
YOUR REIGN OF TERROR IS OVER. YOU EVEN ATTEMPT TO DESTROY ANOTHER WORLD, I'LL BE THERE...
...JUST TO MAKE THINGS COSMICALLY AWKWARD. GET IT?
YES.
THIS EVALUATION IS OVER.
LET THE KREE RETURN TO THEIR WORLD TO RECONSIDER THEIR OPTIONS.
AS FOR
VIN CONNOR,
TODAY'S VICTORY WAS MERELY THE RESULT OF A TECHNICALITY.
IT IS CLEAR YOU ARE UNEQUAL TO THE
ASK OF PROTECTING THE EARTH...AND MAY EVEN CAUSE ITS EVENTUAL DESTRUCTION.
GEE, THANKS.
BALANCE IS RESTORED. YOU MAY GO.
WAIT--
--SO I DON'T DIE... BECAUSE I'M TOO BIG A LOSER TO MATTER?
06

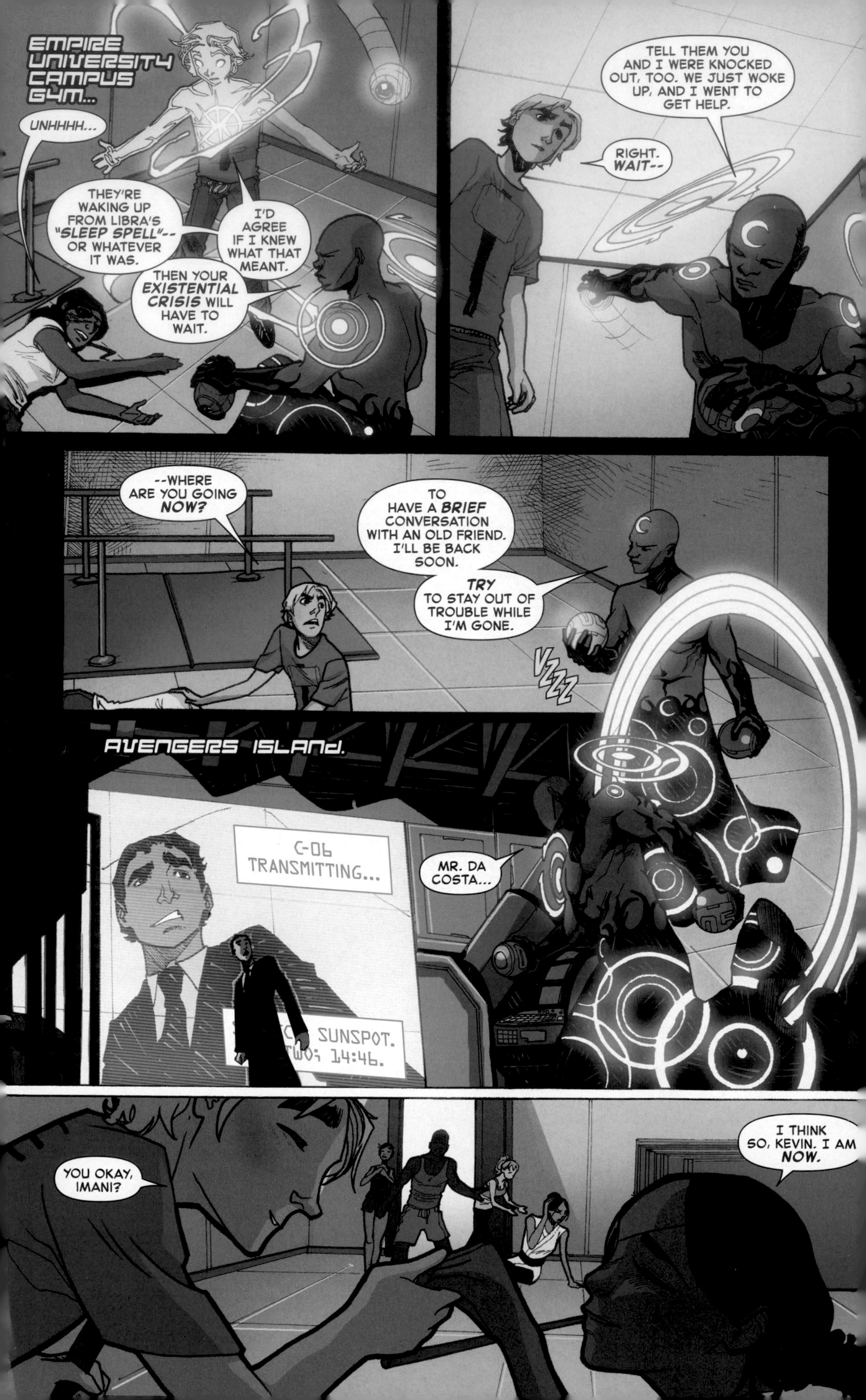
EMPIRE UNIVERSITY CAMPUS GYM...
UNHHHH...
THEY'RE WAKING UP FROM LIBRA'S "SLEEP SPELL"-- OR WHATEVER IT WAS.
I'D AGREE IF I KNEW WHAT THAT MEANT.
THEN YOUR EXISTENTIAL CRISIS WILL HAVE TO WAIT.
TELL THEM YOU AND I WERE KNOCKED OUT, TOO. WE JUST WOKE UP, AND I WENT TO GET HELP.
RIGHT. WAIT--
--WHERE ARE YOU GOING NOW?
TO HAVE A BRIEF CONVERSATION WITH AN OLD FRIEND. I'LL BE BACK SOON.
TRY TO STAY OUT OF TROUBLE WHILE I'M GONE.
VZZZ
AVENGERS ISLAND.
C-06 TRANSMITTING...
MR. DA COSTA...
SUNSPOT.
TWO: 14:46.
YOU OKAY, IMANI?
I THINK SO, KEVIN. I AM NOW.

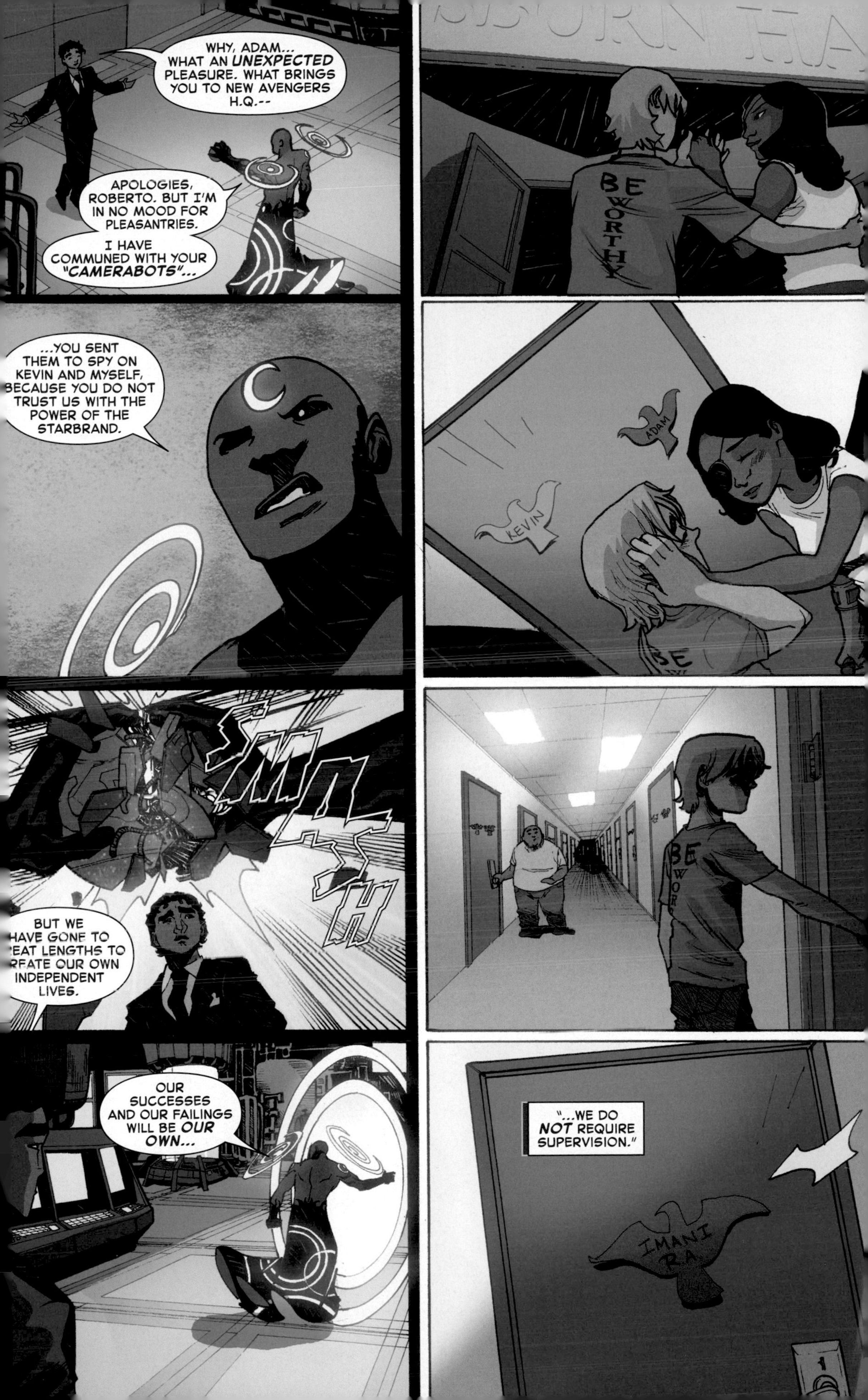
WHY, ADAM... WHAT AN *UNEXPECTED* PLEASURE. WHAT BRINGS YOU TO NEW AVENGERS H.Q.--
APOLOGIES, ROBERTO. BUT I'M IN NO MOOD FOR PLEASANTRIES.
I HAVE COMMUNED WITH YOUR *"CAMERABOTS"...*
...YOU SENT THEM TO SPY ON KEVIN AND MYSELF, BECAUSE YOU DO NOT TRUST US WITH THE POWER OF THE STARBRAND.
SMASH
BUT WE HAVE GONE TO EAT LENGTHS TO REATE OUR OWN INDEPENDENT LIVES.
OUR SUCCESSES AND OUR FAILINGS WILL BE *OUR OWN...*
BE WORTHY
ADAM
KEVIN
"...WE DO *NOT* REQUIRE SUPERVISION."
IMANI RA

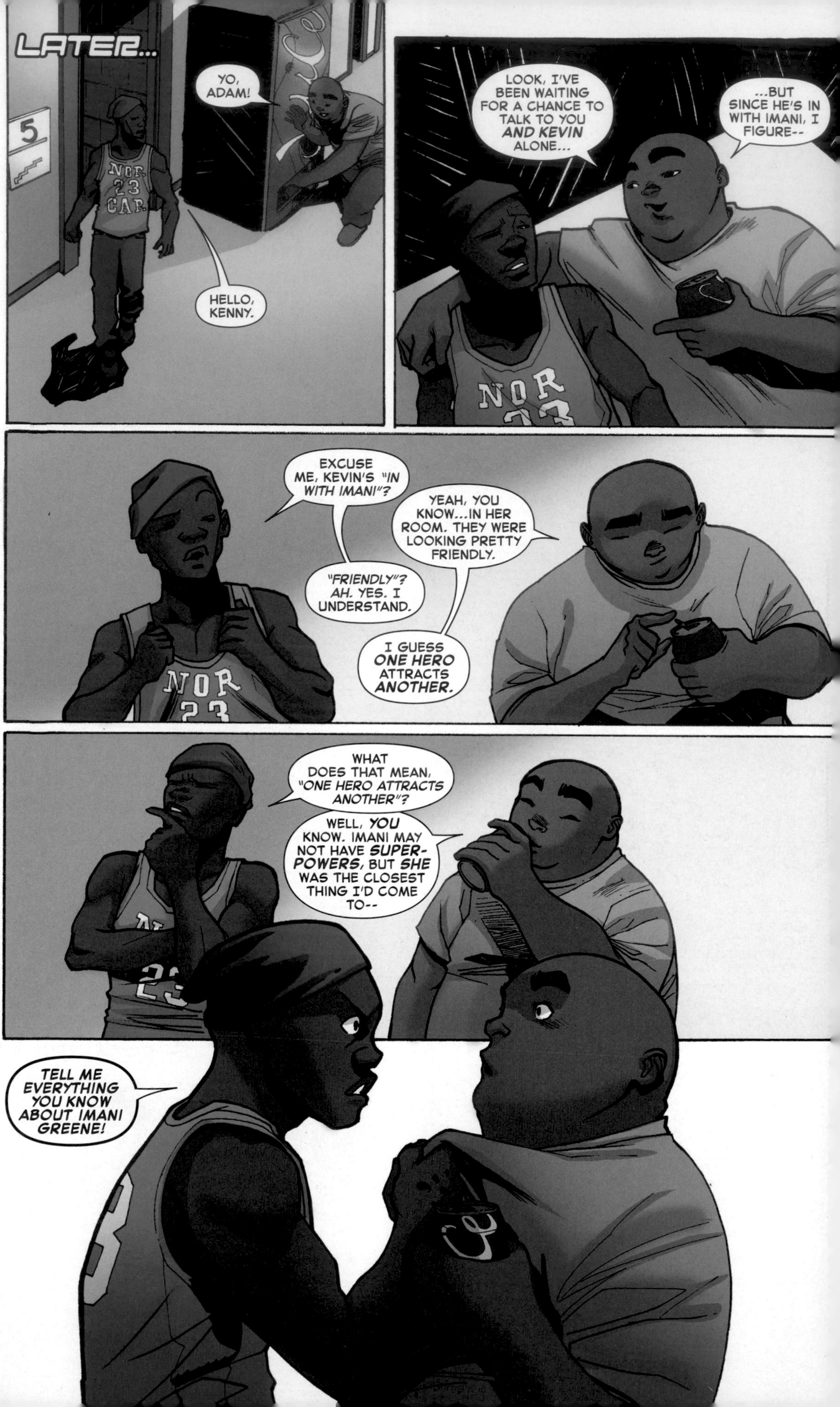
LATER...
YO, ADAM!
HELLO, KENNY.
LOOK, I'VE BEEN WAITING FOR A CHANCE TO TALK TO YOU AND KEVIN ALONE...
...BUT SINCE HE'S IN WITH IMANI, I FIGURE--
EXCUSE ME, KEVIN'S "IN WITH IMANI"?
YEAH, YOU KNOW...IN HER ROOM. THEY WERE LOOKING PRETTY FRIENDLY.
"FRIENDLY"? AH. YES. I UNDERSTAND.
I GUESS ONE HERO ATTRACTS ANOTHER.
WHAT DOES THAT MEAN, "ONE HERO ATTRACTS ANOTHER"?
WELL, YOU KNOW. IMANI MAY NOT HAVE SUPER-POWERS, BUT SHE WAS THE CLOSEST THING I'D COME TO--
TELL ME EVERYTHING YOU KNOW ABOUT IMANI GREENE!

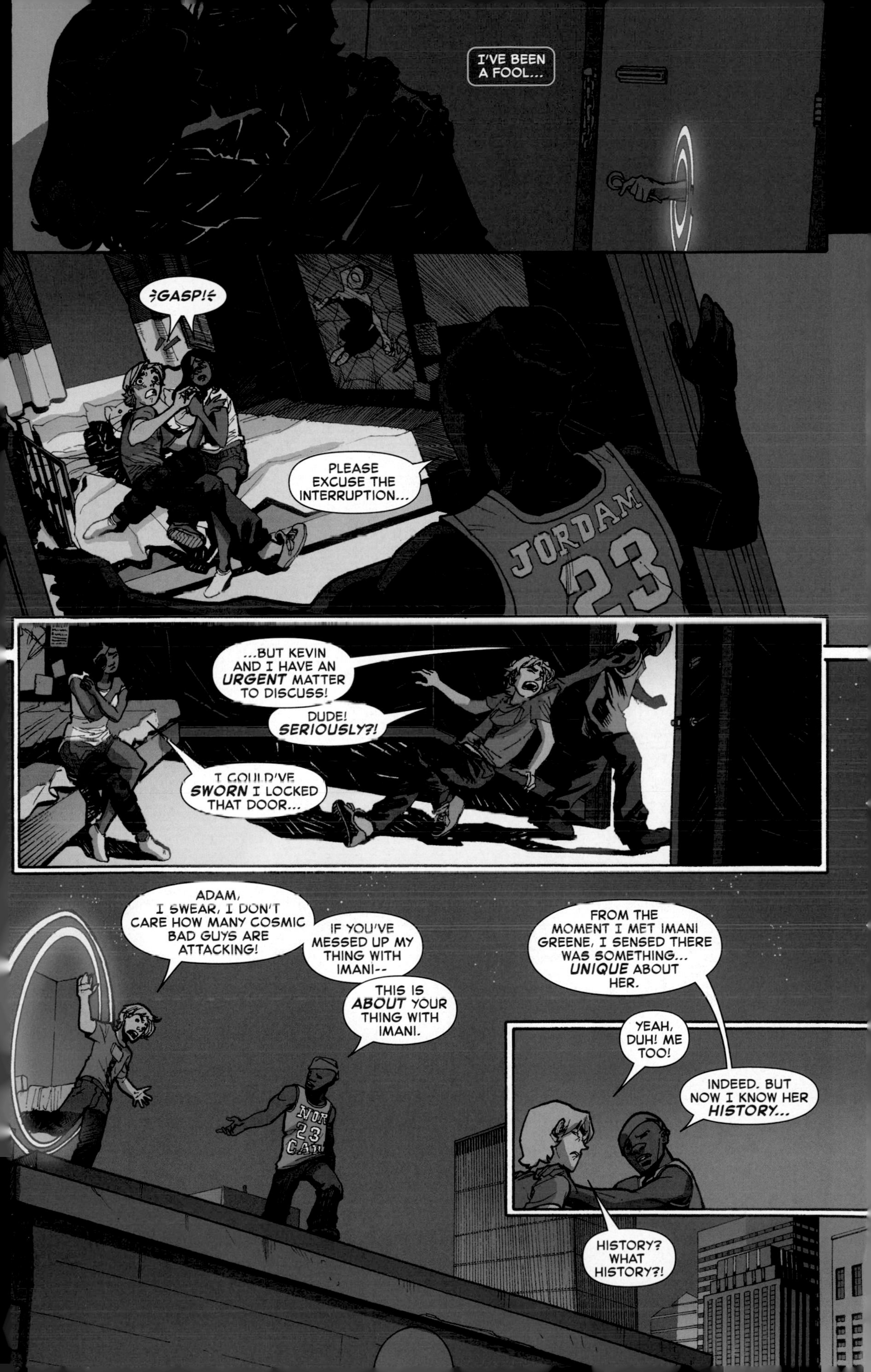
I'VE BEEN A FOOL...
⚡GASP!⚡
PLEASE EXCUSE THE INTERRUPTION...
JORDAN 23
...BUT KEVIN AND I HAVE AN URGENT MATTER TO DISCUSS!
DUDE! SERIOUSLY?!
I COULD'VE SWORN I LOCKED THAT DOOR...
ADAM, I SWEAR, I DON'T CARE HOW MANY COSMIC BAD GUYS ARE ATTACKING!
IF YOU'VE MESSED UP MY THING WITH IMANI--
THIS IS ABOUT YOUR THING WITH IMANI.
FROM THE MOMENT I MET IMANI GREENE, I SENSED THERE WAS SOMETHING... UNIQUE ABOUT HER.
YEAH, DUH! ME TOO!
INDEED. BUT NOW I KNOW HER HISTORY...
HISTORY? WHAT HISTORY?!

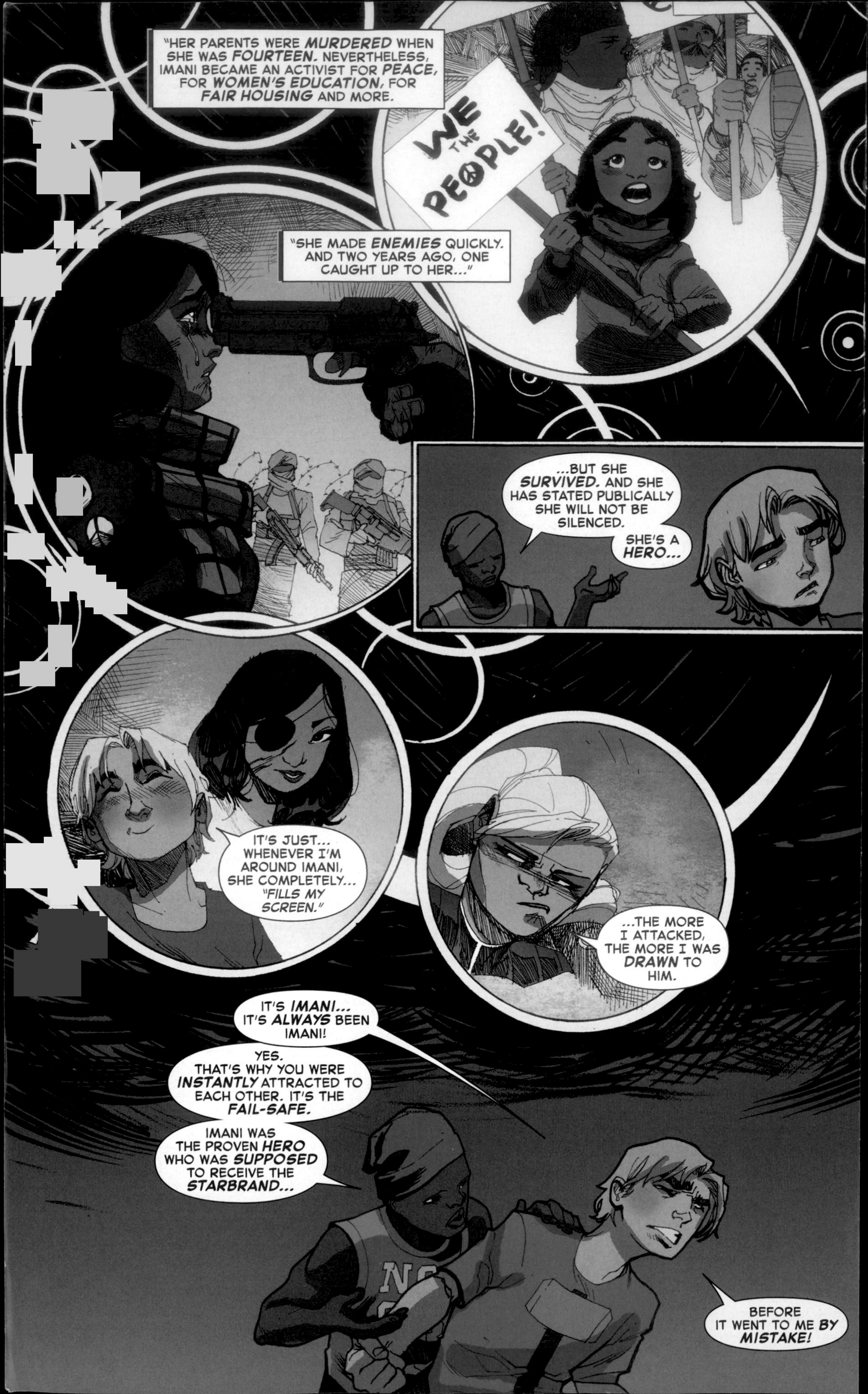
"HER PARENTS WERE MURDERED WHEN SHE WAS FOURTEEN. NEVERTHELESS, IMANI BECAME AN ACTIVIST FOR PEACE, FOR WOMEN'S EDUCATION, FOR FAIR HOUSING AND MORE.
WE THE PEOPLE!
"SHE MADE ENEMIES QUICKLY. AND TWO YEARS AGO, ONE CAUGHT UP TO HER..."
...BUT SHE SURVIVED. AND SHE HAS STATED PUBLICALLY SHE WILL NOT BE SILENCED.
SHE'S A HERO...
IT'S JUST... WHENEVER I'M AROUND IMANI, SHE COMPLETELY... "FILLS MY SCREEN."
...THE MORE I ATTACKED, THE MORE I WAS DRAWN TO HIM.
IT'S IMANI... IT'S ALWAYS BEEN IMANI!
YES. THAT'S WHY YOU WERE INSTANTLY ATTRACTED TO EACH OTHER. IT'S THE FAIL-SAFE.
IMANI WAS THE PROVEN HERO WHO WAS SUPPOSED TO RECEIVE THE STARBRAND...
BEFORE IT WENT TO ME BY MISTAKE!

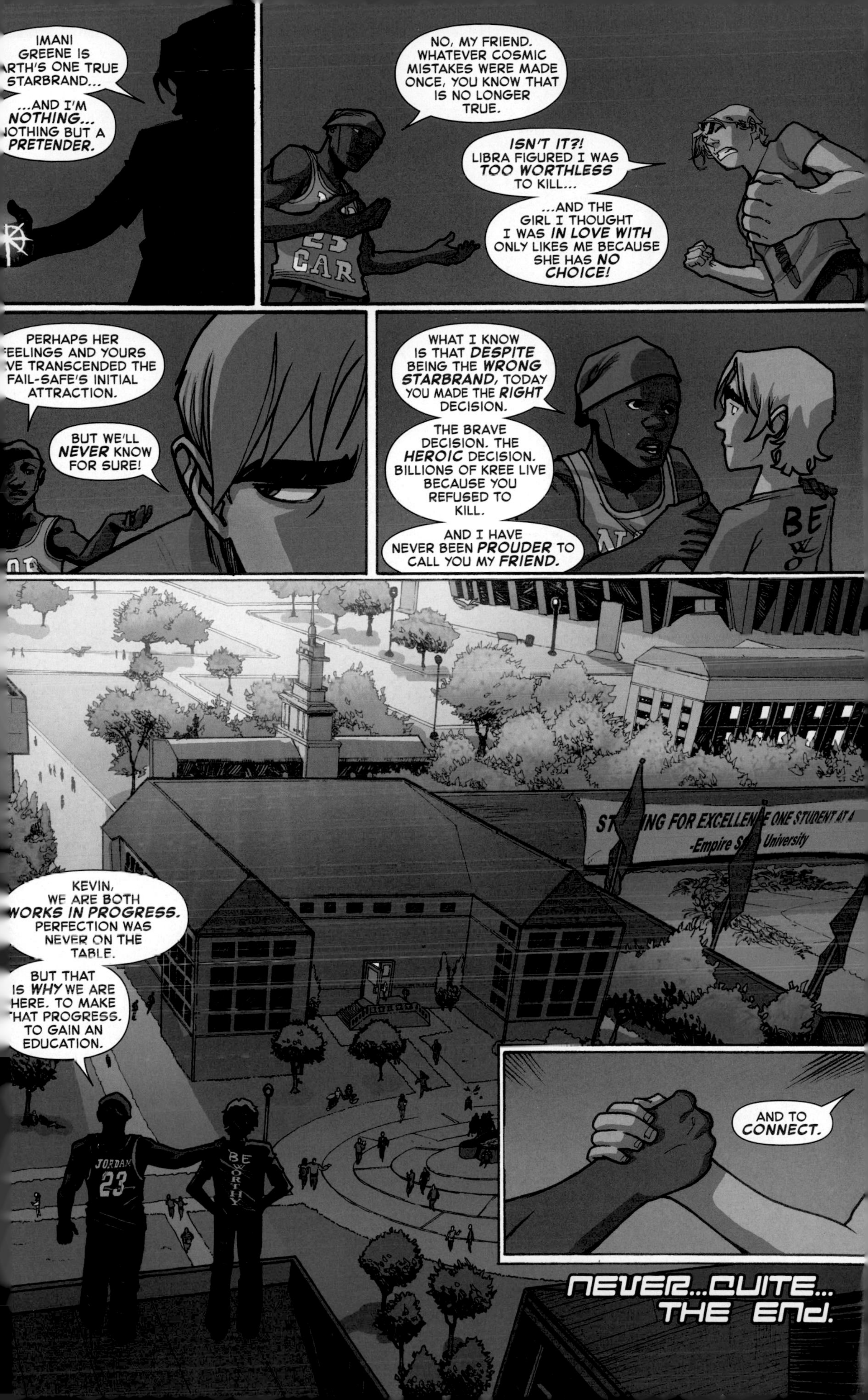
IMANI GREENE IS ...RTH'S ONE TRUE STARBRAND...
...AND I'M NOTHING... ...OTHING BUT A PRETENDER.
NO, MY FRIEND. WHATEVER COSMIC MISTAKES WERE MADE ONCE, YOU KNOW THAT IS NO LONGER TRUE.
ISN'T IT?! LIBRA FIGURED I WAS TOO WORTHLESS TO KILL...
...AND THE GIRL I THOUGHT I WAS IN LOVE WITH ONLY LIKES ME BECAUSE SHE HAS NO CHOICE!
PERHAPS HER ...EELINGS AND YOURS ...VE TRANSCENDED THE FAIL-SAFE'S INITIAL ATTRACTION.
BUT WE'LL NEVER KNOW FOR SURE!
WHAT I KNOW IS THAT DESPITE BEING THE WRONG STARBRAND, TODAY YOU MADE THE RIGHT DECISION.
THE BRAVE DECISION. THE HEROIC DECISION. BILLIONS OF KREE LIVE BECAUSE YOU REFUSED TO KILL.
AND I HAVE NEVER BEEN PROUDER TO CALL YOU MY FRIEND.
KEVIN, WE ARE BOTH WORKS IN PROGRESS. PERFECTION WAS NEVER ON THE TABLE.
BUT THAT IS WHY WE ARE HERE. TO MAKE ...HAT PROGRESS. TO GAIN AN EDUCATION.
AND TO CONNECT.
NEVER...QUITE... THE END.

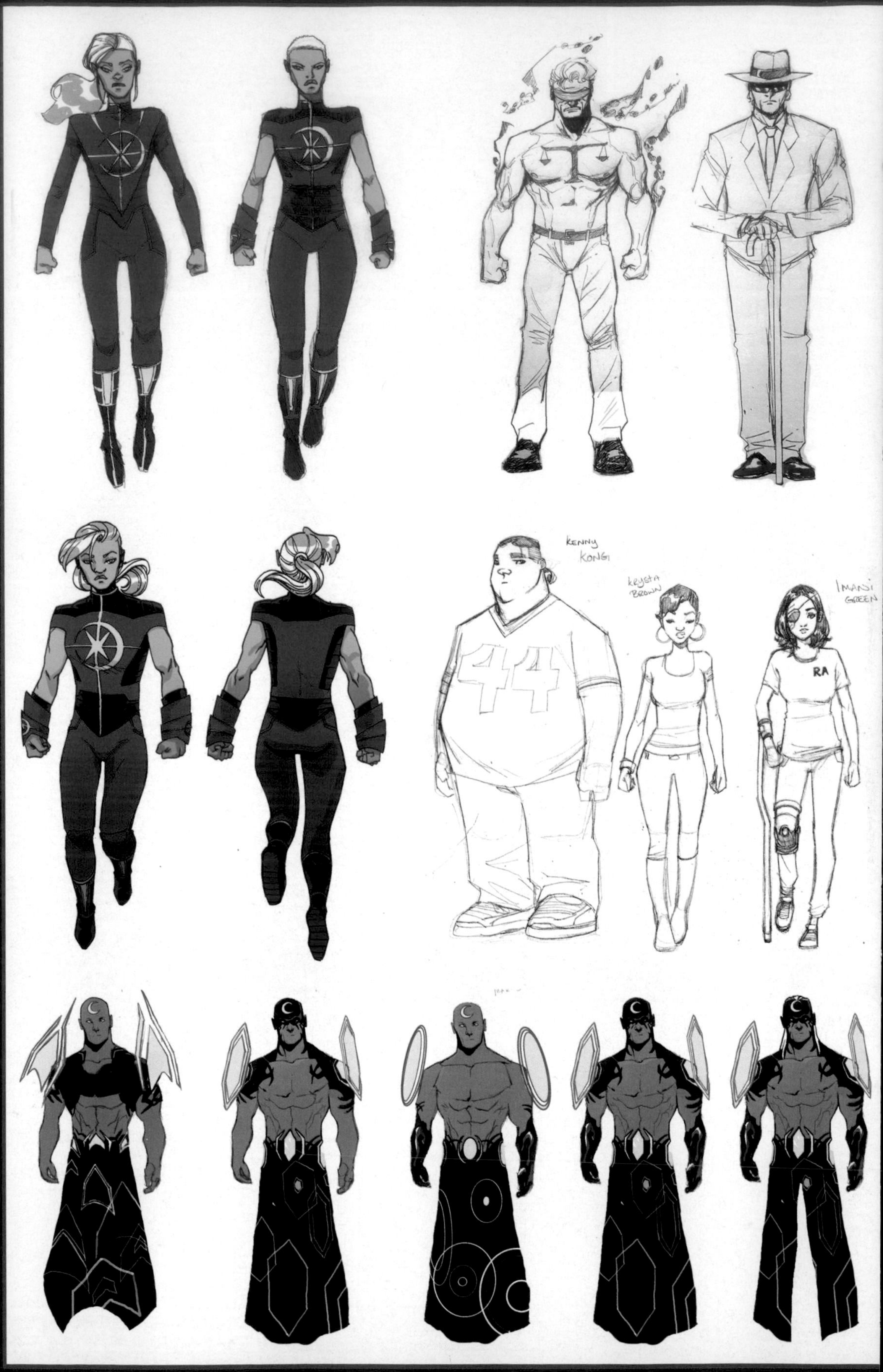
KENNY KONG
44
KRYSTA BROWN
IMANI GREEN
RA

DOMO STANTON
CHARACTER DESIGNS

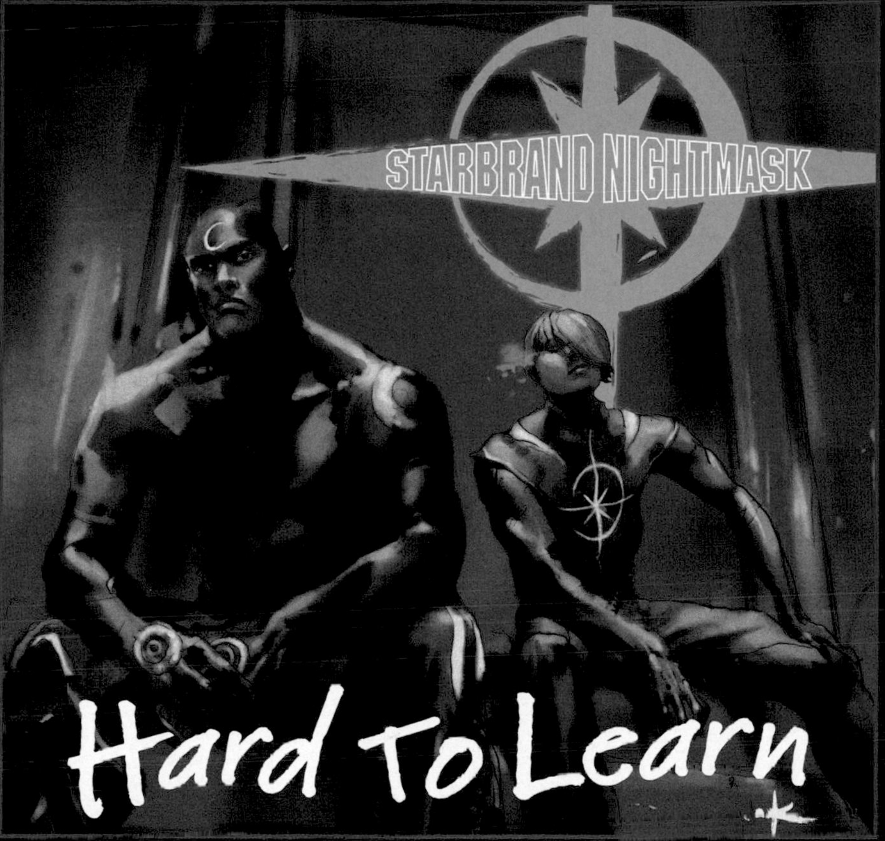
STARBRAND NIGHTMASK
Hard To Learn

KERON GRANT
1 HIP-HOP VARIANT

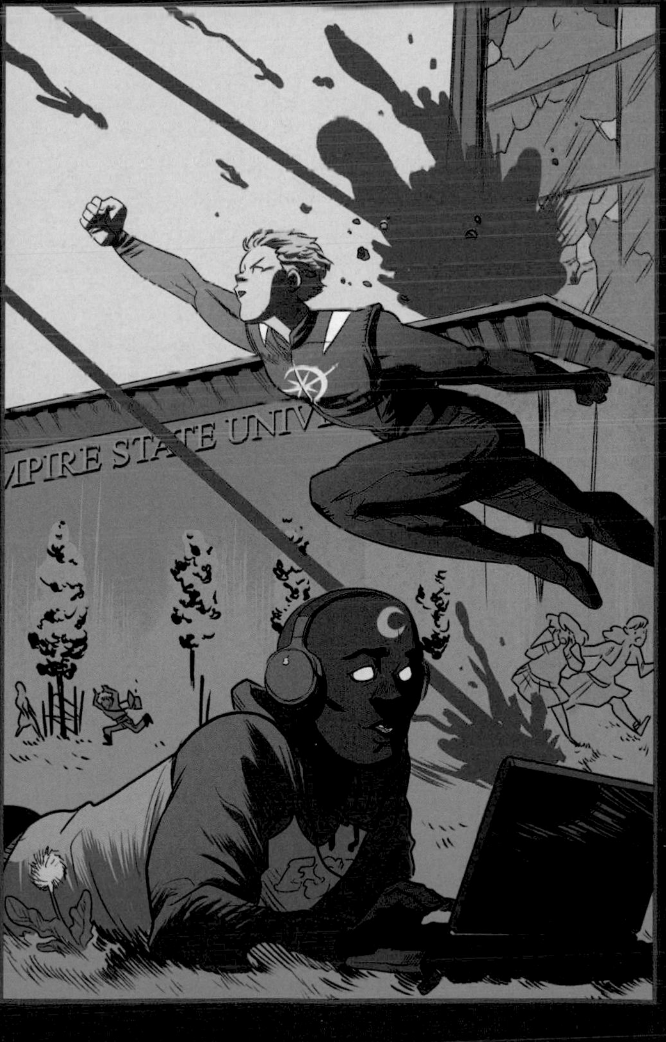
MPIRE STATE UNIV

ERICA HENDERSON
2 VARIANT

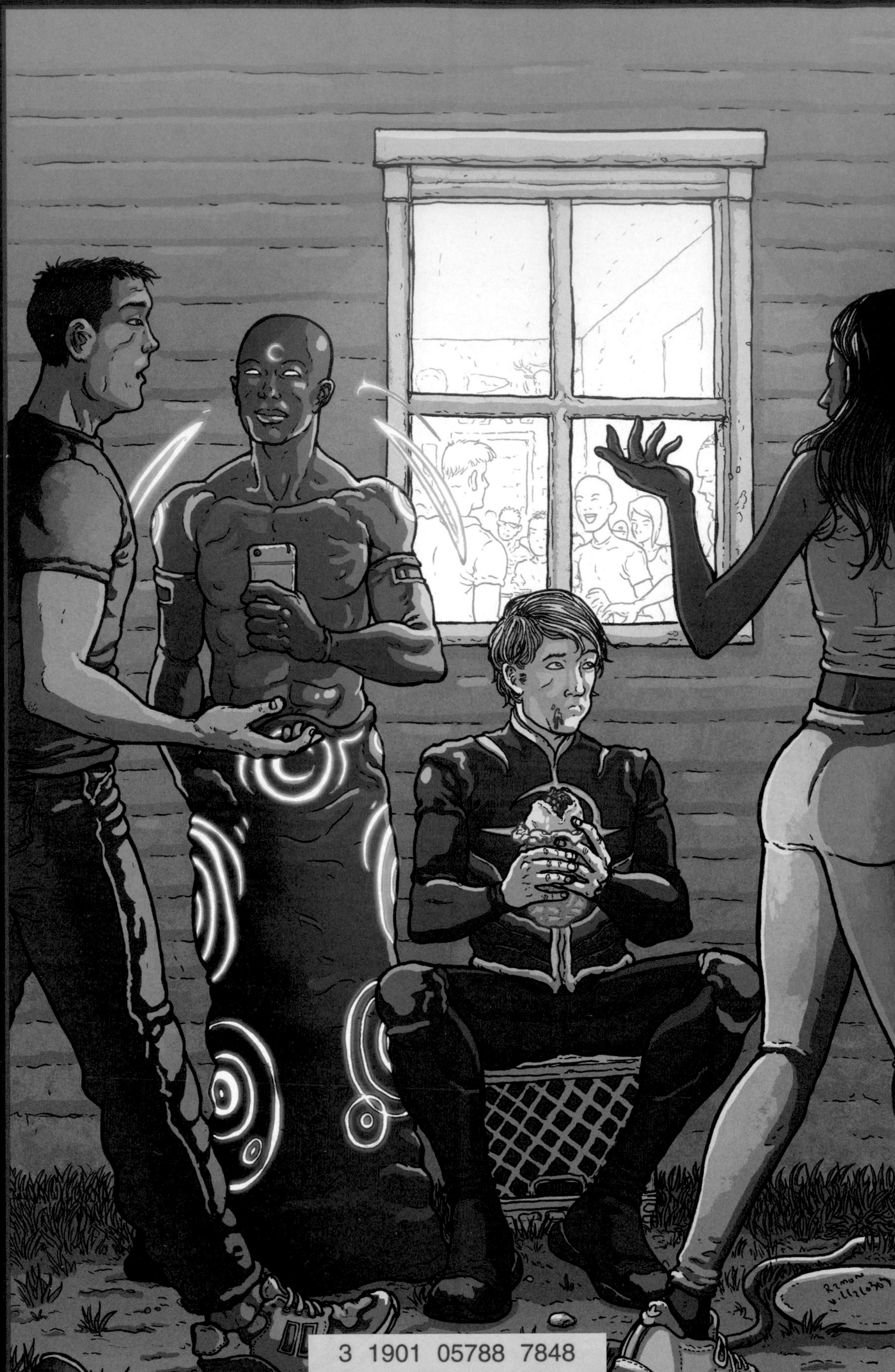

RAYMOND VILLALOBOS & JORDAN BOYD
3 VARIANT